PORTS IN A STORM

INNOVATIVE GOVERNANCE IN THE 21ST CENTURY

ANTHONY SAICH
Series editor

This is the fifth volume in a series that examines important issues of governance, public policy, and administration, highlighting innovative practices and original research worldwide. All titles in the series will be copublished by the Brookings Institution Press and the Ash Institute for Democratic Governance and Innovation, housed at Harvard University's John F. Kennedy School of Government.

Decentralizing Governance: Emerging Concepts and Practices,
G. Shabbir Cheema and Dennis A. Rondinelli, eds. (2007)

Innovations in Government: Research, Recognition, and Replication
Sandford Borins, ed. (2008)

The State of Access: Success and Failure
of Democracies to Create Equal Opportunities
Jorrit de Jong and Gowher Rizvi, eds. (2008)

Unlocking the Power of Networks: Keys to High-Performance Government
Stephen Goldsmith and Donald F. Kettl, eds. (2009)

PORTS IN A STORM

Public Management in a Turbulent World

JOHN D. DONAHUE
MARK H. MOORE

editors

ASH INSTITUTE FOR DEMOCRATIC GOVERNANCE AND INNOVATION
John F. Kennedy School of Government
Harvard University

BROOKINGS INSTITUTION PRESS
Washington, D.C.

ABOUT BROOKINGS
The Brookings Institution is a private nonprofit organization devoted to research, education, and publication on important issues of domestic and foreign policy. Its principal purpose is to bring the highest quality independent research and analysis to bear on current and emerging policy problems. Interpretations or conclusions in Brookings publications should be understood to be solely those of the authors.

Library of Congress Cataloging-in-Publication data

Ports in a storm : public management in a turbulent world / John D. Donahue and Mark H. Moore, editors.
    p.   cm.
Includes bibliographical references and index.
ISBN 978-0-8157-2237-3 (pbk. : alk. paper)
    1. Harbors—Management. 2. Marine terminals—Management. 3. Harbors—Security measures. 4. Marine terminals—Security measures. I. Donahue, John D. II. Moore, Mark Harrison.
    HE551.P837 2012
    387.1068—dc23   2012009158

9 8 7 6 5 4 3 2 1

Printed on acid-free paper

Typeset in Minion

Composition by Cynthia Stock
Silver Spring, Maryland

Printed by R. R. Donnelley
Harrisonburg, Virginia

To the memory of
RICHARD NEUSTADT

Contents

Acknowledgments

The editors of this sort of book have debts to acknowledge, pretty much by definition, since most of the volume's content comes from other contributors. We are grateful for our colleagues' willingness to join us in an unusual (perhaps deservedly so) effort to apply eight different sets of intellectual lenses to the same case. Not only did each contributor deliver his or her own perspective, but all helped to refine the others' chapters in an extended and thoroughly collegial process of rethinking and revision. Special thanks are due to our friend and colleague Steve Goldsmith, who originated the idea of a book displaying a diverse portfolio of Kennedy School approaches to public management. More broadly, we all owe a debt to the giants on whose shoulders we stand—especially Richard Neustadt, to whose memory we dedicate this book—who created and sustained the Kennedy School's capacity to nurture serious intellectual work in the service of practical relevance.

We also acknowledge U.S. Coast Guard Captain Suzanne Englebert (now retired). As citizens, we are grateful for the mix of creativity, patriotism, and dogged persistence that she brought to the mission of improving port security in the wake of the September 11 attacks. As scholars, we are grateful for her generosity and good humor in letting a gaggle of academics look over her shoulder. Relatedly, we acknowledge the contributions of Professor Anne Khademian—who first brought Captain Englebert to our attention and whose prior scholarship illuminates the managerial challenges of national security—and Zachary Tumin, whose written account of the episode at the heart of this book laid the foundation for our analyses. The Kennedy School's extraordinary multimedia producer, Patricia Garcia-Rios, created an elegant video production that has both delivered vivid lessons to many of our students and equipped us, as authors, with images of Captain Englebert in her working world, with her dynamism, determination, and wit on full display.

This project could not have been undertaken without the support of the Smith-Richardson Foundation. We are very grateful for the foundation's continued institutional commitment to the field of public management and for the personal commitment of senior program officer Mark Steinmeyer, whose wisdom and patience have sustained us on the long path to completion of this work. Maureen Griffin and Tim Burke of the Kennedy School's Ash Institute provided skillful substantive contributions and vital administrative support at every phase of this effort. Chris Kelaher, Janet Walker, and Eileen Hughes of the Brookings Institution Press have shepherded the book along the path to publication with their customary professionalism and aplomb.

Our most diffuse but perhaps greatest debt is to the public managers who come to the Kennedy School hoping to improve their practice, requiring us to continually submit our intellectual work to the test of practical usefulness—the truest definition of rigor. We hope that this volume meets that test and thus discharges some small fraction of our debt to the world of practice.

Ports in a Storm

JOHN D. DONAHUE *and* MARK H. MOORE

1

Introduction:
On Management and Metaphor

Metaphors shape and constrain our thinking. We navigate our symbol-ridden, abstraction-drenched civilization using a brain that evolved to escort our ancestors through a bluntly concrete world. The human mind, doing the best it can in a job to which it's not entirely suited, "couches abstract concepts in concrete terms," as the cognitive scientist Steven Pinker puts it. Thirty-five thousand years ago a Cro-Magnon would have used the equivalent of the word *went* to describe the trajectory of a child toddling from her mother to her father. The modern sentence, The traveler *went* from Istanbul to Paris, is pretty much the same thing, scaled up. But the sentence, The meeting *went* from 3:00 to 4:00, is something else entirely, repurposing language that describes concrete motion through space to signify abstract transit through time. Pinker suggests that "a handful of concepts about places, paths, motion, agency, or causation underlie the literal or figurative meanings of tens of thousands of words or constructs."[1] Thus our choice is not whether to think metaphorically—there's no other option; we're simply wired that way—but rather what metaphors will prove most fruitful.

Metaphor and Management

So what sorts of metaphors might we apply to the challenge that a public manager encounters when attempting to use the resources she commands to create public value? Woodrow Wilson's classic dichotomy between policy (properly the task of elected politicians) and administration (the work of unelected administrators) suggests a mechanical—or perhaps more precisely a robotic—metaphor. Decisions made by duly authorized political officials control the actions of administrators, at least when the mechanism

1

is working as it should, as rigidly as instructions encoded in software control the actions of an industrial robot. The implementers exercise little discretion on their own, and the quality of their performance is strictly a function of how accurately they interpret, and how efficiently and fairly they put into effect, the instructions they receive.[2]

The Wilsonian decision/delivery divide, and thus the mechanical metaphor that once came unbidden to many minds when thinking about public managers, have lost considerable ground in recent decades. It is obvious even to casual observers that neither politicians nor administrators are as conscious of their cleanly demarcated roles, nor as disciplined about staying in their appointed lanes, as the Wilsonian image requires. Elected officials trespass into administrative terrain—requiring or forbidding this or that procedural tactic—and, even more chronically, neglect to complete their assigned work of deciding. Instead of resolving empirical disagreements and normative disputes to forge workable mandates, they paper over their differences by issuing superficially attractive but incoherent and incomplete policy directives, which compel administrators, willingly or not, to take up the decisionmaking work left undone.[3]

And even when politicians are able to reach consensus on mandates, they often find it impossible, inadvisable, or both to seek full control over administrators. The context within which a policy is implemented is rarely if ever entirely predictable, or even entirely describable, in advance. Cause-and-effect relationships are seldom sufficiently determinative to obviate the need for continual adjustment during the implementation process. So either political decisionmakers have to hover over implementers, available for continuous consultation. Or robotic implementers must receive their instructions in the form of infinitely nested tangles of if/then contingencies. Or the norm of lockstep, discretion-free fidelity on implementers' part has to yield and, with it, the mechanical metaphor.[4]

Unfortunately, the erosion of this metaphor leaves citizens, politicians, and managers unsettled precisely in areas where they would like to be certain. It is clear that we want government to act with a high degree of political responsiveness and legitimacy and also, no less important, with a high degree of efficiency and effectiveness. The mechanical metaphor divided the desiderata, assigning each to a specialized component of the government, and thus offered reassurance that both ambitions could be served. But if elected representatives cannot construct a coherent, articulate we from the Babel of separate, self-interested voices—and thus cannot give administrators clear guides to action—how can the twin goals of legitimacy and efficiency be advanced?

An alternative metaphor much invoked in contemporary scholarship on public policy (generally invoked implicitly, as metaphors tend to be) emphasizes skillful institutional draftsmanship—choosing from a diverse catalog of organizational models and structuring relationships among them in ways that (in a frequently invoked institutional imperative) "get the incentives right." The implicit metaphor here is not so much mechanical as architectural. A policy goal is set—and many modern writers are less fastidious than Wilson on the question of by whom, implicitly or explicitly letting legislatures, courts, participatory gatherings, or academic experts fill this role—by desiderata derived from philosophy, economics, sociology, or another source of normative wisdom. Achievement of those objectives depends on selecting prudently from the various tools of government to mobilize whatever resources are required to accomplish the task and align motives in ways that induce each actor to contribute its required element to the overall enterprise.[5] Policy draftsmen, who may or may not be elected officials, order up the components their blueprint requires—be they administrative agencies, tax preferences, regulatory codes, tort rules, or financial incentives—to be assembled into a purpose-built construct.

The architectural metaphor invites thought about how different tools of government can be used to alter a broad social production system by redistributing resources, rights, and responsibilities not only across government organizations but also across social sectors. Such an approach is rarely without relevance, and sometimes—particularly when a mission is at once urgent, well-defined, and novel—it is precisely apt. The Franklin D. Roosevelt administration's series of New Deal creations for responding to the Great Depression fit this model. So did the large-scale government investment to develop the applied sciences that built the agriculture and mining industries of the country at the end of the nineteenth century. And so does the campaign launched through the 2009 stimulus legislation to promote electronic health record systems to reduce errors, increase quality, and reduce costs in the health care domain. What makes the architectural metaphor interesting and challenging is that it accepts the idea that the ideal arrangement for accomplishing an envisaged goal will rarely be available. The inventory of components on hand is usually inadequate to realize each detail of any new policy blueprint. As actors—some within government, some wholly outside it—make their responses to the architectural arrangements, they and the architects themselves make discoveries (both good news and bad) about the boundaries of the possible. Together, they find new means, and sometimes even new purposes, for collective undertakings.[6]

The Navigational Metaphor

Without dismissing the frequent relevance and utility of the architectural metaphor, we posit that an even more fruitful image—and one consistent with the scholarly work and professional worldview of many of our Kennedy School colleagues—is neither mechanical nor architectural but rather navigational. (The navigational theme, of course, also comports well with the central example of this book and its Coast Guard heroine.) The image we have in mind is not so much fully modern, GPS-driven navigation, which can itself fit the mechanical metaphor, as (if readers will allow us a bit of historical romance) the golden age of sail, when a captain gliding out of home harbor could anticipate weeks without landfall and months without fresh orders.

This is not to suggest, by any means, mere meandering. Every voyage had its purpose, whether martial or commercial: harvest whales, harass enemy shipping, transport trade goods, seek out new routes, seize territory. But the haze of uncertainty that surrounded each mission at its outset, the impossibility of predicting and programming for each impediment or opportunity, and the infeasibility of consulting authorities at home to resolve each choice as it arose meant that the captain had to wield great discretion. His task was to assess, day by day, his current situation and to choose the route with the best odds of advancing his mission. The modern public manager's situation is similar, in several ways, to that of the wind-driven mariner.

Imprecise Mandates with Retrospective Accountability

Lockstep adherence to advance instructions is no reasonable recipe for accountability when circumstances are fundamentally unpredictable. But that doesn't mean a mariner—or a manager—is free from accountability. At the end of a voyage, the captain of a sailing ship owed a reckoning to his superiors; the admiralty, if a warship; the owners, if a merchant vessel. Literal fidelity to orders was no reasonable touchstone; the orders that were issued long ago, before first weighing anchor, were understood by all concerned to be incomplete and fallible guides to action.

Instead, the ship captain would be judged on his ability to advance the mission he had been given in the face of the opportunities and obstacles that he later encountered. How wisely did he use his discretion, amid a sea of surprises, to advance his principals' interests? So, too, most public managers—at least those with any appreciable degree of seniority—are more accountable for results than for doing precisely what they're told. Legislation, regulations, instructions from superiors, and other embodiments of the public's mandate are inevitably flawed guides to action. A declaration like, "I followed orders but obstacles intruded," is rarely, if ever, an adequate response when called to account by superiors, the press, or the public at large.

Path Dependency

Actions undertaken and events encountered in the past both define the present and bound the future. As a sailing captain pondered what course to plot, his options were constrained by the trajectory that brought him to his current point. Can he accelerate his journey by steering for a latitude where the winds blow fiercely? It depends on whether his sails are new and sturdy or tattered from heavy use since the last refitting. Can he transit an exposed strait fast enough to dodge a looming storm? Not if his hull is encrusted with barnacles and weeds accumulated over the course of the voyage to date. Can he risk encountering an enemy and facing a fight? It depends on whether his crew has been tempered and disciplined, or traumatized and depleted, by actions in the past.

Similarly with public organizations: their capabilities are intimately shaped by their histories. The mighty American military, barely two decades after its triumph in World War II, proved humiliatingly incapable of defeating a ragtag insurgency in Vietnam. There were multiple reasons for the debacle, to be sure, but a major cause was the mismatch between the armed forces' hard-earned operational capabilities and the very different requirements of counterinsurgency. The intelligence services, similarly, proved maladroit when required to pivot from the threat of Soviet communism to the threat of Islamic extremism at the turn of the century.

The past is no straitjacket; agencies can and do change, as the subsequent adaptation of both the armed and the intelligence services attests. But history puts limits on how far and how fast an organization can adapt. As one of us has written, the manager of a public library can quite readily amend the mission from providing access to media to providing a wholesome after-school venue for latchkey children. But there are equally valid public missions—decoding the human genome, deterring substance abuse, scanning space for rogue asteroids—unavailable to the librarian because the path her institution has followed does not equip it to pursue them.

Incomplete Information and Continual Adjustment

A mariner seeking to sail from Madagascar to Mallorca would not simply point the ship toward the northwest and forge ahead, in a straight line, for the days or weeks required to cover the distance. Even if the African continent weren't in the way, he would know the general direction but not the precise bearing he should take. And even if he could be certain of the path from his start to his goal, countless adjustments would be required in the course of such a voyage. Favorable winds or currents might make an indirect course preferable to a straight trajectory. Depleted stores of food and water might mandate a detour for provisioning. The chance to capture an enemy vessel might amply justify a deviation. Even if the captain never makes a choice distinguishable from slavish fidelity to the order to "proceed directly to Mallorca," uncertainty about precisely where Mallorca was, relative to the ship's current position, would require continual corrections almost up to the moment of dropping anchor at the destination. It is no accident that a sailing ship's steering mechanism was organized around a wheel—that shape most capable of adjustments of any scale, from lurching reversals to barely perceptible refinements.

A wise public manager likewise is aware that the only thing he can know for sure is that there are things he does not know that will prove important to the success or failure of his mission. Eclectic opportunism in the face of surprise is a hallmark of effective management in unpredictable public sector settings. Briefly consider two examples.

The New York City parks commissioner, Adrian Benepe, was inclined by temperament and training to provide citizens with excellent parks the old-fashioned way: by hiring city workers to develop and maintain and staff the facilities. But budgetary strictures made the direct approach infeasible. And Benepe realized that parks could become focal points for socializing and status seeking among the city's upper classes and the upwardly mobile. He eventually presided over a network of conservancies, volunteer groups, and "friends of" organizations—utterly unlike what he originally had in mind but successful in advancing his aims.

The Clinton-era labor secretary Robert B. Reich's campaign against garment-industry sweatshops was stymied, at first, by shortages of inspectors. He eventually came to realize that high-profile brands and celebrity endorsers cared far more about reputation than about fines or injunctions. And his team figured out how to exploit that motivation. The anti-sweatshop crusade switched to a strategy of publicly shaming firms and individuals associated with abusive labor practices—a heterodox regulatory model that proved not only cheaper but also more effective than conventional enforcement.

Plan of the Book

Pamela Varley's chapter 2 introduces our prototypical public manager and the problem she faces. In the wake of the September 2001 terror attacks

Suzanne Englebert, a captain in the U.S. Coast Guard, is assigned the responsibility for organizing a national effort—coordinated with international agreements—to improve port security in the United States. On one hand, this can be viewed as a straightforward managerial problem entirely consistent with the mechanical view of public administration set out above. The captain is a midlevel manager in a well-established and hierarchically structured federal agency. The mission of the agency includes managing the security of the ports, both as a target of enemy action and as a portal through which terrorists bent on destruction might pass. Consistent with this mission, she is assigned the task of doing whatever she can think of to do in the material world to reduce threats to, or via, the ports.

But as soon as one begins thinking about what would have to happen to accomplish her material, concrete objectives, much of the mechanical vision has to be abandoned. At the substantive level, the nature of the threat to the port, or passing through the port, remains uncertain. The means for defending against the threats are equally unclear. Standard ideas about what port security means include developing and maintaining a perimeter through clear boundaries, fences, and identity cards, for example. But it is not at all clear that the reproduction of this kind of perimeter control would be the complete, or even the most important, solution to the problem. At the operational and managerial level, Captain Englebert commands little except her own time and capacities. She can leverage these capacities enormously by orchestrating a broad consultative process that simultaneously seeks to comprehend potential threats, imagine useful responses, engage those who could act to thwart the threat in voluntary efforts to do so, and create a regulatory regime that efficiently and fairly distributes the burden of action among the large network of actors who could make a difference. But exactly how to do this, and what the possible results might be, remains uncertain.

Because there is no exhaustive inventory of public management challenges, we cannot say definitively how typical this situation is. Perhaps the problem Englebert faces is at an extreme along some continuum of public management problems, and testing management theories against this challenge would be unhelpful because it represents only a small subset of the problems that managers face. Perhaps the usual problems that public managers face are those that are well described by the mechanical model: the problem of reliably executing a set of well-known policies and procedures to achieve a predictable result. Our sense, however, is that while the problem faced by Englebert may be unusual in the degree and kind of challenge it represents, there are important features of this problem that are typically ignored in the mechanical model and that have become increasingly important in the ordinary day-to-day management of government.

An eclectic orientation toward solving particular substantive problems is now more often the fulcrum of managerial effort than the pursuit of an organizational mission. An exclusive focus on the goals of a single organization is counterproductive when problem solving requires—as it increasingly does require—coordinated action across the boundaries of organizations and even sectors. This, in turn, often requires those responsible for solving a problem to innovate not only with respect to the technical means used to deal with a given problem but also with respect to the governance structures and processes that allow the necessary capacities to be assembled and deployed to achieve the desired results. Both the creation and the maintenance of the new problem-specific governance structures and processes often require a great deal of what can best be described as political (rather than administrative) work. In short, the kind of problem that Englebert faces is a key part of the emerging frontier of public management. The Varley chapter, by arraying with admirable clarity the fundamental facts of the case, enables the analytic work that the rest of the authors undertake.

Malcolm Sparrow, in chapter 3, draws on his extensive experience with enforcement and regulatory agencies to take us deeply into the operational challenges of dealing with risks and hazards that—rather than being targeted narrowly at some particular firm, locale, or demographic group—face the society as a whole. This is surely an important task of government but one that often goes underrecognized and undersupported because it succeeds by keeping everything as uneventful as possible. Being ready for emergencies, acting intelligently to prevent them, and lessening their impact once they occur are activities that (except when they fail) generally escape the notice of citizens at large.

Sparrow concentrates on the heterogeneity of the challenges we face, or more precisely, on the implications—both obvious and less so—of that heterogeneity. It is one thing to deploy against some single threat a response (or array of responses) that is known to be effective against that threat. It is quite another thing to face multiple threats simultaneously and to be obliged to fashion many particular responses to the respective hazards. Sparrow gives us the intellectual framework that an organization charged with mitigating risks would have to deploy to be successful. The world he depicts is one in which the managerial task is to organize structures and processes to support the constant reimagining of a variety of threats and the deployment of idiosyncratic solutions, rather than the creation and maintenance of an organization that can do one preventive strategy with a high degree of reliability.In chapter 4, Robert Behn draws on his extensive research into what he terms performance leadership—a domain akin to, but distinguishable from, more familiar notions of performance measurement and management. He offers insights into how Captain Englebert might be able to convert her unwieldy and ill-defined task into something more manageable by developing objective metrics and a managerial system for using those measures to drive both the short-run performance and the long-run learning of the organization. While it would be nice to have a well-established measure of performance that could capture increments or reductions in objective risk for each port in the United States, Behn reminds us that this is not in the cards. He readily concedes that it would take some time and imagination to create even second-best, proximate performance measures for Englebert's initiative. But even if perfect metrics are unavailable, real-world efforts at performance leadership (inevitably incomplete, inevitably flawed) can help to advance Englebert's goals. It can help those who are part of the system that is trying to improve port security begin to feel accountable to one another and to the wider world for the accomplishment of that mission. Performance leadership can create the forums within which concepts of enhanced port security are debated, measures are constructed, and dialogue is created about the nature of the threats and how they might be prevented.

There is a notable complementarity between what Sparrow and Behn propose. The focus on performance with respect to substantive goals, the reliance on information systems to discover the nature of threats and what could counter them, the creation of forums within which this serious substantive work can be done that is at the heart of Behn's theories can be seen as a useful underpinning for the continuous learning that Sparrow recommends. But there is also a point of potential friction. It takes a lot of time and energy to develop and use a performance management system geared to the accomplishment of some particular set of results. Such systems are also alleged to work better when there are only a small number of measures. Both these considerations can lead to the development of performance management systems that, in the short run at least, become too narrowly focused on detecting one kind of threat or triggering one kind of response to a given threat. The challenge is to create a performance measurement system capable of dealing with threats and other tasks that are both heterogeneous and dynamic.

In chapter 5 Dutch Leonard and Mark Moore present a theory of strategic management in government that seeks to import—and adapt—for public sector use a set of managerial concepts developed in the business world.

While the term *strategic* conventionally evokes ideas like long-run, or big, or ultimate ends rather than means, Leonard and Moore argue that strategic analysis, as it evolved in the private sector, focuses managerial attention on the external environment in which the organization is trying to succeed. In a business setting, the chief feature of the external environment is the market composed of customers, competitors, and financiers. In the public sector, they argue, the most important parts of the external environment include the political authorizing environment, on the one hand, and the task environment, on the other. They also note that both the political authorizing environment and the task environment are heterogeneous and dynamic. Political aspirations and desires change with elections and even between elections. The conditions that public organizations face include many circumstances not easily handled by established routine procedures. Moreover, the conditions they face change with the times. This means that public managers have to think about positioning their organizations for value creation in a complex, changing environment. This puts a lot of pressure on the organizations not only to innovate but also to hold within themselves the variety of tasks they are expected to accomplish and to report against a variety of different dimensions of public value. The challenge for managers throughout is to maintain an alignment among a conception of public value they seek to produce, legitimacy and support for their conception of that public value, and the operational capacity needed to produce the desired results.

In chapter 6, John Donahue and Richard Zeckhauser observe how the capacity to accomplish public purposes frequently resides not in the most obvious unit of government—nor in any single unit of government—but instead is distributed across agencies and levels of government and (particularly) across the meandering and permeable boundary that divides the private sector from the public sector. They argue that an increasingly central task of public management is not the direct control of internal capacity but rather the orchestration of complex networks of capacity diffused across organizational and sectoral boundaries. And they invoke an uncommon metaphor for this work—the tummler, an all-but-vanished profession once ubiquitous in Jewish resorts through the middle decades of the last century. The tummler's job was to forge connections that would trigger the realization of latent collective gains: identifying shared interests, introducing compatible singles, catalyzing the formation of teams and groups of all sorts. Likewise with respect to some public missions—by no means all, but some of the most important—the interests of various stakeholders are reasonably well aligned, and collective gains are (as Donahue and Zeckhauser put it) shallowly latent.

In such settings, the public manager's work is akin to the tummler's task of helping stakeholders discover common goals and overcome impediments to their achievement.

Stephen Goldsmith in chapter 7 continues on the same general tack as Donahue and Zeckhauser. Like them, his point of departure is not a public organization and its assigned mission but a public problem the solution of which is likely to engage a large, diverse, and unpredictable constellation of actors within and beyond government. Goldsmith summarizes the conception of network governance, including the risks, complications, and downsides as well as the undeniable strengths of this approach. He then takes up Captain Englebert's story as an occasion to probe and illustrate some of the subtler and more sophisticated aspects of network governance. He casts the captain in the vital role as convener within the far-flung network—substantively similar to the prior chapter's tummler role, if a bit more dignified—and demonstrates how the convening function becomes the fulcrum for value-creating work in a networked world.

In chapter 8 Elaine Kamarck enlarges the discussion of the range of instruments and institutions that modern government calls upon to advance public missions. Kamarck begins with the uncontroversial theme that classic bureaucratic government is obsolete for many important tasks. But she follows up this conventional point with the less obvious but pivotal theme that Weberian/Wilsonian bureaucracy is being superseded not by any single new model but by a portfolio of alternative approaches to governance. She arrays three of these models: reinvented government, which is structurally similar to but operationally distinct from conventional bureaucracy; government by market, in which public tasks are pursued by weaving skeins of incentives to steer the behavior of private agents; and government by network, a notion akin but not identical to Goldsmith's. The trick, Kamarck observes, is to match public tasks to the right governance model. (In this sense, Kamarck's chapter—along with several of our other offerings—partakes of the architectural as well as the navigational metaphor for public management.) She then arrays the characteristics of port security against the criteria for the various models, in a nuanced and detailed application of her basic assignment approach, yielding lessons not just for port security but also for other urgent tasks.

In chapter 9 Archon Fung and (again) Mark Moore take on the knotty but urgent and inescapable question of where politics ought to fit into our understanding of the work of public managers. Their claim is that doing political work in the form of "calling a public into existence that can understand and act on its own interests" is important for at least three reasons. First, it is only through political consent that we can be sure that the public values being pursued through the use of government assets are, in fact, valued by the public. Second, political consent is an essential condition to the flow of resources to a collective enterprise. Third, political mobilization can build capacities for coproduction that can increase the chance of success. Each of these, to be sure, is an instrumental argument for calling a public into existence. But community, of course, is often seen as valuable in itself, and the instrumental logic can be reversed: A collective enterprise can be valuable in part because it offers an occasion for building community around it.

What emerges from the collective commentary of these different thinkers is a chorus—sung not in unison but (mostly) in the same key—celebrating an appropriately complex conception of public management. This conception takes the perspective of the agent herself—not that of the social scientist—as the dominant analytic point of departure. It orients attention to the public problem to be solved rather than to the mandate of any one governmental organization. It insists upon the application of a diverse analytic tool kit and, in defining and pursuing public value, emphasizes the imperative of painstaking rigor and fidelity to evidence. It takes as an unremarkable norm—not the occasion for surprise or for staking claim to any novel insight—that the capacities of multiple organizations in both the public and private sectors will be engaged in the solution of most problems. And it focuses on the construction and maintenance of legitimacy in citizens' eyes as the indispensable touchstone for valid public problem solving.

However anchored in the practitioner's perspective this conception may be, we readily concede that it offers no fail-safe course to success for aspiring public managers. But that's our point: Any claim to a simple, certain trajectory to effective public management trivializes the task. Our collective conception does provide a polestar or two to aid in orientation. Just as important, we think, it affirms both the value and the difficulty of the manager's work. Our guidance will not, on its own, bring the manager and her mission safely into port. She must do a great deal of careful calculation—and sometimes plenty of dead reckoning—to chart her own true course. Calm days of straight sailing will be rare; endless tacks and threatening shoals will be more the rule than the exception. But the destination is worth the journey, for Captain Englebert and countless committed managers like her. And the rest of us are greatly in their debt. For many of the journeys that define our fate it is better to be in the same boat with our fellow citizens—especially with steady hands at the helm—than treading water, on our own, in stormy seas.

Notes

1. Steven Pinker, *How the Mind Works,* rev. ed. (New York: W. W. Norton, 2009), pp. 352–55.

2. Woodrow Wilson, "The Study of Administration," *Political Science Quarterly* 2 (1887).

3. In an extraordinarily large-scale but otherwise typical example, legislators enacted section 1302 of the historic Affordable Care Act of 2010. The lengthy section ostensibly defines the minimum benefit package that must be offered to count as health insurance under the bill. But beyond some general hand waving, the legislation basically says that the (unelected) secretary of HHS and her (unelected) staff would write regulations defining minimum benefits. When the regulations were released in 2011, they in turn left many of the hard choices up to the separate states.

4. A more tenable variant of the mechanical metaphor may be a cybernetic view of administration. Cybernetics highlights the kind of dense feedback and adjustment mechanisms that facilitate the concentration of decisionmaking authority without sacrificing implementers' advantage with respect to implementation. Interestingly, the word *cybernetic* derives from a Greek word that means helmsman, aligning with our central metaphor here.

5. A canonical text in this tradition is Lester Solomon's sweepingly ambitious edited volume, *The Tools of Government: A Guide to the New Governance* (Oxford University Press, 2002).

6. One of us has invoked a humbler and more realistic variant of the architectural metaphor for public management—that of the handyman who opportunistically exploits available bits and pieces to serve whatever latent goal they best fit—appropriately enough repurposing a metaphor developed by Claude Lèvi-Strauss.

PAMELA VARLEY

2

Sea Change:
Rewriting the Rules for Port Security

On the morning of September 11, 2001, Coast Guard Commandant James Loy and Transportation Secretary Norman Mineta quietly faced a critical national security choice. Terrorists had just hijacked and crashed two commercial jets into the World Trade Center towers and one into the Pentagon. Mineta had grounded all aircraft, marking the first shutdown of commercial aviation in U.S. history. With the scope of the attack still uncertain, should Loy and Mineta also close the nation's seaports?

There was no specific reason to suspect an imminent port attack by al-Qaeda, the Islamic extremist group suspected of orchestrating the jet attacks, but neither was it a farfetched idea. Al-Qaeda had waged sea attacks in the past; eleven months earlier, in the Yemeni port of Aden, the terrorists had successfully attacked a U.S. destroyer, the USS *Cole*. Moreover, a number of large freight ships were thought to have links to al-Qaeda. If the group was now bent on bringing its fight to U.S. shores, might it not, at that moment, be sending a weaponized cargo ship into a U.S. port, set to detonate on arrival? If so, the potential for loss of life and damage was enormous—and senior Coast Guard officials knew all too well that they were ill equipped to detect such a danger in time to stop it.

At the same time, a closure of U.S. seaports would be even more damaging to the day-to-day functions of the country than the closure of the airports. The United States was dependent on the vast quantities of crude oil, liquid natural gas, automobiles, raw materials, manufacturing parts, agricultural products, and consumer goods that daily steamed into its ports aboard huge merchant vessels. Foreign suppliers were dependent on the U.S. dollars paid for them. To cut off that exchange, even briefly, would be globally disruptive and very expensive.

In the end, the Coast Guard's top port officers were given the choice to close their ports, while they took stock of their own port security, or to remain open; many did close briefly.[1] September 11 came and went without a port crisis. But the white-knuckle moment had laid bare an inescapable truth: if terrorists ever decided to target the nation's ports, those ports were eminently vulnerable.

That was not really news. A 2000 report by a specially appointed presidential commission on seaport security had concluded that the ports' "vulnerability to [terrorist] attack is high" but in the same breath noted that "the FBI considers the present threat of terrorism directed at any U.S. seaports to be low."[2] Administration officials and lawmakers knew that any systematic effort to protect the ports from terrorist attack would be difficult, complex, and costly. In the absence of a compelling threat, the issue had remained on a back burner. But after September 11, it vaulted, overnight, to a short list at the top of the national agenda.

The Economic Import of Maritime Trade

At the turn of the twenty-first century, trade represented 25 percent of U.S. gross domestic product. Ships transported 80 percent of global trade, by volume, and 95 percent of U.S. trade with countries outside North America. The United States was the world's leading maritime trader, responsible for 20 percent of global maritime trade. Each year, large merchant ships made some 60,000 port calls at the 100 U.S. seaports with facilities to accommodate them.[3]

A terrorist attack at a major U.S. port therefore posed a threat not only to those directly affected, but to the national and global economy. In fact, a year after the September 11 attacks, an incident on the West Coast illustrated that point. When a labor–management standoff led to the ten-day closure of twenty-nine West Coast ports, the estimated cost to the U.S. economy alone was $20 billion.[4]

At the same time, the idea of imposing a new raft of security procedures and protocols met with resistance. For one thing, maritime experts questioned whether such regulations would, in fact, significantly reduce the terrorist threat. And they argued that the regulations themselves could deal a damaging blow to the economy. In the latter part of the twentieth century, competitive pressures had led shippers to develop new ways to move cargo with greater speed and reliability than ever before. Those improvements allowed manufacturers and retailers to adopt "just-in-time" approaches to inventory management, which reduced warehousing and carrying costs dramatically between 1980 and 2000. Many argued that if the United States began to require ship inspections and cargo screening on a large scale, the resulting delays would wreak havoc with the just-in-time paradigm.

The Nature of the Security Challenge

In considering the security of ports, there were, broadly, three areas of concern: ports, ships, and cargo.

Ports

By and large, U.S. ports were not products of a master design but improvised amalgams of facilities, mostly developed by private capital in fits and starts over decades and centuries and shaped by local geography, local politics, and evolving economic opportunity. Some ports directly joined railroad lines. Some attached to refineries. Some included tank farms, storage facilities, and factories. Some were traversed by public roads and bridges. Many were adjacent to large cities. Ports often encompassed vast swaths of open land, where thousands of people came and went every day. Some lacked even a perimeter fence.

In different locations, the governance of ports had evolved differently as well. Some were owned by state governments, some by county or city governments, some by specially created authorities, and some by publicly established corporations. Most large ports were "landlord ports" that rented out terminals to shipping companies, usually foreign owned, that oversaw the management and operation of their own individual terminals. Their profitability hinged on speed and efficiency.

Some ports were multibillion-dollar enterprises serving as central hubs for transferring and storing cargo. (Fifty of the country's 361 ports accounted for 90 percent of cargo tonnage.) Other ports had different specialties: oil imports, oil rigs, hazardous materials, cruise ships, ferries, Navy installations, grain barges, fishing piers, recreational boating, and so forth. Thousands of private companies were involved in port activities, from ship repair facilities to fueling stations, from taxis to oil spill response companies, from electrical shops to food concessions.

Vulnerability to terrorist attack—and the likelihood of attack—varied substantially according to the nature of port operations. But whatever their focus and physical layout, ports were no more secure than the vessels moving into them and the cargo passing through them.

Ships

In 2000, the United Nations' International Maritime Organization (IMO) counted 87,500 large international ships in the world fleet under its purview. The international shipping system had long been known for a certain rough and lawless quality, exacerbated in the 1980s and 1990s by escalating competitiveness in the expanding global market, which forced shippers to cut their costs and increase their speed to survive.

International maritime law, set and enforced by the IMO, required that every merchant ship be "registered" in a country (its flag state) that would regulate the vessel—inspecting it for safety and environmental controls, certifying its equipment and crew, and so forth. Increasingly, in a bid to reduce their regulatory costs, ship owners obtained "flags of convenience" from countries (some landlocked) happy to offer lax regulations in exchange for registration fees. To a ship owner, that could translate into millions of dollars of annual savings per ship. As competitive pressures grew, even traditional old shipping companies began shifting at least a portion of their fleets to flags of convenience. By the early 2000s, more than half the world's shipping capacity was registered in flag-of-convenience countries, especially Panama, Liberia, and the Marshall Islands.

What's more, with online registration and scant oversight, flag-of-convenience countries allowed ship owners to hide their identity behind fictional corporations and to make frequent changes of name and national allegiance. Ship owners who were in trouble for evading taxes or violating safety standards, for example, were able to repaint a vessel and register it in a new country, under a new name, in order to dodge legal authorities. An uncertain number of large freight ships—estimates hovered in the range of fifteen to twenty—were thought to be owned or controlled by Osama bin Laden.[5]

If some merchant ships were owned by terrorists, others were vulnerable to terrorist takeover at sea. Large and lumbering, merchant ships were typically manned by small, unarmed crews. Thus they had increasingly become prey to pirates, traveling on small, fast-moving boats, especially in shipping choke points such as the Strait of Malacca or hotspots such as the Somali coast. Most of these pirates were small-scale thieves who boarded a ship long enough to steal whatever valuables they could fit in their own small vessels, then sped away. But the 1990s gave rise to a more sophisticated brand of piracy: well-organized groups of bandits that hijacked and "disappeared" an entire ship, either killing or marooning the crew and stealing all of the cargo. In the most elaborate schemes, the pirates repainted and renamed the ship while it was at sea. Some time later, it would turn up in another port, reflagged, renamed, with a new crew and new documentation from a flag-of-convenience state.[6]

From the vantage point of a receiving port in the United States, the wayward side of the shipping world made security difficult. While some ships and captains were well known and reliable, many other ships were, in essence, a black box. Notified of an incoming ship, Coast Guard officials could see who owned the ship on paper and what it claimed to be carrying, but they often had no idea who actually owned the ship, who was crewing it, or what was on board. In some cases—a ship with a suspicious flag or an odd-sounding cargo manifest—the Coast Guard might elect to carry out an inspection at the entrance to the harbor before allowing the ship to proceed into port, but the system was far from airtight. For one thing, such ships were already close enough to inflict considerable damage. For another, commercial developments in cargo containment made it effectively impossible to search a cargo ship for a hidden weapon.

Cargo

A popular late twentieth-century innovation in cargo shipping—the use of twenty- and forty-foot cargo containers designed for easy transfer from ship to train to truck —had led to dramatic efficiencies in transport. But the new containers had also created a pervasive new security risk. A single container might contain cargo from hundreds of companies, destined for multiple customers. It often passed through dozens of different hands, with little or no inspection or oversight, before its ocean passage.

A large container ship might hold 3,000 containers or more, tightly packed and stacked. Nor were the containers necessarily unpacked once they arrived at port. Many were loaded directly onto a freight train or truck and opened only at the destination warehouse or company, which might be hundreds of miles inland. On average, 16,000 containers entered the United States every day. Speed was the lifeblood of the containerized shipping business, and unless the Coast Guard had intelligence indicating that a weapon was hidden in a specific container aboard a specific ship, it could not, practically or politically, undertake a search.

Scenarios for Terrorist Attack

Security experts were especially worried that terrorists might smuggle a nuclear weapon inside a cargo container, triggered to detonate when the ship reached port or when the container was opened at an inland destination. They were also concerned that just as containers were sometimes used to smuggle contraband and illegal immigrants into the country, they could be used to smuggle in weapons, weapon components, or terrorists.

According to a Congressional Research Service report, security experts had also identified several other scenarios for a "high consequence" terrorist port attack. Terrorists might, for example,

—hijack a cargo ship and use it as a collision weapon to destroy a bridge, refinery, or other waterfront structure.

—block a port by sinking a ship.

—explode a large ship carrying a volatile fuel, such as liquefied natural gas, while it was in port.

—take control of a ferry or cruise ship (the latter sometimes carried 3,000 or more passengers) and hold the passengers hostage.[7]

A Multifaceted Approach

After the September 11 attacks, the Bush administration and Congress united to improve port security. The federal government embarked on several initiatives at once.[8]

The International Front

While a port might be attacked from the land, the greatest peril was thought to reside in incoming merchant ships and their cargo. To tighten security on those ships would require international cooperation. The best existing vehicle to address international shipping issues—and by extension, port issues—was the International Maritime Organization, a UN organization of 162 member states. Therefore the Bush administration decided to immediately initiate negotiations at the IMO to add a new maritime security code to the Safety of Life at Sea treaty. The Coast Guard, traditional U.S. liaison to the IMO, took the lead on the negotiations.

At the same time, the administration, well aware of the limited enforcement power of the IMO, pursued other avenues as well. U.S. Customs and Border Protection (CBP), under the Treasury Department at the time, set out to negotiate bilateral, reciprocal agreements with the international "megaports" that sent the greatest number of ships to the United States.[9] The goal was to obtain permission for CBP personnel to work in the ports, reviewing documentation and prescreening U.S.-bound containers at the point of loading. CBP also initiated agreements with private companies, offering them expedited processing in the United States if the companies agreed to comply with CBP measures to secure their cargo containers in a prescribed fashion at every stage of their journey.

The Domestic Front

At home, Congress immediately set to work on developing a new maritime security law, which would establish new security requirements and protocols for U.S. port facilities and ships. In the meantime, the Coast Guard undertook several initiatives intended to improve port security right away:

—It increased its patrolling of U.S. ports and coastal waters with cutters and aircraft. The Guard also increased its security presence in specially identified security zones around high-risk targets such as oil rigs, cruise and cargo ships, and Navy assets.

—It tightened the notice-of-arrival requirement for large ships approaching a U.S. port. Ships were required to give ninety-six-hour (rather than twenty-four-hour) notice and to provide more complete information on the ship itself and its crew, passengers, and cargo. The system was imperfect, relying on accurate self-reporting from the ships, but the Coast Guard used it to identify high-risk ships, which it boarded at the harbor entrance before allowing them to proceed into port.

—It initiated the Maritime Domain Awareness program to actively gather and synthesize information about activities in and near the port from multiple sources.

—It participated in a White House initiative to identify the highest-risk targets for attack in and around the nation's ports.

The Path to New Port Security Rules at Home and Abroad

The Coast Guard had always held the lead role in securing the nation's ports and its 95,000 miles of coastline. But before September 11, that role had mainly involved ensuring safety on coastal waters, preventing illegal smuggling and immigration, providing security to the U.S. Naval assets in seventeen ports, and providing episodic security for special port events. After September 11, concern about port security escalated and the prominence of the Coast Guard—traditionally something of an awkward stepchild within the U.S. Armed Forces—rose abruptly. Rear Admiral Paul Pluta, the top official in the Coast Guard's Marine Safety, Security, and Environmental Protection branch, was given responsibility for recommending new policies for port security.

On the domestic front, fulfilling that responsibility meant working with federal legislators and their staffers to develop a new piece of legislation. Internationally, it meant developing proposals to present to the IMO on behalf of the United States. The Coast Guard found itself scrambling to meet its new responsibilities quickly, without the benefit of staff experienced in navigating the arcane process of drafting international and domestic regulations. In that context, Commander Suzanne Englebert, working in the middle ranks of the headquarters bureaucracy in Washington, D.C., would suddenly emerge as a leader.

The Role of Commander Suzanne Englebert

With an educational background in marine science and engineering, Commander Englebert had joined the Coast Guard in 1980.[10] She worked in operations for her first ten years, spending the greatest share of her time on the inspection of commercial ships. Between 1993 and 1997, she was stationed at Coast Guard headquarters, where she worked to develop complex and controversial federal regulations under the U.S. Oil Pollution Act of 1990, experience that would prove valuable in drafting new port regulations. Englebert returned to headquarters in 2001 as administrative director for Rear Admiral Pluta.

In the wake of the September 11 attacks, Pluta assigned Englebert to head up a team of about ten project managers and economists to draft a set of proposals to present at the IMO's May 2002 conference. Early in that process, Pluta and Englebert took the unprecedented step of inviting more than 300 public and private sector stakeholders in the U.S. port system to a two-day meeting in Washington in late January 2002. There, they solicited advice on how best to improve port security without disrupting port operations— ideas that would inform the proposals delivered to the IMO in May.

In an effort to ensure that new domestic and international port security policies were well aligned, the Coast Guard worked closely with congressional staffers in drafting the IMO proposals. After the May 2002 conference, the IMO held two special sessions in June and August to negotiate the planks of a new IMO security code in multilateral working group meetings. In these international negotiations, the United States succeeded in meeting several of its goals. One was to win agreement that regulations written under the IMO code be performance-based rather than prescriptive to allow each country some flexibility. Another was to obtain an expedited schedule, with regulations written quickly and implemented by July 1, 2004.

The IMO adopted its International Ship and Port Facility Security Code on December 17, 2002. The new IMO code required all large international ships and the ports that served them to develop and implement a security plan. The plan had to establish clear roles for port managers and port industries, to create systems capable of detecting and responding to security threats, and to be able to scale up or down in response to changing levels of security threat. In particular, the plan had to include systems to monitor and control access to secure areas and to monitor the movements of people and cargo.

President George W. Bush signed the U.S. Maritime Transportation Security Act of 2002 on November 25, 2002. The act required the Transportation Department to conduct a risk assessment of all vessels and facilities, on or near the water, to determine which were at risk of attack or accident. All ports, facilities, and vessels with a reasonable level of risk were then required to develop comprehensive security plans that met specific objectives, subject to review and approval by the U.S. Coast Guard. The biggest single problem with the law, in the eyes of its critics, was that the Congress had been unable to agree on a funding method.[11] That was not unusual in the case of broad new legal requirements, but it would increase the chance that port stakeholders would resist the imposition of costly regulations.

The Coast Guard was responsible for developing the detailed regulations necessary to implement the law. At the end of 2002, Englebert expanded her work group to take on this demanding new task, creating four large teams to work on the port security overview, port facilities, vessels, and off-shore installations. With its strict timetables and exacting protocols, federal rulemaking was always a challenging process, but several factors would make Englebert's job especially difficult.

Englebert's Challenge

New federal regulations typically travel a well-worn path before taking effect. They go through an elaborate internal process, with many sign-offs up the chain of command, including a final sign-off from the Office of Management and Budget's Office of Information and Regulatory Affairs. This process produces a draft proposed rule, which is published in the *Federal Register*, and the public is invited to comment for a set period of time. At the end of the comment period, regulators meticulously go through the comments and create a draft final rule, which includes a detailed summary of the comments received and the regulators' rationale for either changing or not changing the proposed regulations in response to the comments. The draft final rule then makes its way once more up the chain of command within the agency and to the Office of Management and Budget (OMB). After the last tweaks, the final rule is published in the *Federal Register* and takes effect on a specified date. Even with only minor substantive complications or procedural detours, the process often takes several years.

Given the urgency of the port security issue, Congress had set July 1, 2004, as the date port security regulations were to take effect, in line with the IMO start date. In light of that timetable, the Coast Guard pursued an expedited process for writing the regulations. However, it would be difficult because the Coast Guard was, over the next year, moving from the Department of Transportation to the newly created Department of Homeland Security. Therefore, proposed regulations would have to move up the chain of command in both departments—the first, which was undergoing a major organizational upheaval, and the second, which was just getting off the ground.

Under the Coast Guard's expedited process, the Guard would not seek public comments before publishing a temporary interim rule no later than July 1, 2003. The rule would take effect immediately, but the public would still have thirty days to comment. If the Coast Guard found merit in the comments, it could make changes before publishing the final rule, which would take effect in November 2003. By conventional standards, however, that schedule allowed very little time for comment, review, and revision. If the regulations proved controversial and generated a raft of critical comments, the Coast Guard would suffer an embarrassment and Englebert would be at risk for missing her deadline. The goal, therefore, was to come up with regulations that all parties would find acceptable.

But avoiding controversy would be difficult. The federal government was requiring security improvements that would cost an estimated $6 billion over ten years. With the funding left uncertain, the maritime industry was tense about the level of responsibility that would be assigned to the various players, public and private, in the maritime economy and the costs that they would incur. Even the requirement to write a security plan could be expensive, and implementing it would be far more so. What's more, once Englebert and her team actually began drafting the regulations, federal law—in an effort to prevent cozy, inside deal making—barred the Coast Guard from consulting with any of the affected parties.

The OMB review added a further layer of complexity. OMB signed off on most new federal regulations, and it had taken the position that the regulator must show, in economic terms, that the benefit of any particular regulation outweighed its cost. In the case of security regulations—intended to prevent something calamitous from happening—passing that test would be especially challenging.

Throughout the process of enacting both the IMO code and the U.S. law, Englebert had been quietly strategizing about how they might be translated into nitty-gritty regulations. In late 2002, she rolled up her sleeves and began working on the project in earnest.

Notes

1. For a more detailed account of this decision, see Zachary Tumin, "From Safety to Security: The United States Coast Guard and the Move to a Global Network of Secure Ports, Cargos, Crews and Vessels," Working Paper, Harvard Kennedy School of Government, 2009.

2. "Report of the U.S. Commission on Crime and Security in U.S. Seaports," Fall 2000 (www.hsdl.org/?view&doc=10562&coll=public).

3. There were 361 sea and river ports, altogether, in the United States.

4. Tim Lemke, "Dockworkers, Shippers Reach Tentative Pact; Dispute Cost U.S. $20 Billion," *Washington Times*, November 25, 2002.

5. "Osama bin Laden is said to own or control up to twenty aging freighters—a fleet dubbed the 'al-Qaeda Navy' by the tabloids. . . . The al-Qaeda ships are believed to have carried cement and sesame seeds, among other legitimate cargoes. In 1998 one of them delivered explosives to Africa that were used to bomb the U.S. embassies in Kenya and Tanzania. But immediately before and afterward it was an ordinary merchant ship, going about ordinary business. As a result, that ship has never been found. Nor have any of the others." William Langewiesche, *The Outlaw Sea: A World of Freedom, Chaos, and Crime* (New York: North Point Press, 2004), p. 39.

6. Ibid., pp. 35–84.

7. John F. Frittelli, "Port and Maritime Security: Background Issues for Congress," Report RL31733 (Washington: Congressional Research Service, May 27, 2005).

8. The information in this section drawn primarily from Frittelli, "Port and Maritime Security: Background Issues for Congress."

9. In October 2002, both the Coast Guard and Customs and Border Protection would be transferred to the newly created Department of Homeland Security.

10. In 2005, Englebert would be promoted to the rank of captain.

11. One proposal—to fund the bulk of the requirements through user fees charged to the shipping companies—was defeated in the face of objections from the shipping lobby.

MALCOLM K. SPARROW

3

Unraveling a Risk-Management Challenge

In the wake of the 9/11 terrorist attacks new measures were implemented to reduce risks to commercial aviation. Congress also demanded assurance that the nation's seaports would be adequately protected, mindful that an attack or serious accident at a major port could result in loss of vital infrastructure and potentially serious economic damage through the disruption of international trade.

U.S. Coast Guard executives knew that commercial shipping was already regulated by a range of government entities—including Customs, Immigration, Agriculture, and the Food and Drug Administration—each of which addressed different categories of risk; but they immediately recognized their own agency's obvious centrality when it came to the task of enhancing port security.

The case narrative shows how Captain Englebert steps forward to lead the effort and immediately confronts the need for a certain type of political action. Chapter 9, by Mark Moore and Archon Fung, distils the essence of such work and examines if and where it fits in relation to traditional views on the role of politics in policymaking and the practice of public management. Captain Englebert envisions and facilitates the emergence of a suitable *mini-public*, using the urgency and importance of the challenge to mobilize support, generate *citizenship*, and galvanize a disparate group of players into concerted action. Moore and Fung observe the particular combination of political skill, diplomacy, and standing within a community that Englebert draws upon in calling this particular *public* into existence.

The purpose of this chapter is to see what difference it makes when the job to be done (by such a consortium) is of the *risk-control* or *harm-reduction* type, as opposed to service delivery or product manufacturing or anything else involving the construction of *goods*. The task here involves the destruction of *bads*. Dangers must be understood. Threats must be identified. Risks—or patterns, clusters, or concentrations of risk—must be scoped and delineated. Terrorist plots, and potential modes of attack, must be detected, anticipated, or imagined. And the American public wants all of these bad things—threats, harms, plots, risks, dangers—to be eliminated, reduced (in frequency or likelihood), mitigated (in effect), prevented, suppressed, derailed, or otherwise unraveled. This task is all about the *sabotage of harms.*

Government agencies find it difficult enough to organize themselves around risks, despite the fact that they exert a high degree of control over their own personnel and resources through formal authority.[1] It turns out to be much easier to organize around *functions, programs,* or *processes.* The work involved in running a functional unit or program is generally well defined, somewhat repetitious, and staffed by fairly stable groups of suitably and similarly skilled personnel. *Process* work is similarly repetitious (and therefore familiar) and occurs within an engineered context designed to deliver efficiency, timeliness, and accuracy. The main challenge in handling processes, once an agency has set them up, is to keep pace with the volumes of transactions that flow in, lest accumulating backlogs embarrass the organization.

In operating *programs* and *processes,* practitioners enjoy certain advantages. The work itself often has a legislative mandate, an established set of supporters, and dedicated funding. Workloads consist of substantial quantities of similar transactions, which make them objectively quantifiable. Good performance is relatively easy to measure, because several of the more obvious dimensions of performance (quantity, quality, efficiency, accuracy, timeliness, and customer satisfaction) lend themselves fairly readily to objective measurement. Moreover, performance monitoring for these types of work is typically *close in* (examining an agency's internal workings and immediate outputs), which avoids all the difficulties of having to observe how the state of the world has changed and trying to explain what role agency operations played in bringing about those changes.

By contrast, organizing around *risks, risk concentrations, threats,* or *dangers* seems vague, amorphous, even optional. A risk-reduction performance is much harder to grasp or to demonstrate convincingly. Risk-control work has little form or structure unless practitioners deliberately *create* a structure for it.[2] When practitioners do attempt to structure such work, it seems they have to invent all the relevant systems, managerial methods, and protocols for themselves. They soon find out that organizational theory has so far paid little attention to the distinctive challenges associated with the task of identifying and tackling risks. Line managers in government agencies, therefore, discover that it is unfortunately up to them

> to figure out the portfolio management aspects of the harm reduction task: whether to organize around programs, or methods, or risk-factors, or types of intervention, or times for intervention, or specific risk-concentrations, or all of these at once. Such practitioners face myriad decisions: how to define their market-niche and distinctive contributions, what competencies to seek out, what type of results to expect, and how to choose when and how to cooperate with others and around what aspects of the task.[3]

Officials from a range of regulatory environments have nevertheless been struggling to pin down and pursue, in some reasonably disciplined and structured fashion, the work of operational risk control.[4] They soon discover, of course, that each one of the myriad choices they need to make (which risks to take on, at what scale, how many, and using which methods) provides yet another opportunity for disagreement and dissent. Colleagues within their own agency, potential collaborators, and a broad range of external stakeholders all bring different views. There were never so many plausible opinions about how to run particular programs or processes, as the available options seemed more mechanistic and limited in number. But for risk-control work the subjective judgments required seem to proliferate, and uncertainty pervades the decisionmaking environment.

Practitioners, nevertheless, must actually reach conclusions and make decisions; otherwise no action will ensue. Herein lies substantial vulnerability for public officials. They are obliged to acknowledge the vast range of contradictory and yet plausible views about risks, about which risks constitute priorities, about how much to worry (or spend), and about whether (in some areas) it is worth worrying at all. Yet they have to proceed in the face of disparate views, or they will get nothing done.

Sometimes the urgency and severity of a crisis helps them over this hurdle:

> This type of work might proceed more naturally on odd occasions when a specific harm stares everyone in the face, demanding attention, and where the shape and nature of the problem is reasonably plain to everyone. But these are the exceptions. The rest of the time practitioners need some guidance to help them navigate the endless choices involved. Without such guidance, the most attractive choice is not to

do this type of work at all, and to revert to forms of work that are more familiar, comfortable, and straightforward.[5]

What happens when we move from a one-agency setting to a multiparty collaborative? Will focusing in a disciplined and systematic manner on risks become easier or more difficult? One might surmise that the temptation to "revert to forms of work that are more familiar, comfortable, and straightforward" would act even more powerfully on people who are already embroiled in complicated, messy, multiparty collaborations. Given the difficulty of establishing common purpose and aligning interests, why would anyone choose to frame the work in a way that was almost bound to provoke a whole new level of dissent? Much easier, surely, to define manageable tasks of a more concrete and predictable nature: for example, "Let us agree a regulatory framework," or "Let us upgrade perimeter controls to some new standardized level," or "Let us agree a new and stricter set of inspection protocols."

It would be an extraordinary accomplishment indeed if the consortium of players assembled by Captain Englebert managed to design and run, among them, an effective risk-control operation. If they had managed that, then they would have succeeded where many others—even with narrower responsibilities and much more formal authority—routinely fail. But if they did *not* manage to design and run an effective risk-control operation, then presumably somebody should, and urgently, in order to protect the ports.

This chapter examines the various ways in which the consortium could formulate its work and considers the choices it seems to have made in terms of picking its portfolio of task *types,* of tasks, and of approaches. This analysis pays particular attention to the *task environment* (that is, to the range of risks Englebert and her collaborators confronted), because doing so reveals a great deal about the relevance of various *tools* or *systems* and the appropriateness of various regulatory *structures* or *regimes.*

Picking apart the task environment also reveals the fact that under the generic heading of "port security" lurk several awkward classes of risks, possessing characteristic properties that substantially complicate the task of controlling them. For example, some of these problems were *invisible* by nature. Some involved *adversaries.* Several were potentially *catastrophic* in nature. A few of the risks Englebert confronted combined several of these qualities at once, posing quite considerable challenges.

Picking apart the task environment also reveals some awkward truths about the use of any one *consortium.* Coast Guard officials might in theory choose one set of partners and a mode of deliberation optimized for tackling one set of risks only to discover that, for other risks, they needed different partners and contrasting regulatory styles. Certain industry groups (or other stakeholders) might turn out to be important partners for some tasks (where their interests align well with the public interest) but simultaneously act as potential *sources* of harm in other risk areas. Consequently, relying heavily on any one consortium might have the effect of imposing some natural limits on the range of risks that Captain Englebert can tackle.

If deliberately adopting a *task focus* brings so much awkwardness and uncertainty, then why should anyone do it? Why not focus instead on tools, systems, programs, and partnerships and make each one work as well as possible? Because there is one potential benefit that goes to the core of the risk-control enterprise: one might actually succeed in identifying harms and controlling them one by one. One might be able to do to specific *risks* what epidemiologists seek to do to specific *diseases:* first to understand them, then to find their vulnerabilities, then to work out how to exploit those vulnerabilities, and, thereby, to defeat the harm. It is this prospect that makes such efforts worthwhile.

> Scrutinizing the harms themselves, and discovering their dynamics and dependencies, leads to the possibility of *sabotage.* Cleverly conceived acts of sabotage, exploiting identified vulnerabilities of the object under attack, can be not only effective, but extremely resource-efficient too. Across the spectrum of harm-reduction tasks, we observe practitioners thinking and then acting like saboteurs. They . . . engage in an analytical search for vulnerabilities of the harm itself: some critical commodity, a pivotal node in a network, an irreplaceable ingredient, or inescapable dependency of some kind. Finding such a vulnerability leads them quite naturally to an action plan which exploits that vulnerability with surgical precision.[6]

Navigating the task environment and organizing attention around the risks themselves provides substantial opportunities to reduce harms. By focusing with greater precision on the task, officials and policymakers can understand more readily what different tools offer, what regulatory regimes might be suitable, and which parties should play what roles. They might also recognize more readily when they have no relevant tools and need to invent them. Let us see how all this plays out in the context of port security.

Enhancing Port Security

Congress was demanding *enhanced port security.* It seemed to be up to the U.S. Coast Guard to figure out what that might actually mean in practice.

There are a great many things that the phrase *enhanced port security* could mean. It could signal the beefing up of existing perimeter controls with taller fences and more frequent patrols. It could suggest the addition of sophisticated systems to supplement security systems already in place. It could indicate the deliberate tasking or refocusing of intelligence operations around the world in order to search for early indications of any threats to American ports. Security enhancements might also include the establishment of information-sharing agreements among various parts of the commercial shipping industry, providing new opportunities for threat detection through data mining and monitoring. Security might also be enhanced if networks of actors were mobilized and organized to deliver collaborative action.

These ideas mostly describe the *means* or *tools* for risk control: systems, capabilities, agreements, protocols, operational arrangements, and regulations. Such enhancements are visible or, at least, observable. But the phrase *enhanced port security* could also signal the accomplishment of *ends*, which—in a risk-control setting—would mean diminution of risk. To be convinced that the Coast Guard's initiatives had actually enhanced *port security*, as opposed to port security *systems*, we would want some evidence that actions taken and systems implemented had actually and demonstrably reduced risks.

The relationship between security systems and security itself is somewhat complex. It is not obvious, at first sight, which additional security investments are worthwhile, particularly when no one knows whether an attack, or what type of attack, might someday be launched against an American port. Measuring progress would be more straightforward, of course, if one could discern a reduction in the frequency of attacks over time as a result of any steps taken; but the benchmark frequency was essentially zero, as no significant attack on U.S. ports had occurred since World War I.[7]

The port security case, therefore, presents something of a conundrum. *Conundrum* is defined "a question or problem having only a conjectural answer; an intricate and difficult problem."[8] The conjecture in this case, satisfying if it turned out to be true, would be that the regulatory structures created, agreements reached, and enhanced security systems implemented as described in the narrative actually *enhanced security* by eliminating, reducing, mitigating, preventing, or suppressing risks.

But the puzzle is indeed intricate and difficult. One cannot resolve the conjecture without exploring the complex relationships among many different types of objects: risks and threats; attacks and the intentions of adversaries; accidents and the safety systems designed to prevent them; detection methods and detection opportunities; regulatory requirements, agreements, and the obligations that flow from them; security systems both technical and human; partnerships and networks. The connections and relationships among these various objects make up a textured and complex landscape, and the challenge of operational risk management is the challenge of navigating that landscape.

Even without resolving the conjecture, one can recognize the Coast Guard's accomplishments post 9/11 as substantial. Captain Engelbert and her colleagues effectively convened, and then established common interest across an extraordinary range of stakeholders. They built a broad consensus around the selection of a particular regulatory structure, which then enabled them to promulgate and implement a new suite of regulations. Using newly established partnerships, they laid the foundation for enhanced information sharing (*maritime domain awareness*) across multiple organizations, both public and private, and straddling national and jurisdictional boundaries. And they accomplished all of this on a remarkably aggressive schedule. This is indeed an impressive story, at least as it pertains to means. This much the case narrative and accompanying interviews make plain.

But to resolve the conundrum means making the connection of *means* to *ends* and making some determination as to whether or not risks, or threats, or some subset of them are better controlled now than they were before. Or, if that determination cannot yet be made, it would be good to know how it might be made at some point in the future. If in fact this conundrum could not *ever* be resolved unambiguously, connecting security means to worthwhile risk-reduction ends, then we might be forced to a depressing conclusion: that officials responsible for enhancing security are condemned to fly blind, relying on guesswork or instinct but lacking navigational instruments sufficient to show progress or set direction.

In terms of risk-control accomplishments, the narrative does leave a great many central questions unanswered. We know that the series of public meetings Captain Englebert chaired produced consensus sufficient to support specific legislative and rulemaking initiatives.[9] But we do not know what else they produced. Did they produce any agreement on which threats or risks constituted priorities for joint action? Did they produce any protocols for organizing collaborative action around any particular threat? Did the various parties to the discussions come away with a clear sense of which risks they would be expected to identify and address by themselves and which ones should more naturally be identified and coordinated by others, or addressed at a different level?

We do know that the meetings produced agreements about information sharing, which provides opportunities for improved threat detection. But we are not told what forms of analysis will now be conducted, or by whom, or how often, in order to derive some operational benefit from the richer data environment. In summary, we cannot tell from the narrative which risks are now better understood and which, if any, have been reduced, or how we might know. Nor can we tell how far the consortium's *rule-making* successes have taken them toward setting up effective risk-control *operations*.

When it came to picking a regulatory structure, the consortium chose the route of *flexibility,* whereby commercial operators propose and develop their own risk management strategies, with a considerable degree of latitude. But did the Coast Guard officials and their consortium partners make this choice because this structure was the best one given the nature of the risks in the ports' environment? Or was the choice simply pragmatic, the easiest way to reach agreement under a tight deadline?

It would be useful to know, also, how many of the stakeholder groups participating really wanted to contribute to better risk control. Any new regulatory regime focused on national security risks would most likely be experienced as a cost for affected industry groups. Were the interests of the various parties actually aligned, if the primary concern was national security? Surely the industry groups would want to know whether risk reductions achieved as a result of these various initiatives would turn out to be worth the price, both in terms of the one-time costs of designing new arrangements and regulatory structures and in terms of the ongoing costs to industry from reporting requirements, delays, and inconvenience. Perhaps interests were better aligned around some other classes of risk, such as theft of cargo or the control of commonplace occupational hazards. One wonders how many of these groups participated in the consultative process purely because they wanted to limit the damage to their own interests that might result from unilateral government action. What else—beyond the particular regulatory structure selected and regulations promulgated—might still be needed in order to provide Congress and the American public the kind of assurance they wanted regarding port safety and security? Has the consortium tackled the ordinary, nitty-gritty, utterly practical questions that pertain to any operational risk-control system: who does what, when, and why, and in relation to which classes of risks?

Exploring the Texture Beneath

In order to make progress on the practical questions—to figure out who should do what, and why—one has to step down a notch and examine more closely the details of the risk terrain. *Threats to ports* are not one, but many. They are not even of one *type*. They inflict different types of harm and have different properties. They are susceptible to quite different types of intervention. Particular security systems and control strategies may substantially mitigate one problem and be completely irrelevant to others. The interests of various parties align much better around some risks than others. One party might be pivotal in the control of one type of risk and at the same time act as a principal source for other problems. And we have learned from other risk-control settings that, to measure risk-control achievements, much promise lies in tailoring metrics to specific problems rather than trying to gauge progress at higher levels and in more general terms.[10]

The *task environment* for risk-control operations comprises the complex, messy, variegated middle ground, populated by objects bigger than individual incidents but smaller than generalities. This is the territory where individual *risks, hazards,* or *threats* need to be spotted, understood, and suppressed before they do much harm; where success, if it is to be had, is made up of specific risks eliminated, reduced in frequency, mitigated (in terms of consequences), prevented, or suppressed.

Effective risk control depends on successful navigation of this task environment. To make some sense of the terrain, we normally aggregate risks where they are sufficiently similar, and it is therefore useful or efficient to group them together. Then we have to disaggregate them where parts of a problem behave differently or require substantially different methods or different coalitions to control them or where the responsibility for problem identification or intervention design belongs in different organizations or at different levels.

The remainder of this chapter focuses on four diagnostic questions, designed to clarify the extent to which the initiatives described in this case map well onto the structure of this particular risk-control environment. (These questions explore the fundamentals of risk-control operations and will hopefully be broadly useful for readers concerned with *enhancing security* or *enhancing safety* in other industries or domains.)

—First, has the risk terrain been adequately surveyed? Do the Coast Guard officials know the full range of risks they need to address? Do they and their consortium partners think about different threats systematically, so that they can design tailored and effective solutions for specific threats; or do they lump them together carelessly in a manner that produces operational confusion? Have the characteristics of specific risks been understood and accommodated insofar as these may affect the locus for risk identification and monitoring, the appropriate locus for intervention design, the types of tools that may be relevant, and the partners that might contribute in each case?

—Second, have they understood the special properties some risks possess, which can complicate or confound risk-control operations in significant ways? Some risks involve *adversaries* (such as terrorists or smugglers), whereas others do not (such as occupational hazards, accidents, and spills). Some risks are *catastrophic* in nature (low frequency but high consequence). Some are *invisible*, so that the underlying extent of the problem is generally not known and authorities can see only what they manage to detect. Such properties have profound implications for the risk-control challenge, and these confounding properties are present in abundance in this setting.

—Third, have they struck the right balance between the *task focus* and a *tool focus?* The former stresses the identification and control of specific threats, whereas the latter focuses more intently on the construction and operation of specific security systems. Both are clearly necessary and valuable, and the two are deeply intertwined. But the tool focus is more concrete and intellectually straightforward and, therefore, too often dominates the agenda.

—Fourth, have the policymakers properly considered the range of regulatory structures open to them? Have they understood which regulatory structures work well for various types of risk? Have they jumped to a one-size-fits-all *structure*, even if they managed to avoid one-size-fits-all rules?

Regarding the first of these, the U.S. Coast Guard was surely no stranger to complex task environments and multifaceted missions. Even without any special focus on port security, and before 9/11, their responsibilities already included narcotics interdiction, safety in commercial shipping, marine environmental protection, crime control, national defense, search and rescue, and fisheries protection. Any one patrol (by boat, plane, or helicopter) might be called on at any moment to contribute to one or another of these various purposes.

Post 9/11 the challenge of defining and enhancing *port security* became more prominent, but the range of issues swept together under that general rubric remained broad. The case narrative, in fact, mentions at one point or another thirteen distinct categories of risk that could all quite plausibly fit under the general heading of port security. The number of categories could be much higher, of course, depending on how finely one cares to distinguish them. These thirteen broad categories, which are laid out and summarized briefly in table 3-1, represent some minimal level of granularity. It is a first, high-level cut, if you like: sufficient to begin to reveal important differences but still leaving plenty of room to subdivide threats further for operational

Table 3-1. *Major Categories of Risk or Threat*

	Category
1	Destructive attack on port: Includes deliberate use of explosives, fire, nuclear devices, crashing a ship into a bridge, sinking a ship to block a waterway, spillage, or other attack on port facilities designed to produce casualties and destruction or economic damage by shutting the port down.
2	Destructive attack on high-value installation: Similar to 1, but the target is a high-value or vulnerable installation (such as a refinery, an LPG facility, a power plant, a naval yard) proximate to a port, rather than the port itself.
3	Transshipment of destructive materials (WMD): Bringing in, through a port, destructive materials (including WMD) for use elsewhere within the United States.
4	Destructive accident for port: Includes an explosion, fire, collision, sinking, or major spill, but by accident or through neglect rather than by malevolent design.
5	Destructive accident of high-value installation: Similar to 4, but it is an adjacent high-value installation rather than the port itself that is damaged or incapacitated.
6	Smuggling through the port: Smuggling of contraband or other commodities (such as drugs, prohibited goods, taxable imports) by criminals but not terrorists.
7	Theft of cargo from port or ships in port: Includes thefts from port storage facilities and thefts by insiders (with authorized access to facilities) as well as by outsiders or intruders.
8	Illegal immigration, stowaways: Illegal immigrants arrive by ship and escape through the port. Not a member of the ship's crew. Crew may or may not be facilitating or aware.
9	Illegal immigration, ships' crew (jumpers): Members of a ship's crew leave the port and do not return, becoming illegal immigrants.
10	Maritime attacks (sabotage or terrorism) at sea: Destructive attack on ships at sea. May target passenger vessels or cargo ships. Purpose may be terrorism.
11	Piracy or theft of ships at sea: Seizing of ships at sea for gain, either using violence or threats of violence.
12	Maritime safety at sea: Includes all classes of accidents at sea, loss of life, injuries, loss of vessels, groundings, and so on.
13	Murder or other crimes on board at sea: Includes all classes of crimes perpetrated on board ship, but at sea.

purposes later on, when risk-control operations prioritize individual risks and set about defining actionable risk-mitigation projects.

Arguably it is categories 1 through 3—the possibility of destructive attacks on ports or marine installations or the transshipment of weapons of mass destruction—that most closely reflect congressional and public concern post 9/11. But all the other ten categories (4 through 13) come up in discussion and seem to affect the consortium's proposals and plans, even though none of these would be construed as new or even much changed as a result of the terrorist attack. There are several possible reasons, though, why one might reasonably expect a broader discussion to arise, even if the newly prominent risks constitute a comparatively narrow set. Here are a few possible explanations why that might happen:

—A generally heightened awareness of the vulnerability of the ports and their critical importance to U.S. commerce might elevate the priority given to existing and familiar risk categories.

—Congress, being a law-making body, had clearly signaled its intention to make law. Legislative proposals relating to port security could not be (and perhaps should not be) so surgically focused that they would touch only risks relating to terrorism. Hence Coast Guard officials and the shipping industry were obliged to reconsider other parts of their business as well, in order to design sensible, broader, regulatory provisions.

—Security systems enhancements, conceived originally in the context of counterterrorism, could turn out to have broader utility in controlling other risks. Hence those other risks are drawn into the conversation because their existence adds value to, and helps to justify expenditure upon, proposed solutions.

—The creation of the Transportation Security Administration and the attempts post 9/11 to "seal the skies" bring to mind the idea, or bring to official notice the possibility, of "sealing the seas" through international cooperation over the control of major access points. This basic idea, whether feasible or not, could affect many risks to commercial shipping operations other than terrorism, and so the discussion broadens to cover them all. (This is a particular version of security systems enhancements, above.)

—Whatever new security arrangements might eventually be implemented, their impact on terrorist risks might be particularly difficult to measure. Their impact on other risks might be easier to identify and assess. Extending the conversation to a broader range of risks might therefore make it easier to satisfy demands for accountability and quantifiable results, even in the absence of detectable changes in terrorist threat levels.

—In order to address the terrorism-related risks, Coast Guard officials sought to develop a broad range of new partnerships. But potential partners come with their own sets of issues. Stakeholder interests naturally encompass a broader range of risk areas. Acknowledging and addressing them all helps make the partnerships more sustainable.

—Proliferation of risks exacerbates tensions over the allocation of time, effort, and resources. Officials might worry that the latest arrivals (terrorism-related risks) could distort the portfolio to the detriment of traditional aspects of the Coast Guard mission and, hence, feel the need to reemphasize all the competing demands.

For any or all of these reasons, it would surely be difficult for Coast Guard officials to isolate discussion of one set of risks from all the others. It is also unlikely that they could tackle novel risk areas efficiently and effectively without understanding how these new risks related to the Coast Guard's existing risk portfolio and to the agency's accumulated repertoire of responses.

At the same time, it would be a huge mistake if officials were careless in navigating the risk terrain and failed to distinguish one risk category from another. Potentially the attractiveness of familiar risk areas, the comparative ease of measuring progress in some areas rather than others, and the miscellaneous interests of stakeholder groups could end up distracting them from their most urgent business—which was to deal with the emergent and least familiar threats.

Developing some kind of risk map, even a crude one like table 3-1, might make it easier for Coast Guard officials to see if and when they spent too much time in certain parts of the risk territory, or overlooked other important areas, or wandered further from their original target than they had intended.

The Character of Different Risks

The puzzle becomes more intricate, and the risk terrain more colorful, when one considers the range of problematic properties that some risks exhibit. The risk literature has already developed an impressive list of descriptors that affect the ways in which people perceive or respond to various risks. Some risks are familiar, others unfamiliar; some exposures to risk are voluntary, others involuntary; some risks induce emotions such as dread or disgust that can affect or distort reactions.

Perhaps the most important class of risk properties for Coast Guard officials to consider, given their professional obligation to design and deliver public protections, are those that tend to confound or complicate the task of control. The three most relevant ones in this (port security) setting seem to be the properties of *invisible* risks, risks involving *conscious opponents* (or *adversaries*), and *catastrophic* risks. None of these are peculiar to Coast Guard operations; but as the subsequent analysis shows, these three properties are present in abundance in this context.

Invisible Risks

Some risks remain for the most part undetected or unreported, even in perpetuity. For these, *you see only what you detect,* and the real challenge is to expose and then grapple with the invisible bulk. Familiar examples of invisible risks include white-collar crimes, consensual crimes such as drug dealing and bribery, political corruption, and fraud schemes designed so that no one ever realizes they took place, even long after the fact. Crimes within the family (such as domestic violence, incest, and child abuse) or between acquaintances (such as date rape) also involve very low rates of reporting or detection.

Where the bulk of a problem remains hidden, control efforts are naturally frustrated. No one knows how prevalent the problem is and, therefore, how much to spend on controlling it. Underinvestment in controls becomes the norm, which leads in turn to low levels of detection, and the cycle continues. Circularity traps abound, where particular parts of the problem might become visible and thereafter attract attention and resources; meanwhile other parts remain out of sight completely, even as they grow in scale. Measuring progress is confounded by the fact that available metrics—such as the number of incidents reported or detected—are inherently ambiguous. An increase in the rate at which incidents come to light might mean that detection methods improved or that the problem got much worse.

For these problems, effective control normally starts with a serious commitment to measuring the underlying extent of the problem, so that control investments reach the right scale. Proactive and intelligence work along with random audits or inspections all play important roles in exposing risk concentrations that would otherwise remain out of sight and in correcting the biases of existing detection systems. Such methods enable authorities to realign their operations with the actual scale and shape of the problem, rather than being deluded by the relatively tiny sliver of cases that come to light.

Risks Involving Conscious Opponents (Adversaries)

Sometimes those responsible for risk control confront opponents who drive the risk, have a malevolent goal in mind, and are determined to defeat the controls. These opponents deliberately evade detection whenever they can.

The control task becomes a game of intelligence and counterintelligence, each side monitoring and adapting to whatever moves the other side makes. Who wins is whoever watches most closely and adapts most quickly and creatively to the actions of the other. Static controls, no matter how sophisticated, quickly lose their efficacy as opponents learn about them.

To control these types of risk you have to get inside the heads of your opponents. That means, preferably, finding out what your opponents are *actually* thinking. And if that is not possible, then (second best) you must figure out what they *might* be thinking. When government fails at the first of these, overlooking or misinterpreting signals about adversaries' actual operations, the American public has learned to label these *intelligence failures.* When authorities fail at the second, allowing adversaries to invent scenarios that they themselves had apparently failed to anticipate, we now call these *failures of imagination.*

Involvement of adversaries substantially alters and complicates the control task, in several ways. For example:

—Probabilistic estimates based on extrapolation from historical data become unreliable or meaningless. An opponent, merely by changing his or her mind, or by having a new idea, can render past history useless (or even dangerously misleading) as a predictor of future risk. What you have seen in the past provides no reliable indication of what you might see in the future.

—Getting inside opponents' heads demands the full spectrum of intelligence methods and capabilities: Humint, Sigint, proactive data analysis, anomaly detection, deployment of tiger teams, covert surveillance, cultivation of informants, and undercover operations.

—Authorities need to think several steps ahead, anticipating opponents' responses to their own control initiatives, and shutting down displacement options ahead of time.

—Some of the default values in government operations, such as *openness, transparency,* and *predictability,* become liabilities. Effective control strategies may require elements of mystery, unpredictability, novelty, surprise, disinformation, and deception. Government agencies working in such territory must retain their capacity to deliver nasty shocks, without warning.

The U.S. Coast Guard, fortunately, was no stranger to risks involving adversaries. In fact, the Coast Guard mission portfolio had always contained a range of them: drug smuggling, people smuggling, waste dumping at sea, illegal fishing, piracy, and theft of cargo in transit or at the ports.

The Coast Guard also deals with a range of risks that do *not* involve adversaries in the same sense. One such area is safety in commercial shipping.

If the Coast Guard successfully controls a particular type of occupational hazard, that hazard does not go looking for another way to kill mariners. Nor is there any malevolent intent or design behind most classes of marine accidents, storm-related dangers at sea, or accidental oil spills. These more benign classes of risk might involve stupidity or carelessness—surely facets of human behavior that involve the brain. But the brains involved with these risks are not acting *adaptively* or *purposefully* in opposing or seeking to defeat the controls. The drunk or reckless generally favor safety, even though their own actions might undermine it on occasions. Smugglers, pirates, and thieves, by contrast, work consciously and deliberately to thwart authorities and undermine controls.

Coast Guard officials, therefore, were already accustomed to confronting a mixed bag of risks—some that involved adversaries and some that did not—and were presumably familiar with the consequences for strategy, tactics, and risk assessment. This mixture surely complicates their lives, nevertheless, as it does for any agency that deals with some of each.

Not all regulatory agencies face such a mixture. The Federal Aviation Administration, for instance, does not count itself responsible for dealing with adversaries. They deal with safety, not sabotage, and focus heavily on technical and maintenance issues. They also deal with human behaviors, as well, insofar as these relate to carelessness, procedural violations, adequacy of training, and potential abuse of drink or drugs. But responsibility for dealing with saboteurs and terrorists (that is, conscious opponents) in the aviation environment now sits with the Department of Homeland Security and the Transportation Security Administration in particular. In large part the TSA's creation was an acknowledgement of the fact that the FAA was not set up to counter adversaries and did not want to take on that responsibility. The FAA focused on airline safety, and had neither the skills nor the mind-set to deal with the potential for attacks. So sharp is this division of responsibilities that the FAA does not even record the fatalities from 9/11/2001 in its statistics on commercial aviation fatalities nor incorporate them into FAA performance metrics—not even the passengers on board the four hijacked airplanes. There is one blip late in 2001 that appears on the FAA's charts of airline fatalities, but that relates to an American Airlines jet that crashed in Rockaway, New York, on November 12, 2001, killing 265 on board. That was an accident. The agency's records for September 2001 show zero deaths, reflecting the agency's position that they were not set up to deal with saboteurs or terrorists; hence the loss of life on 9/11/2001 ought not to count against the FAA's performance record. The subsequent creation of TSA preserves this distinction and the separation of responsibilities. No such luxury for the Coast Guard! They have to grapple with both types of risk

Catastrophic Risks

Some risks materialize very infrequently or never, yet demand attention because of their potentially devastating consequences. Obvious examples of such low-probability but high-consequence threats include the meltdown of a nuclear power plant, nuclear terrorism, global pandemics, and natural disasters such as earthquakes, hurricanes, forest fires, and tsunami sufficiently powerful to cause widespread destruction. In the context of port security, the threats in this category that spring to mind involve weapons of mass destruction or an attack or accident sufficient to shut down a major port for a substantial period.

Catastrophic risks present the following special challenges to a risk-control operation:

—The very small number of past observations is insufficient to provide a reliable estimate of the underlying probabilities. For many risks in this category, no one really knows even the order of magnitude—whether the chance of a particular catastrophic event is one in 10 million, in 100 million, or in a billion. High variance attaches to any point estimate and frustrates the processes of risk assessment, risk comparison, and prioritization.

—Political and budget cycles, short term in nature, do not align well with the long-term perspective required to assess and address such risks. The temptation is to put them off, allowing more immediate concerns and more apparent risks to dominate the public agenda.

—Public opinion, with respect to such risks, is fickle. Either there has been *no disaster lately* (even within living memory), in which case the public displays little tolerance for the costs and impositions of regulatory safeguards. Or there was *a disaster yesterday,* in which case the clamor goes up claiming regulatory failure and government is lambasted for its inability to anticipate and prevent. Public perception of the underlying probabilities and public attitudes about controls lurch from one extreme to the other, all or nothing, based on immediate short-term history. Policymakers have great difficulty establishing an appropriate and sensible level of protection or preparation and sustaining public or industry support for it over the long term.

—Preventive work is of paramount importance and is demanding conceptually and intellectually. There is no pattern of instances available for analysis, in the way that there would be for ordinary crimes or commonplace diseases. Design of controls has to be informed instead by deliberate and exhaustive debriefing of near misses and by analysis of similar or analogous disasters in other jurisdictions. All the preventive work has to be defined, divided up, handed out, and monitored in the realm of precursors to a disaster and precursors to the precursors. In an engineering sense, this means defining a series of contributing or preliminary events—short of the disaster itself—that can be readily counted, analyzed, and reduced in frequency.

—Response operations lack sufficient practice and may turn out to be seriously deficient if and when the time comes. Tabletop exercises and simulations lack realism. The cost of more extensive or frequent exercises is difficult to justify.

Table 3-2 takes the thirteen major categories of risk discussed in the port security case and shows which of them might exhibit one or more of these three complicating properties. So the first column (Invisible risks?) gives a somewhat general answer to the question, Would risks in this group generally pass unobserved, or with a low rate of detection, with the result that the Coast Guard and its partners would not know the true prevalence of the problem? The second column asks whether adversaries are generally involved; and the third column shows which risk groups might include threats generally regarded as catastrophic in nature. Table 3-2's rather basic analysis of the task environment does help to reveal some of the more serious challenges involved in the task of enhancing port security.

First, one cannot help noticing the overall density of the ticks in this chart. Even though it considers only three confounding qualities that risks might possess (out of a potentially limitless list), nearly all the risks considered under the rubric of port security exhibit at least one of these properties. Only maritime safety issues and crimes on board (groups 12 and 13) behave "nicely"; that is, with no unusual complications. These are the risk areas for which a standard Compstat-style approach most naturally makes sense. Data about incidents would generally be available (even if somewhat incomplete) and susceptible to analysis. Clusters or patterns could be identified and the related problems analyzed and reduced one way or another. These are "well-behaved" risks, which neither lurk in the shadows, nor play games, nor strike once in a lifetime with catastrophic impact.

Second, notice the density of ticks in the second column. Adversaries abound in this environment. Most of this work is not about accidents nor casual local criminals of the type that might be kept out by a fence. Success or failure in this environment will depend heavily on the quality of intelligence: the ability of government agents to get inside the heads of their various adversaries. New partnerships, new regulations, new data-sharing

Table 3-2. *Special Character of Different Harms*[a]

	Category	Invisible risks?	Conscious opponents?	Catastrophic risks?
1	Destructive attack on port		✓	✓
2	Destructive attack on high-value installation		✓	✓
3	Transshipment of destructive materials (WMD)	✓	✓	✓
4	Destructive accident for port			✓
5	Destructive accident: high-value installation			✓
6	Smuggling through the port	✓	✓	
7	Theft of cargo from port or ships in port		✓	
8	Illegal immigration, stowaways	✓	✓	
9	Illegal immigration, ships' crew (jumpers)	✓	✓	
10	Maritime attacks (sabotage or terrorism) at sea		✓	?[b]
11	Piracy or theft of ships at sea		✓	
12	Maritime safety at sea			
13	Murder or other crimes on board at sea	?	?	

a. A tick means yes, a blank means no, and a question mark means sometimes or possibly.

b. Probably regarded as catastrophic only if massive casualties result, for example, the destruction of a passenger cruise ship.

agreements, and new perimeter controls will be valuable if and only if they help the law-enforcement and intelligence communities anticipate and undermine the operations of adversaries.

Third, notice the particularly unsettling combination of qualities in the first three rows of the table: that is, the properties exhibited by the risk of destructive attack on port facilities or other critical installations and the potential transshipment of WMD for use elsewhere. It is these terrorist-related threats, rather than the other ten on the list, that provided the initial impetus for rethinking port security and that dominate congressional concerns.

The combination of *catastrophic* with *adversaries* is especially significant. Preventive work on catastrophic risks often occurs in an engineering or highly technical environment. The nuclear power industry, for example, can carefully define a set of precursors to serious failure and then devise monitoring and alarm systems, along with automatic technical interventions, all designed to populate and punctuate any predictable or imaginable path to disaster. Similarly, in aviation safety, the FAA defines near misses and a host of other reportable safety incidents (such as *runway incursions*), all of which fall short of, but are assumed to lie on potential pathways toward, calamity.

This approach provides structure for preventive work. Engineers can successively broaden the range of precursors monitored, moving further back through the chronological chain, leaving more and more safety systems in reserve, reducing the frequency at each gate. This type of analytical mapping enables officials to divide up the work, to monitor progress, and to demonstrate success in enhancing safety.

But when catastrophic risks also involve opponents, the setting for preventive work is transformed. Preventive work remains imperative, of course, given the catastrophic nature of the risk. But the chronological unfolding of the harm no longer takes place in an engineering setting or the observable confines of a power plant. Preparations for an attack are conducted by adversaries out of sight, except where intelligence operations succeed in uncovering them. Near misses represent *plots uncovered* or *missions intercepted,* as opposed to *hazards that arise* in an engineering context. Systems engineering might help us predict *hazards that might arise,* so we can implement technical interventions to prevent mistakes turning into disasters (for example, automatic shut-off valves, collision avoidance systems, and ground proximity warning systems for aircraft). But terrorist missions have no predictable engineering sequence. Preventing them means spoiling the creative plans of another. Even though terrorist attacks are dramatically visible in their final stage, all of the preparations are invisible, by design. Intelligence operations, therefore, form the core of the necessary controls. Without good intelligence, sophisticated technical defenses are unlikely to provide lasting protection. They can all be discovered, tested, corrupted, or circumnavigated by a shrewd adversary.

When adversaries are involved, the intellectual work of prevention takes a different form. In the engineering setting one has to imagine or anticipate undesirable and complex interactions among technical systems. The work is logical and technical. With adversaries, the intellectual work is less about engineering and more about field craft. The preventive work still requires imagination, but imagination of a different type. The intellectual effort has to shift to the intelligence side, fathoming what the adversaries are, or might be, thinking. The most profound conceptual and intellectual challenges revolve around structuring the intelligence task, giving it form and substance, dividing and distributing the work across myriad contributing agencies, and producing in the end some assurance that what can be done, or should be done, is in fact being done. Given the conceptual difficulty of this task, two temptations arise whenever the risk to be controlled is both catastrophic in nature and involves adversaries.

The first temptation is for policymakers to divert the available funds away from prevention and use them instead to bolster reactive capacities. It is intellectually more straightforward (in fact, very little challenge at all) to engage in broadcast dissemination of funds for decentralized investment, rather than figuring out centrally how best to invest in improving intelligence capabilities. The danger, of course, is that the money gets frittered away on an array of locally determined priorities (for example, new mobile command centers or the latest interoperable radio systems), the costs of which can more easily be justified because of the equipment's broader versatility. The resulting investment strategy neglects the principal imperative for this class of risks: to improve prevention.

The second temptation is to retreat from the challenge posed by these poorly behaved risks by referring to a broader class of risks, most of which behave more nicely. In these other areas it is easier to define success, measure progress, and thereby justify the costs and inconveniences imposed on others. Adopting a broader perspective (that is, considering a wider range of risks) may reveal an array of exciting opportunities for collaboration. But that array may, ultimately, be a dangerous distraction from the critical task.

Promoting Wellness or Attacking Disease?

In assessing risk-control strategies and tactics, another useful diagnostic check is to determine where the balance of attention lies: with the *construction of particular systems,* or with the *destruction of particular risks.*

In the field of public health, *promoting wellness* (or *promoting healthy living*) and *disease control* both play important roles and make important contributions. But these two types of work are quite different from each other. Wellness programs promote a range of positive behaviors: adopting a sensible diet, getting enough sleep and exercise, managing stress, adopting safe sexual practices, and generally taking care of oneself and one's physical, psychological, and social needs. Positive (recommended) behaviors can be defined, and compliance with a wellness program or regime will surely deliver some benefits in terms of disease control, reducing the risk of certain illnesses such as heart disease, hypertension, and diabetes. But wellness programs are not organized around specific diseases. Rather they are organized around specific aspects of human behavior, such as diet, sleep, and exercise.

By contrast, epidemiologists organize their analysis and recommendations around specific diseases. They examine pathogens under the microscope, observe their properties, and study their transmission mechanisms.

They use what they learn to find a vulnerability they can exploit. They search for a way to *defeat* the disease. That might mean hardening the target (inoculating potential victims) or removing a vector (such as mosquitoes) on which transmission depends. That might mean isolating an outbreak geographically (for example, through ring-containment strategies) or figuring out how to prevent it from skipping from one generation to the next. Epidemiologists think like saboteurs. They search for a specific vulnerability, something vital to the disease's propagation, and exploit it. They engage in the science of destruction: the *sabotage of harms.*

In many risk-control settings, the positive construction of systems gets a lot more attention than the deliberate sabotage of harms. The two modes of behavior, of course, are deeply intertwined and serve the same overall purposes, at least in theory. But the *system focus* is more concrete and intellectually straightforward than the *risk-control* focus, and therefore the system focus too often dominates the agenda. Systems represent *tools,* and a tool focus specifies *what we shall do.* Risks constitute *tasks,* and a task focus explores *what's out there.* The former (*what we shall do*) is much easier to specify, divide, monitor, measure, and report on than the latter. Even more so when the risks in the task environment display such a dense collection of confounding qualities.

The case narrative mentions a range of systems improvements, but the discussions seem to gravitate toward two in particular: enhanced perimeter controls and better information systems. The consortium spends some time considering what might or might not constitute a good enough fence and whether the rules regarding perimeter controls should be prescriptive or allow for variation according to the context. They also worked extremely hard on establishing protocols for better and earlier information sharing in order to improve what they termed *maritime domain awareness*—which means knowing in real time what, and who, is where—making it easier, potentially, to spot anomalous patterns and unauthorized activities.

Given the broad portfolio of risks under consideration, however, it is worth checking to see which ones might be materially affected by these two systems. The first two columns of table 3-3 indicate which systems seem obviously relevant to which categories of risk. Enhanced perimeter security seems most relevant to destructive attacks (categories 1 and 2) if they come overland and to the theft of cargo from port storage facilities or from ships in port (category 7). Port access controls should also help to control illegal immigration (categories 8 and 9), although they do so by controlling who *leaves* the port, rather than by preventing entry.

Table 3-3. *Other Implications for Port Security*

	Category	Relevance of fences (land-perimeter security)	Relevance of enhanced domain awareness (information sharing)	Role of ships' crews
1	Destructive attack on port	From land	✓	Source of risk
2	Destructive attack on high-value installation	From land	✓	Source of risk
3	Transshipment of destructive materials (WMD)		✓	Either
4	Destructive accident for port		✓	Partner in control
5	Destructive accident: high-value installation		✓	Partner in control
6	Smuggling through the port		✓	Either
7	Theft of cargo from port or ships in port	✓	✓	Either
8	Illegal immigration, stowaways	✓		Either
9	Illegal immigration, ships' crew (jumpers)	✓	✓	Source of risk
10	Maritime attacks (sabotage or terrorism) at sea		✓	Partner in control
11	Piracy or theft of ships at sea		✓	Partner in control
12	Maritime safety at sea			Partner in control
13	Murder or other crimes on board at sea		✓	Either

The column for enhanced maritime domain awareness suggests considerably broader relevance for these information systems and information-sharing agreements than for enhanced perimeter security. But it would still be a mistake to imagine that implementation of this system (with all its substantial and logistical challenges) will lead automatically to the reduction of risk. It merely provides the opportunity for improved threat detection and better informed responses when issues arise. Modern *intelligence failures* seem seldom to involve situations in which the relevant authorities lacked the relevant data. More often they *had* the data but had not done the analysis, or had not connected the dots, or had lacked imagination in figuring out what they should be looking for within the data. It turns out that providing the underlying data infrastructure is very much a *systems* enhancement, a broadly useful positive program, like wellness. But *using* it effectively to spot and suppress emerging threats is by no means guaranteed without proactive exploration of the task environment; that is, deliberate navigation of the textured landscape of risks and threats that might arise. Data richness does not necessarily lead to intelligence richness.

Choosing Regulatory Structures in a Risk-Control Environment

Success, in risk-control operations, means spotting emerging or developing threats early and suppressing them before they do much harm. Choosing a suitable regulatory structure means settling three things: First, who is in a position to identify which risks? Second, who has the capacity to control them, once they have been spotted? Third, which parties might be friend or foe with respect to which risks?

To imagine that the answers to these three questions would be the same for all risks would be to miss some important nuances of the risk-control business. The answers might be quite different for different classes of risk. One party—a company, for instance—might be perfectly capable of spotting some risks concentrated at their level and visible within their data. But they might have no chance of spotting risks broadly distributed across an industry.

Moreover, a specific stakeholder group might be a natural friend (partner) in control of one type of risk and a natural foe (adversary) with respect to others. If one all-inclusive consortium is created to tackle *port security*, and port security in fact comprises myriad different risks, then it is perfectly plausible that, for some classes of risk, this is the wrong consortium. The third column on table 3-3, to illustrate this, looks at the role one might expect ships' crews to play. Of course the Coast Guard should consult with them, generally speaking, to understand their interests and perspectives, learn from their experience, and gain their cooperation as far as possible. But officials should also understand how the nature of the regulatory relationship would vary, given different risks under consideration. Ships' crews are natural partners in risk-control operations aimed at accidents, maritime safety, and attacks on ships at sea by pirates or terrorists (that is, risk categories 4, 5, 10, 11, and 12). But crews or crew members might be conspirators in any destructive attack, or transgressors themselves as illegal immigrants (risk categories 1, 2, and 9). And their role could easily be either friend or foe, depending on the specific scenario, within each of the remaining categories (3, 6, 7, 8, and 13). So the role of different actors can vary by risk.

The narrative suggests that the Coast Guard, as lead agency, considered its newly formed *consortium* a broad positive good. Maybe it was, for a while, and with respect to certain tasks—such as getting legislation passed in a hurry. But in the longer term, as they grapple with the ongoing operational demands of risk control, they will need to think more carefully about who should be at the table when it comes to strategy design. One does not generally want one's adversaries to have a vote, or even to know what you are planning, when it comes to detecting their schemes and thwarting their purposes.

Nor is it clear that one particular regulatory structure would be right for all types of risk. The natural locus for risk identification and the locus for risk control might be different for different risks. Much of the work of (social) regulatory agencies involves spotting and controlling risks of various kinds, the majority of which arise from the conduct of regulated industries. What type of relationship should be formed, then, between regulator and regulated? The answer, when one holds in mind the textured landscape of risks to be controlled, is, It depends. For some risks the interests of regulator and regulated are well aligned, in which case collaboration makes sense, and supervision or oversight may be less necessary. For other risks, private and public purposes are directly at odds, in which case it makes no sense to assume symbiosis or common purpose.

The choice of regulatory structure—and to some degree the style or nature of regulatory interaction—will largely be determined by the answers to two questions: First, who will be responsible for identifying risks? This includes selecting and prioritizing familiar risks, as well as monitoring for novel and emerging ones. And second, who will be responsible for designing and implementing interventions for identified risks? The answers come in various permutations and combinations and give rise to four common models (or structures) of regulatory interaction.[11]

In model 1,

—The regulator takes responsibility for identifying risks.

—The regulator also takes the lead in analyzing and prioritizing risks, and designing the interventions.

—The regulator then stipulates actions required from industry necessary to control the risk.

—Regulatory requirements tend to be highly prescriptive (rule based), and regulatory oversight focuses on compliance and enforcement.

In model 2,

—The regulator takes responsibility for identifying risks.

—The regulator requires industry to control the specified risks, but allows them flexibility in choosing how to do so.

—The regulator stipulates risk-control performance goals for industry, which can be specified for known risks.

—The nature of regulatory oversight tends to be performance based.

In model 3,

—The regulator requires each regulated entity to design, and then operate, its own risk-management system (RMS) or safety-management system (SMS).

—The regulator takes a flexible approach, permitting each company to tailor the design of its RMS/SMS, bearing in mind the company's size, complexity, and the nature of its business.

—The role of the regulator is to approve proposed RMS/SMS designs at the outset and then to audit the operation of them over time, recognizing that each one may well be different.

In model 4,

—An industry association takes the lead in identifying industrywide risks and proposing remedies. The association acts as intermediary between the regulator and the regulated companies, playing negotiating and conciliation roles as well as playing its part in risk-management operations.

—The association may operate industrywide monitoring systems, which will therefore identify some risks that would not be visible to specific companies acting alone.

—Interventions may be designed or implemented either at the association level or at the company level.

—The role of the regulator is to oversee and monitor the combined effectiveness of the association and its industry members in identifying and dealing with the risks that arise within that industry.

It seems from the case narrative that Coast Guard officials have unambiguously selected model 3, apparently assuming that this model will turn out to be equally appropriate for each type of risk they confront. Or maybe they did not assume that at all, but discovered (as Captain Englebert states in an interview) that "flexibility was the key" to getting regulations agreed upon and passed.

Consider for a moment, though, what types of risk one might expect to be well controlled under the structure of model 3. Each organization gets to design its own risk-management system. These vary enormously, given the wide range of different industrial groups and actors. The Coast Guard is subsequently deluged with applications for approval and, to deal with the load, ends up deploying new recruits and inexperienced officers to evaluate the risk-management plans submitted. The way this unfolds suggests the process of getting everything approved was what seemed most important at the time, and that leaves wide open the question of subsequent risk-management effectiveness.

There might be hope, of course, if the public interest in port security and the interests of the myriad private parties were, in fact, well aligned. In that case, the regulator might have some confidence that gentle nudges, good will, and shared concerns would be enough to generate suitable designs and proper operation of risk controls by the regulated entities.

But it is a common mistake in regulatory policy to assume that one structure will deal equally well with all types of risk. In fact, selection of model 3 will likely result in a specific subset of risks being well taken care of with others much less so. This model will likely serve well in tackling the specific subset of risks that

—can be identified through monitoring conducted at the level of a single corporate entity (that is, that they can spot),

—that entity is willing to acknowledge (that is, has no incentive to hide),

—that entity has an interest in controlling (that is, where their private interests align with public interests), and

—that entity is capable of tackling.

Experience in other regulatory professions suggests that this subset turns out to be quite limited. It is also the subset of risks best controlled already, as these are precisely the parts of the risk-control agenda that align well with private parties' interests and capabilities. It seems unlikely, given the genesis of the port security initiative, that these would be the important risks to emphasize at this time. The real challenge during this period lay, surely, with risks that were seldom identifiable from the vantage point of one company and were almost never controllable without higher level planning and substantial interaction with the intelligence community.

Does this mean, then, that decentralized design and company-specific implementations play no useful role in systemwide security? In fact, they do have a role. Decentralized security *systems* contribute to overall security *systems:* like wellness programs, but at a lower level. But do they also contribute to effective risk control and threat mitigation? Yes, they can do that too, but only for a predictably small subset of risks, as discussed above.

Is this therefore a suitable approach to building a risk-control apparatus focused primarily on issues of national security? Certainly not. Parceling security work out among corporations is not the same job as structuring an intelligence operation in a way that makes sense given the nature of the potential threats.

Conclusions

The purpose of this analysis is to clarify—from an operational risk-management perspective—what the Coast Guard and its partners have already achieved and what remains to be done. To that end, this essay explores the risk terrain, beginning the work of teasing apart the multiplicity of risks, contemplating their various properties, and testing the relevance of particular tools (security systems) for the control of different risks. It also considers the balance of attention paid to specific security systems, as opposed to specific security threats. Finally, it considers a range of regulatory structures and questions the appropriateness and potential motivation for the choices Coast Guard officials actually made.

Clearly much has already been accomplished, and valuable groundwork has been laid for improved risk control. Equally clearly, much remains to be done to give form and structure to ongoing risk-control operations. The following five achievements are noted, each with its disclaimer.

—*Achievement:* On the positive side, Captain Englebert and her extraordinary array of partners forged a consensus sufficient to support passage of regulations and to get that job done within a remarkably short period. *However:* The ways in which the consortium will actually work together in the ongoing business of risk identification and control have yet to be specified or developed. The case narrative does not describe effective collaborative action aimed at, or organized around, any specific risk; nor has it developed any protocols for tackling work of that type in the future.

—*Achievement:* The network of relationships formed, spanning an extraordinary range of interested parties, should provide a basis for improved communication and information sharing in the future. *However:* It is not yet clear if or how this network has been or can be deployed around any specific risk-mitigation tasks or projects. It is not clear if there is any continuing schedule of meetings for this purpose or a clear understanding about who has the responsibility for setting the risk-control agenda, prioritizing the issues to be addressed, and calling together the right set of players in each case.

Achievement: The initiative focused on the enhancement of specific security systems, notably, perimeter controls and *maritime domain awareness* information systems. *However:* The case narrative reveals very little attention to the core task of identifying and mitigating specific threats or risks. A task focus, in this setting and given the nature of the principal threats faced, demands a much stronger emphasis on intelligence networks and links to the rest of the international intelligence system and possibly less reliance on physical security.

—*Achievement:* The consortium was able to reach agreement on a specific regulatory structure, which emphasized flexibility and avoided the inefficiencies of one-size-fits-all rules. *However:* The regulatory structure selected deals effectively with only a subset of the risks confronted and is not optimal for many others. Coast Guard officials may have fallen into the trap, in the short term, of adopting the same regulatory approach for all categories of risk. In time, one would expect more careful examination of different risks to lead to more insightful judgments about who can spot them and who can suppress them. Such insights, in turn, should lead to a more nuanced view of relevant regulatory structures and styles.

—*Achievement:* Officials have perhaps been artful in using the urgency, post 9/11, to upgrade their information systems and secure better data sharing across the industry. The enhanced *maritime domain awareness* is a valuable and significant accomplishment and provides useful opportunities relevant across a broad range of threats. *However:* A data-rich environment by no means guarantees an effective analytic operation. It provides the opportunity for enhanced vigilance but does not itself constitute or lead to the exercise of analytic vigilance. Intelligence does not spring forth naturally from fertile data sets; it has to be deliberately extracted. Nor does analysis blossom by itself, no matter how data rich the environment; it has to be designed, planted, nurtured, and practiced. Relevant analyses will be commissioned and good use made of analytic products only if the analytic operations are embedded within a well-designed intelligence structure.

Hopefully these summary observations serve to illuminate the distinction between *enhancing security systems* and *enhancing security,* perhaps not entirely resolving our conundrum but revealing enough of its intricacies and texture to provide some clearer sense of the work still to be done.

Notes

1. For an examination of the challenge of operational risk control in the context of social regulatory agencies, see Malcolm K. Sparrow, *The Regulatory Craft: Controlling Risks, Solving Problems, and Managing Compliance* (Brookings Press, 2000).

2. The management systems (or infrastructure) required to help an agency organize risk-control tasks are described in ibid., chap. 11. See also Malcolm K. Sparrow, *The Character of Harms: Operational Challenges in Control* (Cambridge University Press, 2008), chap. 7.

3. Sparrow, *The Character of Harms*, p. 15.

4. A collection of regulatory innovations of this type is presented in Sparrow, *The Regulatory Craft*, chap. 6. A more recent collection is described in Sparrow, *The Character of Harms*, pp. 5–7.

5. Sparrow, *The Character of Harms*, p. 69.

6. Ibid., p. 27.

7. For an account of the attack on the Black Tom Arms Depot in New York Harbor, July 30, 1916, see Zachary Tumin, "From Safety to Security: The United States Coast Guard and the Move to a Global Network of Secure Ports, Cargos, Crews, and Vessels," Working Paper (Harvard Kennedy School of Government, 2009), p. 1.

8. See the definition at www.merriam-webster.com/dictionary/conundrum.

9. ISPS Code, MTSA 2002, and the Port Security Act 2006.

10. For a discussion of performance measurement in the context of risk control, see Sparrow, *The Character of Harms*, chap. 6.

11. My co-authors, during the course of our project discussions, raised the possibility of a fifth model, which one might call "risk control without a top." Such a model assumes no one necessarily in charge and reliance on a wide range of actors and deliberative processes to do the work of identifying risks, prioritizing them, and forming coalitions around them. Other chapters in this volume explore that idea more fully and examine the conditions under which it might or might not provide adequate protection.

ROBERT D. BEHN

4

Portstat: How the Coast Guard Could Use the PerformanceStat Leadership Strategy to Improve Port Security

In 1994 the New York City Police Department, under the leadership of Commissioner William Bratton and Deputy Commissioner Jack Maple, created CompStat, the NYPD's leadership strategy for reducing crime in the city by improving the performance of the department's seventy-six precincts. Since then, numerous police departments have created their own versions of CompStat. Moreover, a variety of other public agencies have adapted the CompStat leadership strategy to improve their own performance. In New York City these include JobStat and ChildStat; elsewhere, they have names such as KidStat and SchoolStat. Moreover, a number of governmental jurisdictions have adapted the strategy to improve the performance of all of their agencies, including Baltimore's CitiStat and Maryland's StateStat.

Collectively, I call these leadership strategies PerformanceStat. This covers various AgencyStat strategies (such as CompStat and SchoolStat) as well as JurisdictionStat strategies (such as CitiStat and StateStat). All of these leadership strategies are designed to improve performance by producing better results.

At the national level, however, few U.S. departments or agencies have sought to employ this approach to performance leadership.[1] This raises a question: *Could* the United States Coast Guard (USCG) adapt the PerformanceStat leadership strategy to help it improve security at the nation's ports? And if the answer to this question is yes (or even maybe), it raises a second question: *How* should the USCG incorporate and *adapt* what *core concepts* of the PerformanceStat approach to achieve its specific purpose?

What Is PerformanceStat?

Unfortunately, too many agencies and jurisdictions create what can only be called MimicStat—a superficial mimicry of CompStat's most visible components. They miss one or more of the core concepts that help to make this strategy effective. Consequently, to separate out those adaptations that have the potential to improve performance from those that are much less likely to do so, I have created the following definition:

> A jurisdiction or agency is employing a PerformanceStat *leadership strategy* if, in an effort to achieve specific public *purposes,* its leadership team *persists* in holding an ongoing series of *regular, frequent, integrated meetings,* during which the chief executive and/or the principal members of the chief executive's leadership team plus the director (and the top managers) of different subunits use *current data* to *analyze* specific, previously defined aspects of each unit's past *performance;* to provide *feedback* on recent progress compared with *targets;* to *follow up* on previous decisions and commitments to produce *results;* to examine and *learn* from each unit's efforts to improve *performance;* to identify and solve *performance-deficit* problems; and to set and achieve the next *performance targets.*

This definition is not all that constraining. Nevertheless, it does include several key features that can separate a potentially effective PerformanceStat strategy from the pretenders:

—Leadership's focus on specific public purposes;

—Leadership's use of current data that relate to that purpose and help reveal whether performance is improving or not;

—Leadership's conduct of regular, frequent, integrated meetings at which efforts to improve and progress are examined in a way that promotes organizationwide learning; and

—Leadership's persistent effort to improve performance.

Operationally, when designing a PerformanceStat leadership strategy, the agency's or jurisdiction's leadership team would need to:

—specify the public *purpose* they are trying to achieve,

—identify specific *performance deficits,*

—establish specific *performance targets* for particular *results* to be achieved,

—decide what performance *data* they will collect,

—build a small staff (and organizationwide capacity) to *analyze* these data,

—determine how they will conduct the *meetings,*

—assemble the necessary *infrastructure,*

—build the requisite *operational capacity,*

—create explicit mechanisms to provide *feedback* on progress and to *follow up* on the problems identified, solutions proposed, and decisions made at the meetings, and

—think through carefully how they need to *adapt* the features and principles of other versions of PerformanceStat to their own purposes, problems, and circumstances.[2]

Adapting PerformanceStat to Create PortStat

In an effort to improve the security of the nation's ports, the commandant of the United States Coast Guard could choose to create a PerformanceStat approach for the entire nation. Or to improve port security in one of the USCG's nine districts, its commander could (without any nudging from USCG headquarters) create its own PerformanceStat. Or to improve security at one of the USCG's forty-five port zones, the captain of the port could create its own PerformanceStat. Indeed, USCG headquarters, or a district, or a port could choose to employ a PerformanceStat strategy for any of its eleven statutory missions.

Still, the mission to which the Coast Guard devotes the most resources is "ports, waterways, and coastal security."[3] Moreover, for each port, Congress has designated the USCG's captain of the port to be the federal maritime security coordinator (FMSC) who "leads the collaborative and collective efforts of the Federal, state, local, and private entities who share responsibility for protection of the maritime transportation sub-sector."[4]

Thus the USCG—because of both this congressional mandate and its reputation for competence—is the obvious candidate for creating a PerformanceStat strategy to improve port security. Indeed, at all three levels the Coast Guard could take the initiative to create its own PerformanceStat: undertaking an enhanced effort to improve its own performance on those aspects of port security that it (mostly, primarily) controls or, at least, influences; learning how to improve its own performance on this specific problem, thus learning how to improve performance in general; and then convening others to think about how to improve performance on problems that require collaboration with other organizations (both public and private).

Before, however, the Coast Guard could engage other organizations in a collaborative, PerformanceStat-like effort to improve port security, it needs first to figure out how to make the strategy work internally. It needs to create a platform upon which to build a collaborative strategy.[5] Moreover, whenever an organization seeks to employ a strategy developed by others, it needs to determine the principles that underlie that strategy and then figure out how to *adapt* these principles to its own unique circumstances. In many ways, the USCG is not the NYPD. Consequently, if the USCG decides to develop its own PerformanceStat leadership strategy, it would need to *adapt* the NYPD concept to its own purposes, resources, and culture.

Thus the USCG's first step could be to concentrate strictly on improving its own performance on port security. This could be an even narrower focus than an AgencyStat; you can think of it more as ProblemStat, using the strategy to improve performance on just one of the organization's many responsibilities.[6] This would focus less on improving ongoing operations and more on eliminating (or at least mitigating) one very specific and very serious problem. In the process, the USCG—not just its top leadership, but the entire organization—would learn how it could make the strategy work internally to pursue more effectively all of its eleven statutory missions.

Unfortunately, the commandant does not run the nation's port security alone. Neither does any one of the nine district commanders solely run port security in his or her own district. And none of the forty-five captains of the port solely runs security at his or her port. Numerous other public safety agencies at the local, state, and federal levels have some responsibility, as do a variety of private-sector organizations, such as port authorities, shipping firms, and liquified natural gas (LNG) facilities. Thus any comprehensive effort to improve port security will necessarily require a collaboration among a variety of organizations.

Still, all of those organizations will not automatically cooperate, let alone collaborate. Someone—some organization—has to take on the inaugural responsibility for leadership. And the Coast Guard is the logical candidate. (See Stephen Goldsmith, chapter 7, this volume.) Indeed, at each of the USCG's forty-five ports, the U.S. Office of Management and Budget emphasizes the responsibilities of the USCG's federal maritime security coordinators:

> Each FMSC exercises authority by empanelling an Area Maritime Security Committee (AMSC) with an all-inclusive maritime membership that draws from responsible federal, state, local, and private entities (stakeholders) and ensures their participation in antiterrorism planning and preparedness activities.[7]

Consequently, once the USCG has used an internal PerformanceStat strategy to produce better results on its own efforts to improve port security, it could engage other organizations in achieving this important public purpose in a more collaborative approach, to create something that would look like CollaborationStat. In this chapter I suggest how the USCG's commandant might adapt a PerformanceStat approach to help the Coast Guard achieve its statutory mission for "ports, waterways, and coastal security" and how it might build on this internal platform to create a more collaborative approach—to create something that would look like CollaborationStat.[8]

Call this comprehensive leadership strategy PortStat.

Purpose

Always start with purpose.[9] And what public purpose might the USCG use a PortStat strategy to achieve? For this illustration, I propose that the purpose is to "protect every port from a terrorist attack and to protect the rest of the country from an attack that results from terrorist individuals or weapons being smuggled through a port."

This is a very ambitious mission. After all, there exist a heterogeneity of ways that a terrorist could attack a port and perhaps even more ways that a terrorist could smuggle weapons or individuals through a port. Nevertheless, this is one of the USCG's eleven statutory (and quite uncontroversial) missions. This purpose will generate little debate either within the Coast Guard, among the members of the Area Maritime Security Committees, or among U.S. citizens.

Data

Any attempt to improve the performance of any organization requires data. It needs data to identify its performance deficits—the problems along its value chain (from inputs to processes to outputs to outcomes) that are preventing the organization (and its collaborators) from producing better results.[10] It needs data to reveal whether its performance is improving or not.

If the USCG is to create a PortStat (or any other) strategy to improve performance, what kind of data would it need? What kind of data would help the USCG detect important patterns that jeopardize port security, compare (and learn from) the security-enhancing efforts of different USCG districts and ports, and assess whether security is improving? (Note: when an effort to improve performance requires cross-organization collaboration, the members of the collaborative need to agree not only on the purpose or purposes that they hope to achieve but also on the data that they will employ to identify problems and measure progress.)

Unfortunately, when it comes to collecting relevant, useful data, the NYPD has several advantages that the USCG lacks.

—In the normal course of business, each of NYPD's precincts collects the same, common set of data that are directly related to their purpose: data on arrests (outputs) and data on a set of standard and common crimes (outcomes). In contrast, the USCG faces unknown threats; thus it is not obvious what data the USCG should collect, let alone how it might collect them.

—Every day, the NYPD gets a large number of individual data points, a data point for each arrest and a data point for each reported crime. Even if the USCG could get some kind of data on terrorist activities in one of its ports, it might not have the large number of data points necessary to facilitate analyses that reveal vulnerabilities and patterns.

—The NYPD gets data for a large number of subunits: seventy-six precincts. This facilitates comparative analysis of the effectiveness of different tactics. A small number of data points distributed over the USCG's nine districts or forty-five ports does not permit an easy comparison of effectiveness.

Obviously, in attempting to improve port security by employing the principles of the NYPD's CompStat, the USCG will need to make some significant adaptations in its search for data.

The Potential of Near-Miss Data. The problem that the USCG has in collecting data that can reveal how well it is doing in preventing a terrorist disaster is similar (though not identical) to the problem that the Federal Aviation Administration has it collecting data that will reveal how well it is doing in preventing an airplane disaster. Actual disasters are very rare. But the FAA does have access to a kind of data that it finds useful: data on near misses, collected by Aviation Safety Reporting System.[11] U.S. airlines have very few airplane disasters, but they have many more near misses. And if the FAA can collect near-miss data, analyze these data, and use the conclusions of these analyses to drive down the number of near misses, it can reduce the probability (though not the certainty) of actual disasters.

This is, of course, a theory. Near-miss data are not outcome data. There is no guarantee that reducing near misses will automatically reduce the number or severity of airplane disasters. Nevertheless, an analysis of a near miss, or of a series of near misses, can reveal some performance deficits. Indeed, underlying this approach is the assumption that those events that are classified as near misses (according to some definition) have the potential, if the miss was a little nearer, to cause a serious accident. Thus the cause-and-effect theory is quite specific if unproven: If we reduce the number of near misses, we will reduce the potential for accidents and thus the number (and severity) of actual accidents.

Perhaps the Coast Guard could employ similar data. Perhaps it could collect near-miss data on the number of terrorist attacks that *almost* happened.

Perhaps it could collect data on the number of terrorists or weapons that were almost smuggled through each port and each district. If so, perhaps it could focus its efforts on reducing such near misses and, as a consequence, reduce the probability of a terrorist attack both in a port and within the United States.[12]

Of course, if the Coast Guard were collecting such data, it would not give them to me. And if it did give them to me, it would not permit me to publish them. So I have to invent some kind of near-miss data that may or may not be meaningful to the Coast Guard's efforts to improve port security, something like the characteristics of unauthorized breaches of security perimeters of critical facilities within ports.

The USCG's commandant and his leadership team might immediately dismiss such data as completely irrelevant to their most significant port-security problems. The commandant could easily decide that some other performance deficits (about which I know, and should be told, absolutely nothing) would be a more logical focus and a more advantageous first initiative for a PortStat strategy.[13] I focus on near misses not because I know they are very important but because they present an understandable problem that can illustrate the development of a PortStat leadership strategy.

Still, the breaching of security perimeters at U.S. ports is not automatically a trivial problem. Actually, most breakdowns in security involve some type of breach, whether it is a computer hacker breaching an information-technology firewall or a suicide bomber breaching a building's defenses. Indeed, the last dozen years have witnessed a variety of physical breaches of security boundaries:

—In December 1999 the "millennium bomber," Ahmed Ressam, nearly smuggled through Port Angeles, Washington, four times the quantity of explosives used to destroy the Murrah Federal Building in Oklahoma City. Ressam's target was the Los Angeles International Airport, but he was caught by customs and immigration officials.[14]

—In December 2009 Michaele and Tareq Salahi breached the security perimeter for a White House state dinner. Indeed, in less that thirty years, various individuals breached the security perimeter established by the U.S. Secret Service to protect the president and other dignitaries ninety-one times.[15] That's an average of three breaches a year. Indeed, given the large number of locations and dignitaries (both U.S. and foreign) that the Secret Service must protect, the opportunities for such breaches are obviously very high.[16]

—In January 2010 Hiasong Jiang snuck past a guard from the Transportation Security Administration and simply walked through an exit into the secure part of Newark Airport, causing the airport to be shut down for six hours.

—In November 2011 Delvonte Tisdale breached security at Charlotte Douglas International Airport, stowed away in the wheel well of a Boeing 737, and when the pilot put the landing gear down as the plane approached Boston, fell to the ground and died.

Obviously, the threats to the security perimeters at U.S. ports—from a multiplicity of small, unregulated boats to millions of cargo containers—are diverse and numerous.[17] Thus the opportunities for breaches in port security are countless and recurrent.

I am using security breaches at U.S. ports and near-miss data only as an example. I do not claim that this is the most important port-security problem faced by the Coast Guard or even the best way to launch a PortStat strategy. Instead, my purpose is to suggest how the Coast Guard, if it chose to, could use the problem of unauthorized breaches to launch a PortStat leadership strategy, learn from it, and adapt it. As USCG leaders in Washington—plus in the nine districts and forty-five ports—seek to learn how to employ the strategy, they could experiment with a series of adaptations to ensure that the strategy fits their organizational needs and cultures. Then they could further adapt the strategy to concentrate on the most important port security threats. (For an analytic framework for identifying the most important port security problems, see Malcolm Sparrow, chapter 3, this volume.)

Data and Quick, Small Wins. Moreover, I believe that any effort to improve the performance of any organization ought to begin with some small but quick wins. Any organization (public, private, or nonprofit) is skeptical of any new initiative. From their personal experience, many people will rely on the Lincolnian wisdom: "This, too, shall pass."[18] They will assume that they don't really need to put much effort into the latest new initiative, because they know, again from personal experience, that it will soon be superseded by the next new thing. Why bother? Thus in the spirit of Karl Weick's "strategy of small wins," the commandant might begin not necessarily with one of the most important security problems but with a problem that satisfies three criteria.[19] The problem is one that is very significant, for which the Coast Guard can produce some quick results, and from which it can learn.

Other problems, accompanied by other forms of data, might also satisfy these three criteria (significance of problem, results, and lessons). For example, terrorists could use a small boat to attack a larger ship (as they did with the USS *Cole* in Yemen) or a facility on the water's edge. Indeed, the recent

USCG commandant, Admiral Thad Allen, believes that small boats are the biggest waterborne risk to port security.[20] At a meeting of the International Maritime Association, Allen observed, "If you look at piracy, the terrorist attacks in Mumbai, as well as the use of self-propelled semisubmersible vessels to smuggle narcotics, the common thread is the use of small, unregulated, and unmonitored vessels. . . . We must raise awareness of small vessel movements so we can identify the few hostile vessels from the thousands of legitimate recreational and work boats that ply our shores."[21] Thus the USCG could choose to launch a PortStat strategy by focusing on reducing the threat from such "small, unregulated, and unmonitored vessels." This is, I think, a much more complex problem.

If this is true, it might make more sense to start with a simpler problem (barrier breaching is only one such possibility). This would permit the USCG to *experiment* with a PortStat leadership strategy for just one aspect of port security and *learn* how to make it work in the Coast Guard. Then it could make the necessary adaptations that result from this learning and apply this revised strategy to more complex problems. Having experimented, learned, and adapted again, it could then take on the even more demanding challenge of collaborating with other organizations that have a role in ensuring port security.

Consequently, to illustrate how the Coast Guard might initiate and evolve a PortStat leadership strategy, I have chosen to use the example of barrier breaches. The data for such breaches may not now exist, though it is possible to envision how such data for this near-miss category might be collected. Thus I can use such (potential) data to help illustrate how the Coast Guard could develop a PortStat leadership strategy employing such data or whatever data it found more relevant.[22] In doing so, the USCG could develop the organizational capacity to apply its PortStat approach to more demanding security problems as well as uncover other security vulnerabilities that it could seek to reduce or eliminate.

Collecting the Data. To obtain near-miss data, the USCG would first need to decide what exactly counted as an unauthorized breach of a security perimeter of a critical facility. Thus data collectors need several definitions. For example:

—A *critical facility* is any area within a region of a port that a terrorist could use to inflict significant harm or to which it could cause significant harm. (For example, a LNG tank farm.)

—A *security perimeter* is the border of a critical facility that is somehow secured. (For example, a fence around a LNG tank farm.)

—An *unauthorized breach* is any crossing of the security perimeter of a critical facility by someone who is not entitled to do so. (For example, a drunk college student climbing over the fence around a LNG tank farm.)

I have no idea how many such unauthorized breaches of a security perimeter of a critical facility might occur in a large, tier 1 port (such as Long Beach or New York). There might be five a year; there might be five a day. If there are only five a year, it will be difficult to analyze the data to detect patterns, to determine what ports have developed a better approach to preventing such breaches, or to assess whether efforts to prevent such unauthorized breaches were improving security. (In this case, the USCG should focus first on a different near-miss problem.) If however some ports average five such breaches each day—or even just one breach each day—there will be enough data for analysts to begin looking for patterns, comparing different districts and ports, and assessing macrotrends.

Finally, note that these data would not just include the number of unauthorized breaches during a week or month or quarter. Rather, each such data point would (just like each data point for crime) include a variety of different dimensions. For example,

—Type of facility breached
—Date, day of week, and time of day of the breach
—Location on the security perimeter of the breach
—Method used to commit the breach
—Characteristics of the facility that was breached
—Characteristics of the specific segment of the barrier that was breached
—Depth of the breach
—Seriousness of the breach
—Characteristics of the person or persons who committed the breach
—Reason (if any) given for making the breach

Some of these data points might be for breaches committed on Saturday night by drunks on a dare, drunks who were not engaged in any act of terrorism. These data should not be discarded, for they too would be helpful. This is because every breach suggests a vulnerability. It could be a simple, single vulnerability (such as a hole in a specific fence) that could be easily fixed. It could be a complex pattern of vulnerabilities (such as security guards from numerous firms who fall asleep at 4:00 a.m. on Saturday morning) that would require a more systematic response.

There exists one other mechanism for generating data on the vulnerability of various kinds of barriers to a breach: a "red-team" attack on a facility or a port. Of course, for such an exercise to generate useful data and learning, the red team has to guess imaginatively: What are a port's real vulnerabilities? If the red team doesn't guess well, it will test a vulnerability that potential terrorists have ignored in favor of a more penetrable barrier or a more significant target. (For a discussion of this approach, see Elaine Kamarck, chapter 8, this volume.)

Output Data versus Outcome Data. Unfortunately, the data the Coast Guard would really like to have are not just output data but outcome data. The USCG would like outcome data that tells it how safe a port really is. Yes, a decrease in the number of breaches at a port might suggest that the port is getting safer. But it also might suggest that the terrorists have invented more nefarious tactics for attacking a port—tactics that do not require the breaching of barriers or, at least, not the barriers on which the Coast Guard has focused.

This is a common dilemma. It faces, for example, the FAA. Near misses, which are just outputs, may go down; this, however, does not guarantee that flying is safer. A drop in near misses merely suggests that flying is safer; it does not prove it. On January 19, 2009, Chesley "Sully" Sullenberger "landed" US Airways Flight 1549 "safely" in the Hudson River—"safely" meaning that no one died. Did this, however, imply that the efforts of the FAA and the airlines had made flying more safe or less safe? And given that this crash was caused by a flock of geese flying into the airplane's engine (or by an airplane flying into a flock of geese), *who* should be responsible for doing *what* to prevent this "breach" of an airplane engine from happening again?

Moreover, even comparative outcome data may not prove anything. On safety, Southwest Airlines has some very impressive outcome data. In over 18 million flights, Southwest has never had a fatal crash. But does that prove that Southwest is a safer airline than either American with six fatal events in over 20 million flights or United with six fatal events in over 16 million flights?[23] It certainly looks that way. If you have a choice of flying from city A to city B on Southwest or American or United, it might be safer (and cheaper too) to fly on Southwest. But the character of routes that American and United fly are different from those flown by Southwest. Moreover, the caveat found in the advertisements for every mutual fund also applies to these data: "Past performance is no guarantee of future results."

Analysis

Thus any PerformanceStat strategy requires analysts who will probe, scrutinize, and interrogate the data. Ideally, this kind of thinking would be done both by a group of PortStat analysts in USCG headquarters in Washington and by at least one PortStat analyst in each district (and perhaps even by a PortStat analyst in each of the seventeen tier 1 ports, if not all forty-five ports). Regardless of where these PortStat analysts sit, however, they will be looking for information that will help them

—Distinguish between singular vulnerabilities that can be directly eliminated by unique actions and patterns of vulnerabilities that require systemic remedies,

—Identify such patterns of security breaches and suggest possible systemic solutions that could be applied portwide, districtwide, or even nationwide,

—Compare the operational effectiveness of different ports or districts in reducing the number and seriousness of unauthorized breaches in an effort to develop systematic evidence of what operational tactics and strategies are working, so that every unit can learn and improve.

There exists no formula for this kind of analytic work. It requires creative people who are willing to muck around in the data, rummaging for patterns that others don't see, foraging for insights into the potential behavior of potential terrorists who might discover potential vulnerabilities, dissecting coincidences for something more than pure randomness, delving further into an observation that generates a "that's funny" reaction.[24]

The analyst is looking for something but doesn't know what that something is. The analyst might have a theory—perhaps something based on experience with some apparently similar data or perhaps a guess about what might be important if a connection can be found. Yet while pursuing this personal theory, the enterprising analyst is alert for other possibilities: blips in the data, things that don't add up (mathematically or metaphorically), something that doesn't quite look right. Indeed, when the ingenious analyst comes across something that generates a "that's funny" reaction, he or she is curious enough to go looking for what is behind the funniness.

Unfortunately, people with this kind of imaginative, innovative, and ingenious mind-set are rare. Indeed, they are often viewed by their more serious, sober, and staid colleagues as certifiably crazy. Yet this kind of analyst may be able to mine the data for insights that their more dignified peers will miss.

I assume neither that all of the knowledge about port security is located in USCG Washington headquarters nor that all of the learning will happen there. Any PerformanceStat approach—while focusing on specific results—delegates significant responsibility and discretion for producing those results to subunits in the field. This leadership strategy is not based on the assumption that all of the leadership, all of the knowledge, and all of the decisions (about both the problems on which to focus and the ways to deal with these problems) come from headquarters.

Initially, the Coast Guard's Intelligence Coordination Center in Washington might well have the primary responsibility for analyzing the data on breaches of security perimeters. For a PortStat strategy to be effective, however, each of the districts needs to also possess the capacity to analyze its own data. After all, there is no reason to believe—for breaches in security perimeters or for any other aspect of port security—that the nature of this problem will be the same in the Seventh District, headquartered in Miami, and the Seventeenth District, headquartered in Juneau. When launching any PerformanceStat initiative, one challenge is not to permit subunits to believe that all of the responsibility—for analysis, for strategy, and for leadership— resides in headquarters.

Searching for (and Learning from) Patterns. What would a pattern look like? This isn't obvious. It could consist of a time of day: a lot of breaches occurring between 2:00 a.m. and 5:00 a.m. It could consist of a type of breacher: drunk college students. It could consist of a type of facility: LNG tank farms. Or a pattern could be found mapping the data, as the NYPD did with crime. Yet detecting such a pattern doesn't automatically happen. If the data do not include any demographic information about the breachers, no analyst can discover that they are drunks, or college students, or illegal immigrants, or. . . . The analyst's ability to identify a pattern depends upon the data, either data that are automatically collected or data for which the analyst (based on some kind of hunch) goes looking.

What can be learned from an identified pattern could be even less obvious than the pattern itself. Suppose the data revealed that 15 percent of the breaches were drunk college students scaling the fences surrounding LNG tank farms on Saturday nights. What might be learned from this? A simple lesson could be that the LNG tank farms are not well protected; after all if drunk college students (who presumably did little advance planning before they set out on Saturday night to climb a fence) can breach the security boundary so frequently, LNG tank farms need to make major security improvements. These data might reveal a more significant insight, but only if the analyst is energetic and creative enough to go looking for it.

Comparing (and Learning from) Subunit Performance. The initial level of this analysis is relatively straightforward. The USCG has (presumably) chosen to collect data that relate to the performance of its districts and ports. For example, such data could include the number of breaches each month, the number of people (and their demographic characteristics) involved in each breach, the time of each breach, and the type of facility breached. From such data the PortStat analysts at USCG headquarters might discover that

Districts K and Z have had, during the past six months, significantly fewer LNG breaches than Districts J and W (with the numbers for Districts Q, T, U, V, and X falling somewhere in between).[25] This suggests that there might be something that can be learned from what is happening in Districts K and Z, something that Districts J and W (and the others) could employ to reduce their breaches.

Such data—perhaps simply displayed on a bar chart—capture everyone's attention. Comparative data (if the analysts have done the work necessary to make the raw data comparable) can reveal who is performing well and who isn't.[26] And they authorize almost anyone to ask the questions that are super-ficially objective but fundamentally about leadership: Why are Districts K and Z performing well? Why are Districts J and W not performing well? Indeed, everyone who looks at the comparative data is asking, if only silently, these same two questions. The commanders of Districts K and Z know this. And they recognize that, without a coherent and convincing explanation, their per-formance will be attributed to pure luck. The commanders of Districts J and W also know this. They recognize that, without some significant improve-ment, they will be evaluated by everyone else as inadequate, even incompetent.

Moreover, these data suggest that there might be something that can be learned from what is happening in Districts K and Z, something that Districts J and W (as well as Districts Q, T, U, V, and X) could employ to reduce their breaches. What, however, might be learned? This is not obvious. After all, the data do not speak for themselves.[27] In this case, the data do not reveal what (if anything) Districts K and Z are doing that could be profitably adapted by the other districts. These two districts might simply have fewer LNG tank farms or fewer college students to get drunk. Or the data could simply be random, so that we could expect both Districts J and W and Districts K and Z to regress toward the mean suggested by Q, T, U, V, and X; if so, next year the districts that post above average and below average results could be com-pletely different.

There are, however, analytical strategies for testing these explanations. The number of breaches could be divided by the number of tank farms or by the number of college students or by anything else that might distort comparisons among districts. And of course data collected over three years are less vulner-able to pure randomness than data collected over three months. Once, how-ever, the explanations that have nothing to do with the behavior of USCG dis-tricts have been eliminated, it is necessary to go looking for other possibilities.

The first step is simply to ask the "positive deviants" (the districts with the better data) what they are doing.[28] This might well be informative. District

K might have mapped out a specific strategy designed to deal with the patterns of LNG breaches that it had detected over the previous two years. Or District K might only offer a muddled explanation that is not in the least bit helpful. District Z might have no idea what (if anything) it was doing that might affect its low numbers. Or District Z (in an effort to affirm its managerial wizardry) might concoct an explanation that, upon examination, has little validity. Moreover, the actual relevance of either district's tactics won't really be known until some of the other districts adapt one of these tactics and discover whether or not it has any impact.

Meetings

The thinking that drives an effective PerformanceStat is not, however, done exclusively by a group of analytic wonks working in the basement of some headquarters annex. Much of the analytical and strategic thinking has to be done collectively by the organization's leadership: by the USCG commandant and his leadership team as well as by the commanders of the nine districts and their key staff. Moreover, a good deal of this analysis—debate, discussion, and learning—will need to take place at periodic meetings, when they all get together to examine their data and their strategies. Otherwise, the analyses would be little more than a technical exercise that fails to have any significant impact on operations. The regular meetings of any real PerformanceStat—the discussion among the organization's leadership team, the director, and the top managers of the subunits—converts what might be a weird wonkdom of enigmatic data and nerdy analysts into an opportunity for real performance leadership.

What are the operational requirements for these meetings? What is necessary to convert an ordinary gathering of top officials into a potentially effective PerformanceStat session? The several important features of these meetings include timing; leadership and participation; data, analysis, and performance deficits; learning; performance targets; and the essential, but often missing, follow-up.

Timing. PortStat meetings need, in some way, to be regular—perhaps quarterly, maybe monthly (though obviously no more frequent than updates of the data). The meetings could all be held at USCG headquarters; or during the year, three could be held in Washington and the other nine rotated among the nine districts. It might make sense to schedule them on, say, the second Friday of each month, so that the previous month's data would have been available for analysis by both headquarters and the districts. The primary intention behind this regularity is to establish the clear expectation that these meetings are the basic mechanism that the organization is using to ensure that all operational units are thinking analytically about how to improve specific aspects of their performance and acting intelligently on the learning generated by these analyses.

Leadership and Participation. PortStat meetings need to include the USCG commandant and his leadership team and the nine district commanders and their key staff.[29] The commandant needs to chair these meetings (at least initially) to establish that these sessions are, indeed, a core component of his effort to manage the organization and produce better results. After a year, or maybe even six months, the commandant could delegate responsibility for chairing the meetings (even if he was in attendance) to his vice-commandant or chief of staff—provided that this delegation is accompanied by an unambiguous signal that this individual speaks for the commandant.

Data, Analysis, and Performance Deficits. Effective PerformanceStat sessions usually begin with a presentation (either by the primary analysts or by a member of the organization's leadership team) reviewing the recent period's data and offering some analytical observations. The other option is to permit the subunits whose data are being examined to make an initial presentation.[30] Regardless of who begins the discussion by reviewing what data, the chair of the meeting needs to ensure that discussion focuses on three issues: the performance improvements that need to be made, the "performance deficits" that are revealed by the analyses of the data, and the possible actions that subunits or the entire organization could take to learn from the improvements so as to reduce or eliminate the deficits.

Learning. Different people can, of course, think of any particular PerformanceStat in different ways—as a practice, process, procedure, technique, system, model, or simply approach. And many people think of many PerformanceStats in terms of accountability—as primarily about imposing top-down accountability on the directors of subunits.[31] Indeed, at meetings of some versions of PerformanceStat, the questioning of subunit directors can be brutal. Implicitly, the underlying assumption is that this subunit director is indifferent to the need to improve performance or incompetent to do so. Thus the subunit director needs to be "held accountable."[32]

Yet to be truly effective—to help all subunits produce improved results—a PerformanceStat has to be at least as much about learning. Rather than simply berate the directors of subunits that are lagging, the leadership team needs to help them learn how to improve. For an AgencyStat—with each of the subunits having similar responsibilities—this learning is easier than with a JurisdictionStat. That is, if Districts K and Z have had significantly fewer breaches than other districts, the commanders of these two districts could be asked to explain *what* they are doing and *why* they think it works. Moreover, if the performance of Districts J and W is inadequate, the commandant could suggest that the commanders of these two districts ask those from K and Z for some advice. (And, if the formal and informal rewards are not limited, the commanders of Districts K and Z have no reason to withhold their insights.)[33]

Performance Targets. The PortStat session needs to conclude with some clear decisions about future actions. What is to be accomplished next? Who is responsible for making this happen? By when? Next year? Next quarter? Next month?

Given that the USCG is divided into nine districts (and forty-five ports), these are the subunits to which these operational responsibilities should be delegated. These are the units for which specific performance targets should be established. And, of course, these responsibilities and targets also need to be specified in the meeting's follow-up memo.

Follow-Up. Any PerformanceStat session has two foundations. The most obvious is the most recent period's data (and the insights revealed by the analyses of these data). There is, however, a second, less visible, yet essential foundation: What transpired at the previous meeting or meetings? What performance deficits were analyzed? What actions, tactics, or strategies did what units suggest could reduce or eliminate these performance deficits? What did different subunits report they learned from the discussion, and what new approaches did they say they would try? What other new approaches were proposed to deal with what performance deficits? And—perhaps most important—what *commitments* were made?

The first follow-up step needs to happen soon after each meeting, even by the end of the day. A PortStat analyst needs to prepare a detailed, follow-up memorandum that is then reviewed and signed by the commandant. This memo summarizes the discussion: what patterns and performance deficits were analyzed, what learning was derived from what the data revealed about the relative effectiveness of different subunits' efforts, what new approaches were suggested, and who made what commitments.

A simple follow-up memo serves several functions. It keeps everyone focused on both the long-term, underlying purpose and the short-term actions that need to be taken before the next PortStat meeting (and beyond). It creates an additional basis for future analysis and learning. It provides a foundation for the questions and discussion at the next meeting. And it reminds everyone that PortStat is not some fleeting fad; PortStat is here to stay.

Too often, organizations that claim to be employing their own version of PerformanceStat miss the importance of the follow-up.[34] They conduct each meeting as an independent activity, with little connection to the problems analyzed, issues examined, and commitments made at previous sessions. This is particularly true if the subunit directors are permitted to run the meetings; for if they want to escape both accountability and the need for learning, they can ensure that their next meeting is completely disconnected—in terms of both data and problems—from everything that has been discussed at recent sessions. This limits the opportunity for follow-up questions linked to past discussions and decisions.

If PortStat meetings are not to be a succession of disconnected discussions—if they are to build on each other as the commandant and his leadership team as well as the district commanders and their key executives analyze, learn, experiment, adapt, and improve—then they need to be connected both analytically and operationally. To ensure that this happens, the commandant needs to build follow-up into every meeting.

Infrastructure, Capacity, and Commitment

Even if the commandant's leadership team is enthusiastic and committed to its PortStat leadership strategy, there is no guarantee that the rest of the organization will come on board. The leadership team may be professionally and psychologically prepared to launch PortStat, but the rest of the organization may lack the necessary physical infrastructure, results-focused mindset, analytical bent, or organizational and personal commitment.

Infrastructure

Any organization that seeks to employ a PerformanceStat strategy needs some essential (though quite minimal) infrastructure. It needs an apparatus for collecting data. It needs the computers and software with which the analysts can probe the data.[35] It needs a room in which to conduct its PerformanceStat meetings. And it needs some technology to display data and other information so everyone in the room is looking at precisely the same information. For an organization as large as the U.S. Coast Guard, the financial resources that it must invest in creating this infrastructure is almost inconsequential compared with the truly significant investment that it must make: the *time* of its leadership team.

Moreover, this infrastructure is not the essence of the PerformanceStat strategy. Certainly a meeting room plus some technology for displaying data are important. They are, unfortunately, the most visible aspects of the approach. So those who visit a PerformanceStat before creating one of their own tend to faithfully copy the infrastructure while missing the less visible leadership concepts, which are much more essential in creating the strategy's potential for improving performance.

Results-Focused Mind-Set

The U.S. Coast Guard has built a reputation as a mission-driven organization. Unfortunately, many of those who rise to positions of authority in large public agencies do so by assiduously following the rules, not by producing results. In most bureaucracies, the typical rewards and punishments encourage people to focus on the rules more than on the results. Consequently, some of those upon whom the commandant will need to rely to improve performance at the district and port levels might have "learned"—through years of experience—that their primary job is to follow the rules and stay out of trouble.

Some people may find a focus on results intriguing but confusing: "Sure there exists some evidence that this new results-producing idea—what do they call it? PortStat?—is very effective in *other* districts. But I don't know how these other districts get away with it. If we did the same thing, we will clearly be in violation of OMB's Regulation #7002XOS/4002DER." Of course, the new idea might not be in violation of any rule. Or it might only *appear to be* in violation of some regulation. In a risk-averse world, it makes little difference. Why risk a career-damaging reprimand for a small (and maybe fleeting) improvement in results?

No one is opposed to improving performance. Everyone likes the idea—in principle. Yet all improvements necessarily come with some costs: the opportunity costs of tasks ignored; the personal costs of careers jeopardized; and the intellectual costs—the need to understand how to switch from an easy-to-interpret, quite-precise, rule-driven system to a difficult-to-comprehend, rather-experimental, more-ambitious, and also much-more-ambiguous, results-based culture.

For the Coast Guard to create PortStat, the leadership team will need to develop a performance-focused mind-set throughout the organization. This may be particularly important for middle managers, who have learned to salute all of the rules obediently.

Analytical Bent

The commandant may find it even more difficult to infuse analytical thinking into the everyday behavior of the districts and ports. The managers at this level may lack the mental framework necessary to examine and draw conclusions from relevant data let alone to determine what data might be relevant.

But why? Why might public managers lack the analytical capacity necessary to use data to improve performance? There are, I think, four causal contributors: the reason why people enter any of the public-service professions, the professional training they receive, the type of daily work they are asked to do, and the nature of their organizational (that is traditional bureaucratic) life.

First, people tend to choose a public-service profession to do it, not to analyze it. Few people enter the United States Coast Guard because they want to analyze data to determine what port-security strategies are most effective. Those who decide to join the Coast Guard do so primarily to do port security (or to pursue one of the USCG's ten other statutory missions). Primarily, the individuals who choose a public-service profession do so because they want to help people. They like doing it (or they will find another profession). They get their professional kicks from doing it—not necessarily from thinking about it philosophically or analyzing it abstractly.

Second, managers are trained to *do* it, not to *analyze* it. At the Coast Guard Academy they take a variety of analytical courses covering probability and statistics, mathematical modeling, and experimental design. These courses may have even helped them get their initial postings. Still, most of their pre-career and in-career training is apt to focus on the doing, not the analyzing.

Third, when they take that first, entry-level job, it won't involve doing much analysis. Primarily, they will be asked to simply do it. Doing it doesn't mean analyzing it. Particularly in a high-risk organization such as the Coast Guard, whose effectiveness often depends upon across-the-board coordination, doing it means that everyone does what the standard operating procedures require. It means following the procedures and routines of the organization.

Fourth, as they grow in experience and show the capacity to accept more responsibility, their organization will give them additional assignments. Some may be analytical tasks. Often, however, they will be bigger and more demanding versions of the same, doing-it assignments. In most organizations, people tend to be promoted for their demonstrated professional abilities, not necessarily for their skills at management or leadership, let alone analysis. This hardly encourages or reenforces an analytical bent in aspiring managers.

Organizational and Personal Commitment

Some middle managers may respond quickly to a shift from rules to results and attempt to augment their skills in analysis and sharpen their focus on results. After all, a number of USCG junior officers attended graduate school, earning an M.B.A. or a master's in operations research. Still, most will remain sensitive to future changes in both the direction and the intensity of the commandant's attention. If they sense that the leadership team is lessening its emphasis on port security or is curtailing its dedication to its PortStat strategy, they will adjust their behavior accordingly. Without the personal, visible, and persistent commitment of the Coast Guard's commandant and leadership team, PortStat will deteriorate into another bureaucratic exercise.

"The Imperative of Adaptation"

No other organization on the planet is identical to the United States Coast Guard. Thus when seeking to create an effective PortStat leadership strategy, the USCG commandant cannot simply copy the NYPD's CompStat or any other PerformanceStat. The commandant has to adapt the strategy to the needs and capabilities of today's Coast Guard.[36] This adaptation needs to reflect all of the specifics of PortStat, from the purpose or purposes it is designed to help achieve, to the kind of data that can be (and might be) collected, to the frequency, structure, and style of the meetings. There is no one best way to employ a PerformanceStat strategy. Thus the commandant needs to customize the various aspects of the strategy to mesh with the needs and resources of the Coast Guard.

For example, what style should the commandant employ when questioning district commanders at the PortStat sessions? Should he, following the NYPD's well-established reputation, be very aggressive?[37] Or should he be completely nonconfrontational? The choice needs to reflect the commandant's personal style, the culture of the organization, and the behavior of district commanders. The Coast Guard, with its organizational structure built around official ranks and definitive commands, might want to conduct its PortStat meetings in a way that is not as brutal as the NYPD's but not as bland as others. There is no universally correct answer to this design question. Every agency or jurisdiction that creates its own PerformanceStat needs to figure out how to balance the brutal and the bland.[38]

The Final Adaptation: CollaborationStat

If PortStat is to be truly effective, the Coast Guard will eventually have to expand it from AgencyStat to CollaborationStat. And any form of CollaborationStat cannot be brutal. In a very hierarchical, quasi-military organization, such as the NYPD, superiors can be very demanding, aggressively and repeatedly questioning subordinates about their strategies for improving their subunits' performance. But when the PerformanceStat strategy is going to be implemented by a collection of collaborators, none of whom reports to any of the others, all of the participants have to take a cooperative posture toward their colleagues.

After all, accountability within any such collaborative is reciprocal, not hierarchical. Each of the collaborators has voluntarily entered into a "compact of mutual, collective responsibility."[39] The Coast Guard may have enough status to attract organizations and individuals to join the collaborative, but it has limited ability to impose new obligations on them. It has to convince a variety of private partners—firms that ship cargo, that own LNG tank farms, and that manage port facilities—and other governmental units that it is in their own best interest to participate in an extension of PortStat.

Thus as the USCG attempts to expand a strictly internal PortStat to include other organizations, it will need to make a variety of additional adaptations. It will be able to anticipate some of these adaptations, but other challenges will be completely unpredictable. Consequently, an expansion of both participants and scope will require much experimentation. Who exactly is responsible for what? Who disagrees with whom about what? How can the Coast Guard ensure that all participants stay focused on PortStat's purpose: to protect each and every port from a terrorist attack?

And how should the Coast Guard launch this expansion? Whom should it first ask to join the expanded and collaborative PortStat? Should it select a specific individual organization to become the first outsider to participate in the strategy? Or should it invite several organizations to join simultaneously? Then, what performance deficit should it suggest that these collaborators tackle first? Or should it first pick the performance deficit on which it will focus next—on the first small win on which it will seek to build future collaborative successes—and only then select the collaborators who can contribute the most to achieving this target?

These questions reflect the challenges that Eugene Bardach, in his analysis of social service collaboratives, calls platform building and momentum building. The creation of "interorganizational collaborative capacity," he argues, is a dynamic process. It requires the collaborators to create specific capabilities, such as trust, intellectual capital, and a communication network. It also requires them to employ its successes to build momentum: "any sort of success represents an opportunity to create even more success in a self-expanding cycle of effects." And one of the key components of both platform building and momentum building is trust—"interpersonal trust" among the individuals who do the collaborative's work.[40]

Yet, as Bardach emphasizes, there exists no magic sequence for either the platform-building process or the momentum-building process. The collaborators figure this out as they "grope along."[41] Nevertheless, the Coast Guard does have the legal mandate, the institutional capacity, and the informal status to take the lead. Indeed, any expansion of PortStat—from AgencyStat to CollaborationStat—to include non-USCG participants significantly (and necessarily) expands the nature of the Coast Guard's leadership responsibilities.

From BreachStat to PortStat

The danger of a small-wins strategy is that the organization never moves from small wins to bigger wins. Initially, a small-wins strategy makes a lot of sense. A few quick, small wins help an organization learn—learn *how* to produce some results and learn that it *can* actually produce results. In many organizations—and certainly for many collaboratives—this is a significant accomplishment.

Unfortunately, if the organization is not attentive, it can become stuck in a small-wins phase. After all, it has accomplished something. It has bragged to the world about this accomplishment. And the world—surprised that the organization could accomplish anything—has praised the organization for this new (significant if small) achievement. At this point, chasing more ambitious wins, or even chasing different but still small wins, looks dangerous. Why mess with success?

Thus the USCG and its collaborators could get stuck on a narrow Breach-Stat plateau and fail to pursue a more comprehensive PortStat strategy. Fortunately, for this collaborative, two factors may work to prevent the collaborators from failing to see beyond the problem of unauthorized breaches.

First, the problem of port security is not going away. Breaches of security barriers are not the only danger. Indeed, terrorists will undoubtedly launch new attacks that will reveal other vulnerabilities. Thus while those who launch PortStat may choose to concentrate initially on breaches to security barriers, and while they may receive credit for their accomplishments, they will face vocal, public demands to move beyond this narrow focus.

Second, the members of this collaborative will each have their own, specific concerns. At any port, the USCG's key collaborators, the members of the Area Maritime Security Committee, will represent quite diverse interests. Moreover, these different interests will also be present in any effort to create PortStat at the national level. Initially, these constituents may be willing to suppress their own concerns so that the collaborative version of PortStat can achieve some small wins and can learn how to create bigger ones. They will not, however, do so forever. Eventually, they will want the PortStat collaborative to address the vulnerabilities that they find most dangerous.

Finally, as the convener of PortStat, the Coast Guard has the responsibility to keep everyone focused on its purpose. Not only does any effort to improve performance have to start with purpose, it also has to keep constantly focused on purpose. Indeed, that may be the best way to ensure that the collaborative moves from a narrow BreachStat to a full PortStat.

Leadership

There exists no PerformanceStat model. There is no formula, no template. No public executive can create a PerformanceStat system, push the start button, and walk away, thinking that everything will work wonderfully on automatic pilot. Anyone who thinks this leadership strategy is little more than an organizational process will end up only creating one more senseless bureaucratic routine.

An effective, performance-enhancing PortStat will require the constant attention of the commandant and the Coast Guard's leadership team. After the initial period of experimentation, learning, and adaptation, they cannot walk away, leaving subordinates to sustain its energy and effectiveness. They will need to frequently rethink whether they are, indeed, focused on those port-security problems that most warrant their attention. They will need to be personally engaged in everything from thinking through the connection between the purposes and the data to the mundane monthly follow-up memos. They will need to reach out to other public agencies and private organizations to create a CollaborationStat-type approach to port security. And they will have to do this at USCG headquarters, in each of the districts, and in each of the ports. For if they don't demonstrate that they care—if they don't spend their most valuable resource, their own time—no one within the Coast Guard and none of the collaborators will believe it is for real.

PortStat—and indeed any effort to improve port security—requires the active leadership of the commandant, the USCG leadership team, the nine district commanders, and their key staff.

The PerformanceStat Potential

A PerformanceStat leadership strategy has the potential to improve the results produced by any public agency or government jurisdiction. But only the *potential.* There is no guarantee. Moreover, PerformanceStat—as epitomized by the NYPD's CompStat and Baltimore's CitiStat—is not the only leadership approach that can help improve performance.

Nevertheless, a PortStat leadership strategy could help the Coast Guard achieve its national security mission (or any of its other ten statutory missions). This, however, will not happen automatically. It will only happen if the commandant and the USCG leadership team think carefully and thoughtfully about the purposes they are trying to achieve; the data they will use to help them assess whether port security is improving; the analyses they will employ to detect patterns and compare operational effectiveness; the meetings they will conduct to learn and motivate improvements; the follow-up they will employ to keep everyone focused; the infrastructure, operational capacity, and organizational commitment that they will have to create; the adaptations that they need to evolve; and the leadership that they will need to personally demonstrate.

Notes

1. The Environmental Protection Agency employed EPAStat, the Federal Emergency Management Agency created FEMAStat, and the Food and Drug Administration developed FDA-Track.

2. These design considerations are adapted from Robert D. Behn, "Designing PerformanceStat: Or What Are the Key Strategic Choices That a Jurisdiction or Agency Must Make When Adapting the CompStat/CitiStat Class of Performance Strategies?" *Public Performance and Management Review* 32, no. 2 (2008), pp. 203–32.

3. The U.S. Coast Guard has eleven statutory missions (listed here in the order of their percentage of USCG operating expenses: ports, waterways, and coastal security; drug interdiction; aids to navigation; search and rescue; living marine resources; marine safety; defense readiness; migrant interdiction; marine environmental protection; ice operations; and other law enforcement (www.uscg.mil/top/missions/).

4. U.S. Office of Management and Budget, "Program Assessment: Coast Guard: Ports, Waterways, and Coastal Security" (www.whitehouse.gov/omb/expectmore//detail/10003635.2006.html).

5. For a discussion of the importance of platforming in building a collaborative, see Eugene Bardach, *Getting Agencies to Work Together: The Practice and Theory of Managerial Craftsmanship* (Brookings Institution, 1998), esp. pp. 270–76.

6. Actually, all PerformanceStats are ProblemStats. To improve performance, an organization needs to identify, then eliminate or fix, problems that are preventing it from producing better outputs and outcomes. The NYPD doesn't attack crime as a whole; it attacks each individual pocket of crime, all the while looking to learn from its successes either microstrategies than can be adapted to combat other pockets of similar crimes or macrostrategies that can combat a variety of crimes.

7. U.S. Office of Management and Budget, "Program Assessment: Coast Guard."

8. Robert D. Behn, "Collaborating for Performance: Or Can There Exist Such a Thing as CollaborationStat?" *International Public Management Journal* 13, no. 4 (2010): 429–70.

9. Robert D. Behn, "On Why All Public Officials Need to Follow the Basic Rule: Always Start with Purpose," *Bob Behn's Performance Leadership Report*, vol. 9, no. 4 (December 2010) (www.hks.harvard.edu/thebehnreport).

10. For a discussion of the concept of a performance deficit, see Robert D. Behn, *Performance Leadership: 11 Better Practices That Can Ratchet up Performance* (Washington: IBM Center for the Business of Government, 2004), pp. 10–11; Robert D. Behn, "On Why Public Managers Need to Focus on Their Performance Deficit," *Bob Behn's Public Management Report*, vol. 4, no. 1 (September 2006) (www.hks.harvard.edu/thebehnreport).

11. ASRA, created in 1976, is voluntary, confidential, and anonymous, and (to ensure its independence) is actually operated by the National Aeronautics and Space Administration.

12. One example of adapting the concept of near-miss data to help identify other problems, is in medicine. A variety of hospitals have created near-miss reporting regimes. For example, see Paul Barach and Stephen D Small, "Reporting and Preventing Medical Mishaps: Lessons from Nonmedical Near-Miss Reporting Systems," *British Medical Journal* 320, no. 7237 (2000): 759–63; Rachel Sorokin and others, "The Near-Miss Resident Conference: Understanding the Barriers to Confronting Medical Errors," *Seminars in Medical Practice* 5, no. 1 (2002): 12–19; Erin DuPree, Loraine O'Neill, and Rebecca M. Anderson, "Achieving a Safety Culture in Obstetrics," *Mount Sinai Journal of Medicine* 76, no. 6 (2009): 529–38; Lucian L. Leape, "Reporting of Adverse Events," *New England Journal of Medicine* 347, no. 20 (2002): 1633–38. In 2000 the U.S. Department of Veterans Affairs contracted with NASA to develop the Patient Safety Reporting System, or PSRS (similar to ASRA), which "invites everyone who works in a healthcare facility to voluntarily report any events or concerns that involve patient safety" (www.psrs.arc.nasa.gov/faq.html#accept_anonymous_reports). These practices are not, however, completely uncontroversial. For a discussion of the differences in the incentives for reporting near misses in aviation and in medicine, see Charles H Andrus and others, "'To Err Is Human': Uniformly Reporting Medical Errors and Near Misses," *Journal of the American College of Surgeons* 196, no. 6 (2003): 911–18. In this chapter, I do not examine how to design the data-collection incentives to ensure that the near-miss data are complete, accurate, and usefully classified (would a LNG tank farm report a breach of its security barrier to the Coast Guard if that could result in some kind of sanction?). For a discussion of such data-collection incentives, see (in addition to Andrus and others) Michal Tamuz, "Learning Disabilities for Regulators: The Perils of Organizational Learning in the Air Transportation Industry," *Administration & Society* 33, no. 3 (2001): 276–302. Another effort to learn from near misses—to "prevent 'history from repeating itself'"—was initiated in 1998 by a group of firefighters. "In order

for firefighters to survive the dangers of the job," FirefighterCloseCalls.com explains, "we must learn how other firefighters have had 'Close Calls' and even been injured or killed" (http://firefighterclosecalls.com/mission.php).

13. Some other possible performance deficits include the absence of communication interoperability among the various agencies (public and private) in a port; poor training of personnel from the Coast Guard and other public and private organizations in, for example, "behavior pattern recognition"; and inadequate detection or other types of equipment. A vulnerability analysis could identify specific performance deficits for specific ports and well as performance deficits that are common to all ports.

14. Stephen Flynn chronicles the "many lucky breaks"—"the border-control equivalent of winning the lottery"—that lead to Ressam's capture. Stephen Flynn, *America the Vulnerable: How Our Government Is Failing to Protect Us from Terrorism* (New York: Harper Collins, 2004), pp. 20, 136–37. Flynn's book is full of examples of breaches in security boundaries.

15. Spencer S. Hsu, "Secret Service Counts 91 Breaches: 2003 Report Has Been Used as a Training Tool," *Washington Post,* December 7, 2009, p. A1.

16. The Secret Service reports that, in 2008, it protected 34 U.S. officials and 222 dignitaries at the United Nations, plus spouses and relatives in thousands of locations in the United States and abroad. Ibid.

17. In 2002, 8 million cargo containers entered U.S. ports. Flynn, *America the Vulnerable,* p. 93.

18. Abraham Lincoln, "Address before the Wisconsin State Agricultural Society, Milwaukee, Wisconsin" (September 30, 1859), in *The Collected Works of Abraham Lincoln,* vol. 3, edited by Roy P. Basler (Rutgers University Press, 1953), pp. 481–82.

19. Karl E. Weick, "Small Wins: Redefining the Scale of Social Problems," *American Psychologist* 39, no. 1 (1984): 40–49.

20. Rob Margetta, "Small Vessels, Big Threat," *CQ Weekly,* November 2, 2009, p. 2496.

21. See www.uscg.mil/comdt/blog/. See also Thad Allen, "Friend or Foe? Tough to Tell," *Proceedings* 134, no. 10 (2008), U.S. Naval Institute, pp. 14–18.

22. I considered starting with other possible security threats as illustrated by other categories of data, such as the number and type of people taking unauthorized pictures of critical facilities. I concluded, however, that this would not provide useful, near-miss data. Lots of people who took such pictures would be ordinary citizens or tourists, not terrorists. Meanwhile, terrorists who wanted really excellent pictures of a critical facility could avoid being detected by buying a camera with a telephoto lens and renting a hotel room from which take the desired pictures. Thus the collectable data on unauthorized pictures of critical facilities would miss many (or even most) of the cases about which the USCG would care the most and would reveal little about major vulnerabilities.

23. These data on fatal airline "events" come from the website planecrashinfo. com, which emphasizes that "these accident rates are not safety ratings."

24. Isaac Asimov, the biochemist, popular science writer, and author of numerous books of science fiction, is often quoted as saying, "The most exciting phrase to hear in science, the one that heralds the new discoveries, is not 'Eureka!' (I found it!) but 'That's funny.'" Asimov didn't mean, "That's funny, ha-ha." He meant, "That's funny, strange"—strange enough to warrant further investigation. Read Montague, *Why Choose This Book? How We Make Decisions* (New York: Dutton, 2006), p. 108.

25. To avoid any suggestion that some of the USCG's nine districts (numbered 1, 5, 7, 8, 9, 11, 13, 14, and 17) are better than the others, I have chosen to label nine districts with nine letters—J, K, Q, T, U, V, W, X, Z—and to not connect these letters with an existing district or even with any geographic area.

26. For a discussion of the value of comparative data, see Robert D. Behn, "Steering with Comparative Data: How the Bar Chart and 'The List' Might Help to Steer Social Integration," paper prepared for the 2010 Conference of the International Public Management Network, New Steering Concepts in Public Management: Working toward Social Integration, Erasmus University, Rotterdam, The Netherlands, June 28–30, 2010.

27. See Robert D. Behn, "On Why Public Executives Need to Remember That the Data Don't Speak for Themselves," *Bob Behn's Public Management Report*, vol. 6, no. 7 (March 2009).

28. Gretchen M. Spreitzer and Scott Sonenshein, "Toward the Construct Definition of Positive Deviance," *American Behavioral Scientist* 47, no. 6 (2004): 828–47.

29. If a PortStat session were conducted at one of the USCG's district headquarters, it would make sense to include the captains of the ports in the districts in the meeting.

30. The meeting should not be wasted on issues that are not central to improving performance. The time that several dozen people are spending in a PortStat meeting has a significant opportunity cost. If a subunit director begins the discussion, the danger is that he or she will waste everyone's time on extraneous issues, diverting them from key performance deficits on which they need to concentrate.

31. On Google, the two words *citistat baltimore* generated 17,100 hits. The three words *citistat baltimore accountability* generated 7,600 hits (or 44 percent of the 17,100 total), while *citistat baltimore learning* produced 4,050 hits (or 24 percent of the 17,100).

32. For more than you want to know about accountability, see Robert D. Behn, *Rethinking Democratic Accountability* (Brookings Institution, 2001).

33. Robert D. Behn, "On the Characteristics of Friendly Competition," *Bob Behn's Public Management Report*, vol. 1, no. 3 (November 2003).

34. For a detailed discussion of the importance of follow-up, see Robert D. Behn, "PerformanceStat as a Leadership Strategy: It Don't Mean a Thing if It Ain't Got That Follow-Up," paper prepared for the Twelfth Annual Conference of the International Research Society for Public Management, Brisbane, March 26, 2008.

35. Most agencies and jurisdictions find that off-the-shelf computers and software are perfectly adequate.

36. Robert D. Behn, "On Why Public Managers Need to Remember the Imperative of Adaptation," *Bob Behn's Public Management Report,* vol. 3, no. 12 (August 2006).

37. A report by the Police Foundation finds that New York's CompStat had "a reputation among line officers as brutal and punitive rather than collaborative and creative." James J. Willis, Stephen D. Mastrofski, and David Weisburd, *Compstat in Practice: An In-Depth Analysis of Three Cities* (Washington: Police Foundation, 2003), p. 21.

38. This is the seventh error in Robert D. Behn, "The Seven Big Errors of PerformanceStat," policy brief (Cambridge, Mass.: Rappaport Institute for Greater Boston and the Taubman Center for State and Local Government, 2008).

39. Behn, *Rethinking Democratic Accountability,* pp. 125–28.

40. Bardach, *Getting Agencies to Work Together,* pp. 276, 277 (also pp. 270–76).

41. Ibid., pp. 42–44, 204. See also Robert D. Behn, *Leadership Counts: Lessons for Public Managers from the Massachusetts Welfare, Training, and Employment Program* (Harvard University Press, 1991), chap. 7; and Robert D. Behn, "Management by Groping Along," *Journal of Policy Analysis and Management* 7, no. 4 (1988): 643–63.

HERMAN B. LEONARD *and* MARK H. MOORE

5

Pursuing Public Value: Frameworks for Strategic Analysis and Action

For many years now, the Harvard Kennedy School of Government has introduced public managers to a particular framework designed to help them manage "strategically" in government.[1] By strategic management we mean something very simple but very important: the cognitive capacity to figure out what is worth doing and how that particular value proposition might be achieved in the particular circumstances a manager confronts. The core idea is straightforward: in order for a contemplated initiative to be worth a manager's time, that initiative must incorporate three elements. It has to be

—publicly valuable,

—socially legitimate, politically authorizable, financially sustainable, and

—operationally feasible and substantively effective.[2]

At one level, this idea is embarrassingly simple. Of course it is true that a successful enterprise in the public sector has to be valuable, authorizable, and doable! What could be more simple and obvious than that? Yet however simple in theory, aligning these three elements in practice is often distressingly difficult. This shouldn't be too surprising. After all, there is nothing in the world of public managers that naturally aligns judgments as to public value with the necessary political support and operational capacity to achieve the desired results. If these three elements of a strategic calculation are to be aligned, it will only be through some process of close environmental diagnosis, inspired value-creating imagination, and hard managerial work.

The idea of strategic management in government is not only practically challenging but also philosophically suspect.[3] As a concept, it invites *all* managers in government—not just elected executives and politically appointed executives but also career civil servants—to have ideas about valuable *ends* that government could serve as well as efficient means for achieving ends decided by others. It also invites managers to consider actions that could strengthen the legitimacy of a government effort and increase resources available to pursue that effort. And it invites managers to experiment with innovative operational methods whose results cannot be perfectly predicted.[4]

In these respects, the concept of strategic management challenges the traditional conception of public administration. That conception sharply distinguished between the *political* tasks of mobilizing popular support and defining the public values to be pursued by government, on the one hand, and on the other hand the *operational* task of organizing the means for achieving those objectives. The first was the task of elected legislatures and elected political executives (assumed to have established their right to define public value by winning popular elections). The second was the task of civil servants (assumed to be administrative and substantively expert but strictly neutral on important questions of public value and politically inert).[5]

That traditional conception also downplayed the potential importance of operational innovations and the political and substantive risks such innovations generally entailed.[6] It was commonly assumed that the professional expertise of civil servants was sufficient to banish any uncertainty. When new methods were required, and the civil servants were unable to eliminate the uncertainty, political authorization would be required to assume the risks of experimenting with something other than well-established methods. On this view, the strategic responsibilities for innovations were vested in legislatures or the top of the executive branch agencies, not in midlevel bureaucrats.

In this chapter we stake out our concept of strategic management and then apply it to the case of Captain Englebert. The aim is to see whether and how that framework could usefully inform her particular managerial calculation and how the concept might reshape our ideas not only of managerial practices but also of the organizational structures within which and from which public managers operate.

If the traditional conception of public administration were accurate, this would be a short essay. If strategic thinking is not for midlevel bureaucrats, then our strategic management framework would be of little use to Captain Englebert who—far from being a senior political official—is not even at the top ranks of the civil service! She is a midlevel, career official in a hierarchical military organization, accountable to her bureaucratic superiors, who are themselves accountable to political executives and the Congress of the United States, and through them, to the American citizenry as a whole. She has a mandate from that chain of command to execute a particular technical task: improve port security in the United States. In all these respects, she looks like a functionary, not a strategic manager.

Yet on close examination there is much about her position that seems to require her to think and act as a strategic manager. One can claim that her mandate requires her to execute a specific, concrete, and operational mission. In the execution of that mission there is little room for philosophical issues of public value, or political processes of legitimating the claims she is making on others, or the use of imagination to create and evaluate alternative ways of proceeding. Yet even the most casual reflection shows that none of this is true.

The situation she faces looks less like a simple technical operational calculation of means to specific ends and more like what our colleagues Ronnie Heifetz and Marty Linsky would call an adaptive challenge.[7] As Malcolm Sparrow shows in chapter 3 of this volume, there is a great deal of uncertainty about the task Englebert has been assigned. Is the goal to protect the ports, or to exploit the ports as a location that could be used to thwart attacks headed to other targets, or some combination of the two? What is the range and most likely form that threats could take? Similarly, Bob Behn (chapter 4) and Elaine Kamarck (chapter 8) show the difficulty of capturing her performance in such specific and concrete measurements that her superiors and their overseers could know how well she was doing and how she might improve. In seeking an effective response to terrorist threats, a great deal of policy analytic and program design work needs to be done, work that focuses on defining the ends to be pursued and on weighing the values at stake in choosing one line of action over another. In short, the problem she faces is thick with the challenges of innovating and of being able to see and calculate the important values at stake.

In addition, it becomes quickly apparent that if she is going to succeed in her assignment Captain Englebert will have to find the means to stretch her influence well beyond her formal authority. As Stephen Goldsmith (chapter 7) and Elaine Kamarck observe in this volume, achieving the goal of enhanced port security will depend on actions taken by thousands of organizational units and individuals spread across levels of government and across public, private commercial, and private nonprofit organizations.[8] Very little if any of that effort can be commanded; it will have to be induced through some combination of self-interest, a sense of duty, and a vision of the common good to which those other actors are asked to contribute. Even worse, the particular form such efforts will take will vary greatly from one port to another. In this situation, the common forms of leverage—command-and-control regulatory authority and federal contracts that link public expenditures to particular activities or to results to be carried out by the contractor—are mostly unavailable. What leverage can be gained will have to come from the mobilization of a broad social and political process that activates a powerful norm that will influence thousands of decentralized actors to take steps they deem necessary to improve port security.[9]

Finally, it seems clear that that Captain Englebert will have to become visible in the community she seeks to influence and find the means to orchestrate larger policy development and political processes. As Mark Moore and Archon Fung observe in chapter 9, she will have to deal with the media and will have to design consultative mechanisms with key stakeholders both to find effective means of enhancing port security and to build a commitment to those means. She will have to create and develop—and then work tirelessly in—collective deliberative processes that can build norms that guide actors toward enhanced port security. She will have to work with more particular initiatives at the level of individual ports where the general rules don't work. In short, she has to assume the strategic leadership of the effort, even though she has little direct authority over it.

In sum, her assignment seems to require her to think and act as a strategic manager in all the following senses:

—She has to be concerned with giving more particular concrete definitions to the ends of her work and with searching for effective means for achieving those ends. She has to imagine possible unintended consequences of her proposed actions and to bring those concerns about values and ends to both her overseers and her design teams. The ends are intertwined with the means.

—She has to use not only tried and true operational methods but also her professional experience and her imagination—and to use these in consultation with others—to develop plausibly effective, innovative means for advancing the purposes assigned to her and to be able to identify the risks of the unproven methods.

—She has to use political (in the broad sense of relying on persuasion and negotiation) rather than command and control methods to extend her effective influence beyond her formal authority to meet the challenge of the task she faces.

—She has to be an effective participant in policy processes convened by others and to convene policy processes of her own that will allow her to find and build legitimacy for the policies and programs she develops.

In this respect, the case presents an anomaly in public administration theory: Doing the job Captain Englebert has been assigned to do within a tight bureaucratic hierarchy seems to require her to behave in a highly strategic way. This suggests that the strategic management framework we have been developing might indeed have wider application beyond politically elected or politically appointed government executives. In this brief chapter we can at least explore this question with respect to one particular public manager.

Strategic Management in Government

Our conception of strategic management in government was developed at a time when many important ideas about good management were passing from the private sector to the government, including a focus on customers, the use of performance metrics, and creating pay-for-performance incentive systems for managers and frontline workers.

Significantly, the biggest idea in private sector management—the idea that occupied pride of place in business schools, in consulting practice, and in the performance of the best-managed firms—did not pass as quickly or directly to the public sector. That idea is the concept of corporate strategy.[10] Those who advocated for and taught the techniques of developing a corporate strategy claimed (on the basis of both logic and some empirical evidence) that, in order to succeed, a business needed to develop and execute (and revise as necessary) a functionally integrated, forward-looking strategy that set out the products and markets in which the business planned to compete and also needed to identify the key investments (and disinvestments) it would have to make to be able to execute the envisioned strategy.

Corporate Strategy: Adapting a Key Concept in Private Sector Management

Given the current enthusiasm for all things private, one might have expected that the biggest idea in private sector management would move most quickly to the public sector, particularly since concepts of strategy originated in the governmental world of military operations. But despite its importance and origins, the concept did not make the transition easily.

Of course, the word *strategy* has been around for a long time and has been widely used in government management. When used in government, the idea of strategy meant all of the following: oriented to the future, focused on the big picture, emphasizing ultimate substantive ends rather than intermediate procedural means, and coherence and synergy among different distinct activities. These were certainly the important parts of the concept of organizational strategy, and they gave much useful guidance to those who sought to act as professional managers in government. But as we considered the concepts of business strategy in the context of public management, what seemed important was a different idea: namely, that organizations could not succeed in either the short or long run unless they were *fitted to the environment in which they were operating*.

On this view, the challenge facing government managers was not simply shortsightedness, or getting bogged down in details and process, or pursuing ultimately inconsistent goals; *the challenge was to carry out a close diagnosis of the environment in which the organization was operating in the short and long run and to formulate an idea about how an enterprise that held particular assets and capacities might best be positioned in that environment to create value for society*. That insight, in turn, raised the important question of exactly what pieces of the external environment that strategic public managers faced required their closest attention.

The business world, of course, knew the answer to that question.[11] It looked at *customers* (understood to be individuals with desires and with money to spend who might be attracted to the particular goods and services that the business could supply). It also looked at *competitors* (who could offer similar products at lower prices). It also considered *suppliers, financiers,* and (often reluctantly) *government policy*. In short, corporate strategy in the private sector was built from a diagnosis of how a particular firm was positioned to compete in a competitive market environment.

Government managers and those advising them were much less clear about how they should diagnose their situation. To many government managers who pride themselves on their professionalism in meeting the operational demands of fulfilling their mission and have little patience for politics, the key part of the external environment to consider was their *task environment*—the material conditions that existed in the world that they had been asked to improve. On this view, professionally oriented public managers—generals, public health officials, city planners, job training specialists—needed to take the long view of how social conditions would alter the tasks they were called upon to do in performance of their assigned mission and to make the investments necessary to improve their ability to respond. Yet these task-focused public managers despaired of the possibility of doing this because they thought their efforts would be undermined by the fickle movement of political forces and by the short time horizons of politicians. If only politics and politicians would stop intruding, the professional public managers could actually engage in strategic planning! Until that occurred, most strategic planning efforts were doomed to failure.

What this perspective ignored, however, was a fundamental feature of strategic management in democratic government. Since all government management relied on the use of the collectively owned authority and money of the state, all management activity would be subject to review by elected representatives of the people and other forms of political accountability. If political oversight and review was a permanent feature of the environment that public managers moved in—and if a fundamental precept of strategic management was that these managers had to pay attention to that environment—then it followed that the political process could not be kept outside the strategic concerns of public managers. The political environment they faced *had to be viewed as a key part of the external environment that had to be diagnosed and integrated into any plausible strategic plan.* In short, the political processes that directed and provided the resources to sustain government operations were not *outside* the strategic calculation, threatening to undermine it; they were *inside* the strategic calculation as a key element of the external environment to which government organizations had to be "fitted."

The key importance of the political authorizing environment was founded on both practical and philosophical considerations. As a practical matter, those actors in the political authorizing environment—legislatures, courts, interest groups, media, and so forth—could and did routinely demand accountability from public managers at all levels of the system. As a philosophical matter, in a democratic society, these actors and their complex interactions with one another are constitutionally enshrined as the arbiters of the public value that guides the use of state assets.

Strategic management therefore required public managers (at all levels) to stare unblinkingly at two important pieces of their external environment beyond the cozy confines of their government: the *task environment* (defined in terms of the concrete conditions that they were being paid to transform) and the *authorizing environment* (which provided them with the money and authority they needed to do their work and told them what values they should pursue through their actions). A key question was, What would they find when they did so? Would they find simple and stable conditions in which they could work to perfect their organizations? Or would they find complex and dynamic circumstances that would force them to manage complex, highly innovative organizations?

The Task Environment

As noted above, many public managers felt keenly responsible for monitoring the task environment they faced. That was a key part of their professional competence. What remained uncertain, however, was exactly how complex and dynamic that task environment was and how fast they would have to innovate to adapt it.

Complexity of the Task Environment. The complexity of the task environment can be measured along two dimensions: the degree of familiarity and similarity in the tasks that public managers confronted and the degree to which the problems they faced could be solved with resources held within the boundaries of a given public organization. The more unfamiliar and varied the work, and the more that success depended on mobilizing work from many individuals and organizations, the more complex the task environment.

The hope, of course, was that processes like fighting crime, educating children, and reducing environmental hazards could be standardized and kept primarily within a government organization committed to those goals. The aim was to keep costs low and performance high through the use of standard operating procedures. Indeed, citizens liked standard procedures: they are both efficient and cost-effective, and furthermore they ensure that like cases were being treated alike—a publicly valued characteristic of government services in itself.[12]

Unfortunately, in many public sector environments the task environment is very complex, and effective responses are not easy to standardize.[13] It is also true that for many public purposes—including those described above—much of the required operational aspect lies outside the government organizations.[14]

The operational implication seems straightforward: the more complex the task environment and the more varied the organizational response, the more the performance of the organization would be dependent on the initiative and imagination of the frontline workers and the more discretion would have to be delegated to operational-level personnel. The more the capacity to accomplish the mission lies outside the organization, the more important it is for those in the organization—at top, middle, and bottom—to leverage the capacities of those outside actors through more political than administrative systems of influence.

Dynamics of the Task Environment. The dynamics of the task environment could take three distinct forms. First, the task environment could stay relatively constant in terms of the specific operational challenges the organizations faced, but the relative importance of one kind of task could grow dramatically compared to others. For example, a police department might not see a new kind of crime, but the relative importance of shootings and aggravated assaults could change relative to burglaries or traffic offenses. Second, the task environment could produce some new challenges. For example, a police department post 9/11 might face a task environment that included terrorists—a problem previously unseen. Third, the task environment could include simultaneous changes, such as the emergence of new threats and also significant changes in the relative importance of the usual conditions.

Again, just as the *complexity* in the task environment puts pressure on the organization to develop more *varied* responses, so *dynamics* in the task environment put pressure on the organization to develop *new* responses to deal with the emergence of new threats. In a dynamic task environment, the rate of innovation becomes critical to the success of the organization. The need for innovation, in turn, means that the organization has to experiment with methods that it cannot be sure will work. And if the ordinary expectation for accountability in the public sector is that organizations should know what they are doing, and not gamble with other people's money and lives, then there will be a tension between the idea of professionalism as knowing everything and the idea of professionalism as a continuous process of learning.

Strategic Management, Accountability, and Innovation. The need to build organizations that can respond to complex and dynamic task environments conflicts with the usual methods that ensure accountability in the public sector.[15] A complex, dynamic task environment demands varied and innovative responses. Public accountability often demands standard operating procedures rooted in what is assumed to be established professional knowledge.

The most common solution to the problem of complexity is to allow discretion. The most common solution to the problem of dynamism is to carry out a few pilot programs. But these measures typically result in a level of adaptation and innovation that is far lower than required by the real characteristics of the task environments that many public managers face.

In the traditional theory of public administration, a clear distinction was made between the kinds of innovation in government activities that could be introduced into a public organization at the initiative of—and with the sanction of—both democratically elected and appointed officials and professional civil servants. Generally speaking, only political sanction could change the ends of a public organization. Mere professional credentials had weight only in the area of the means to the ends.

But it doesn't take much imagination or experience to see how quickly the distinction between mission-changing ends (on the one hand) and mission-improving means (on the other) can become blurred. When a library chooses to use its capacity to lend books—and have them be returned for use by others—to lend other things such as videos, or framed pictures, or even tools, has its mission changed? Or has it simply found a new use of its capabilities? A similar question might be raised when a library uses its physical facilities to hold public meetings and conferences, or concerts and poetry readings—that is, when it starts to operate as a kind of indoor park where individuals can come to be with one another even when it is rainy or cold. The point is that the lines between the activities that support an old mission, the activities that improve the ability to perform an old mission, and the activities that take advantage of a latent capacity of an organization to produce something more valuable for the community, given changing circumstances, are less clear than they first appear.

Moreover, it is not at all clear that society is well served by insisting on this particular boundary, with politicians concerned only about ends and professional public managers concerned only about means. In the private sector, society relies upon managers with value-seeking imaginations to keep thinking about new and more valuable uses of the organizations they lead. That is the engine that has driven productivity. Moreover, in the public sector, senior career officials are given policy responsibility, which might mean imagining valuable uses of existing assets for new purposes as well as imagining new means for achieving old purposes. But it makes citizens very nervous to think that they might benefit from having public managers with restless, value-seeking imaginations. The reason they worry is that they think that unaccountable public managers will seek to feather their own nests at the public's expense or that they will pursue some idiosyncratic view of public value. The only way to keep this from happening, people may think, is to keep the officials under firm democratic, political control. But then they worry that such control discourages the initiative and imagination that are so desirable in officials who have policy-level responsibilities and that it drastically slows the rate of innovation and productivity.[16]

The Authorizing Environment

Observations about the potential conflict between actions that seem consistent with, on the one hand, responding appropriately to a dynamic and complex task environment and, on the other, meeting public demands for accountability bring us face to face with the second feature of the environment that managers face: their authorizing environment. Because the idea of strategic management took the external environment seriously, and because it viewed the political authorizing environment as an important part of that environment, the idea of strategic management in government reclaimed the critically important role of democratic politics in legitimating governmental action.

Specifically, the idea of strategic management insisted that the only way to know for sure that one was engaged in creating public value was through a political process that conferred legitimacy and support on that particular conception. Moreover, to the extent that the concept of strategic management focused attention on the fact that the resources required to achieve public purposes would come through political processes that provided money, authority, and social legitimacy to the purposes that public managers were expected to achieve, political processes were given important standing. Once questions of democratic accountability and resource mobilization for achieving specific public purposes became important, however, the idea of what constituted politics began to change in important ways.

Defining the Authorizing Environment. In the traditional view, the important politics governing public organizations were those that elected individuals to governmental offices in legislatures and executive branches. And it was precisely because elected officials had (in Sam Erwin's memorable phrase) "suffered the indignity of running for election" that they had acquired the right to make powerful, legitimate judgments as to what constituted a publicly valuable purpose or accomplishment. Of course, the elected officials soon discovered that winning the election simply gave them the right to begin shaping and implementing public policy from a powerful position; it did not, as one disappointed elected executive observed, "change all the laws we disagree with."

To do that, even elected political officials had to engage in what might be viewed as policy politics.[17] They had to make proposals in legislative and administrative arenas and have these proposals vetted by opposing politicians, interest groups, the media, and (well in the background!) the views of ordinary citizens, taxpayers, and voters. And they often enlisted career public servants in these activities in an effort to bolster the legitimacy that comes from democratic election with the legitimacy that comes from professional expertise and knowledge of the law.

In fact, as the legitimacy of government faltered in the last decades, and as efforts have been made to make government more responsive to citizens, the overall effort to engage citizens in policy politics as well as electoral politics has increased.[18] This has extended politics—particularly policy politics—beyond the realm of elections, and even beyond of the domain of legislatures, into the heart of public administration. It has also pushed responsibility for engaging in politics further down into bureaucracies.

None of this should be surprising. If public managers were being encouraged to take lessons from private, commercial enterprises and focus on the external market in which they were trying to operate, it would be natural for them to pay closer attention to the political forces that washed across their organizations. While it was tempting to see the important part of the external environment that public managers faced as the individuals with whom they interacted as clients and the social outcomes they were mandated to achieve, it was undeniable that the political overseers who superintended government operations, and the political forces to which they were accountable, were an equally if not more important part of the authorizing environment.

The Complexity and Dynamism of the Authorizing Environment. The next questions, of course, are whether the political authorizing environment as construed above is simple or complex and whether it is constant or dynamic. In the traditional theory of public administration, politics was supposed to shape the action of public managers through the medium of a policy mandate. However turbulent the underlying politics of a given policy domain, it was assumed that politically elected and appointed officials did the hard political work of developing a clear, consistent, and stable policy mandate. That mandate, in turn, gave guidance to public managers about what they should do and how they would be called to account. The policy mandates could and should change with elections, or with the passage of new legislation, or sometimes with the signing of executive orders or the filing of a policy report or white paper. But the policy guidance to public officials was supposed to be coherent and stable in the intervening periods, and when it changed it was supposed to change all at once and remain clear and coherent.

Unfortunately, while this was good in theory, it hardly ever happened in practice. The external political authorizing environment remained stubbornly fragmented and contentious. Fights over both the ends and the means of government might have been temporarily resolved for some issues through elections, but they soon started up again.[19] Demands made on public officials by legislators, by interest groups, by the media, and by officials at other levels of government were incessant, insistent, incoherent, and changeable. In that situation, democratic policymaking can often be aided by some public leader who steps forward and offers both an end and a means of pursuing the end that succeeded in organizing the complex political world. This could happen in the large, in national elections. But it also could happen in the small, when managers nominated concepts of public value that the organizations they led could produce.

Why Strategic Management in Government Is Important and Possible

What was important about the idea of strategic management in government, then, was the idea that there were managers with value-seeking imaginations, who had the right and the responsibility to look out into the environments they faced—both the task environment and the authorizing environment—and to start asking themselves questions about how they could make better use of the organizations they led, the positions they held, or the assets they controlled to create public value. While it made many individuals nervous to think that public managers—elected, appointed, and career—might be encouraged to develop restless, value-seeking imaginations, this could be one of the important paths forward for government performance. This, after all, was understood to be what the best private sector managers provided to their organizations—a way forward toward value creation in environments that were both complex and dynamic. The ideas that emerged from such considerations had lighted the path to progress in the private sector. Why not in the public sector?

In considering this question, it is important to remember that the invitation to public managers to use their value-seeking imaginations is hardly a wide-open one. Private sector managers were expected to be disciplined by the realities they faced—the realities of customer demand, competitive pressures, and investor caution. Public sector managers, for their part, would be disciplined by the realities *they* faced—the politics that defined their desired ends and placed restraints on appropriate means and the material realities of poverty, ignorance, ill health, and so on that government operations were supposed to transform. In short, what disciplined the imaginations of public managers and brought them back from reckless adventurism to sober, conscientious work were the realities they faced on the political side, on the substantive side, and on the administrative and operational side. Their imagination could not release them from the real world in which they lived; it could only reveal more or less promising actions in that concrete world.

Toward a Strategic Framework for Public Managers

In this section we develop our framework for strategic management in more detail. We start by laying out the elements of good strategy formulation in government. This includes the claim that strategy begins with a clear-eyed diagnosis of the external environment in which managers find themselves.

But it goes beyond that to the challenge of imagining a plausible value proposition that could be pursued and the specific steps that a strategic manager (or more likely, a strategic management team) would have to take to execute the strategy over time—and to revise it as necessary.

The transition from environmental diagnosis, through envisioning public value, to executing the imagined strategy is aided by two graphic representations of public value, operational capacity, and legitimacy and support, which are the core concepts in our strategic management framework.

Finally, we identify the fruits of applying this framework in particular situations: stimulating imagination, avoiding characteristic errors, locating levels and kinds of risks, and identifying the key steps that managers must take to exploit the opportunity they have seen to create public value.

Elements of Good Strategy Formulation and Execution

In our view, strong strategy formulation requires a method that encourages managers to successfully complete six key elements. These are, first, a diagnosis of the external authorizing and task environments; second, a public value proposition consistent with the environmental diagnosis; third, proposals for sources of legitimacy and support for the public value proposition; fourth, proposals for ways to deploy assets to realize the public value proposition; fifth, a sequence of specific and leveraged actions to implement the strategy; and sixth, a process for evaluating progress and making adjustments.

Diagnosis of the External Authorizing and Task Environments. Central to the analysis of the authorizing environment is the identification of those particular actors who can formally authorize public managers to act *or those who can influence those who have the formal authority.* Also important is understanding the laws that sustain and guide the enterprise, the political currents that legitimate or undermine support for a particular course of action, and so on. It may even be important to know the ideas in good currency that exist in a policy domain. Anything that could help strengthen or weaken the legitimacy of a contemplated action demands attention.

Equally important is the capacity to identify and size up the interests and capacities of those social actors who control key assets or operational capacities necessary to achieve the imagined benefits of a contemplated action. This list of actors is generated by a process of imagining the concrete actions that would be necessary to achieve a desired result and locating particular actors who have the assets and capacities required to take the necessary actions. These implementing actors obviously include the organization one leads, but it can also include many partners and coproducers who are beyond the scope of a manager's authority. School superintendents need the support of parents to educate the children. Welfare-to-work programs need strong partnerships with employers. Fire departments need property owners to invest in fire retardant materials. And so on.

Also central to this effort is a clear-eyed view of the material conditions the manager seeks to transform and knowledge about specific actions that could be reasonably expected to improve these conditions. This knowledge could be rooted in social science and program evaluations, but it might also be rooted in professional knowledge or hard-won experience.

A Public Value Proposition Consistent with the Environmental Diagnosis. A strategy must ultimately settle on a particular concept of public value—a "destination" vision—that gives an account of the particular ways in which the individual and collective quality of life will be improved by a particular course of action. In a dynamic environment in which individual wants and needs, political aspirations, and operational capacities are all changing of their own accord, the vision of public value should not be considered predetermined or fixed; rather, it should be seen as iteratively constructed, as the organization and its progress under its strategy interact with both the task environment and its authorizing environment. There is an opportunity for everyone to learn about what is both feasible and desirable as experience accumulates. But there must be a conception of a particular state of the world that is desirable: a valuable social outcome.

Legitimacy and Support for the Public Value Proposition. A strategy must locate the sources of social legitimacy, political support, and financial resources as well as the means to tap them to give the strategic manager a reasonable chance of success. Ideally, this would not be a problem for strategic public managers. If they have an existing mandate, consistent with an attractive value proposition, anchored in legislation, political agreement, and common sense, there may be no problem. But if the mandate is threatened, or contested, or does not cover new ideas about value creation, there must be some conception of how the social legitimacy and political support can be mobilized to ensure the necessary flow of resources.

Deploying Assets to Realize the Public Value Proposition. A good strategy will have an associated operational conception that describes (in more or less specific terms) how the publicly valuable goal can be achieved (given some assumptions about the level of political and financial support). This includes an idea about how assets under the direct operational control of a strategic public manager will be deployed. But it also includes ideas about how work by partners and coproducers might be mobilized to contribute to the cause as well. Having such a conception not only gives operational focus to a strategic public manager but also provides assurance to the authorizing environment that a goal is feasible; it provides a way to monitor progress even if the achievement of the ultimate goal is far into the future.

Specific, Highly Leveraged Actions to Implement the Strategy. A strategy will have not only a vision of the value to be produced, the sources of legitimacy and support, and the required operational capacities; it will also have at its core a detailed planned sequence of actions to be taken by the strategic public manager or team that takes responsibility for executing (and, when necessary, revising) the strategy. Strategy cannot be simply an abstraction (though it may be motivated and guided by abstract descriptions and ideas). And broad strategies cannot be executed all at once (though it is often useful to create some urgency about the execution of a strategy).

Strategies become real and concrete only as managers and their teams take highly leveraged action to build the political support and to deploy the operational capacities they need to accomplish the desired goals. Ultimately, the organization's strategy is not what it says it is—*it is what it actually does.* And that strategy cannot be changed without a managerial team taking specific actions that are reliably linked to advancing the newly imagined vision and goals; that are coherent, in the sense that each action supports the other; that are well paced and coordinated in time; and that are feasible, given the resources and skills of the managers and the leadership team.

Evaluating Progress and Making Adjustments. For managers to be successful in a changing, demanding, and sometimes hostile environment, they need not only an initial plan but also a concrete picture of what they should be seeing as they take actions to implement the imagined strategy. They need not only to track progress over time on each element of the strategy but also to know what the developing success or failure in one element of the strategy implies for the other elements. If a particular element is going badly, does that mean they should redouble the effort with respect to that element? Or work harder with respect to another element to compensate for the problems in the first? Or scale back overall ambitions in light of new information about how hard the task actually is?

Without an interim process evaluation (one rooted in an image of what results or indications they expect to see from the strategy as a whole—and from each of its major components—and when they expect to see them), managers cannot use the valuable feedback that the collision with the real world provides to them.

Figure 5-1. *The Strategic Triangle*

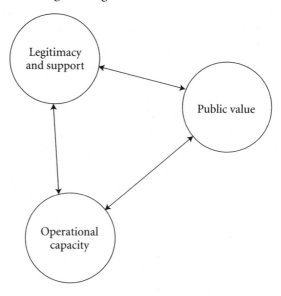

A Strategic Management Framework with Two Applications

We believe that the core concepts we introduced at the beginning of this chapter—public value, legitimacy and support, and operational capacity—guide the observations and structure the calculations of managers to meet the tough standards set above. So far our argument has been primarily that these categories will aid in diagnosing the external environment. Here we go farther and explain how the concepts can be used to stimulate creative imagination and to provide tests of what imagined actions would be worth doing. Two graphic means of representing the core strategic concepts help push us along this path.

The Strategic Triangle: Exploring and Exploiting Causal Links. Figure 5-1 presents one way in which the core concepts have been graphically displayed. We call this the strategic triangle. By separating the three concepts, the figure emphasizes the importance of answering questions about each of the core concepts: What is the public value to be produced? From what sources will legitimacy be derived? What operational capacity is needed to achieve the desired results?

But the separate circles are also connected: arrows show how each point of the triangle relates to the others. These arrows connote causation. On this view, a proposal to create a particular kind of public value, or the actual production of a particular kind of public value, will cause public legitimacy and support to wax or to wane. The recruitment of a new constituency to support a proposed initiative might change the purposes of the initiative, but it will also increase the resources available to the initiative. The development of a new capacity for producing a certain public value can build legitimacy and support for that effort. And so on.

Taking this causal account of the strategic triangle seriously allows a manager to use the strategic triangle in both a rigorous planning mode and a focused action mode. In the planning mode—the realm in which one thinks, tries to anticipate consequences, and so on—one can begin with a vision of what public value should ideally be produced and then map backward from that idea to determine what operational capacities would be required to achieve the desired results and what kind and level of resources and public enthusiasm would be required to produce that effort. The requirements for operational capacity and legitimacy and support can be compared with what would be naturally forthcoming, and a managerial plan can be made to ensure that the political and operational requirements could be built from present circumstances through managerial action.

In the action mode, a manager can act in two ways: both to build operational capacities and public legitimacy and support on behalf of a vision of public value and also to check with reality to see whether the plan worked. Did the vision build enough support? Did the efforts beyond articulating the vision succeed in legitimating the effort and sustaining a suitable level and kind of resource? Did the moves made to transform the operations of the organization and leverage the capacity of partners and coproducers actually produce the desired results?

On this view, the strategic triangle not only emphasizes an independent diagnosis of each part of the strategic management framework but also seeks to identify—and exploit—the causal connections among the different elements. The process is something like the following musing reveals: I just had an idea about a dimension of public value that could be advanced. Does that help or hurt with my authorizing environment? What does it mean for the work I have to do to build operational capacity? Gee, I see that we can produce that dimension of public value relatively easily, but it creates a problem for me in my authorizing environment.

Thus strategic managers try to shape and rearrange the elements until they get something that is both consistent and valuable.

The VCS Visualization: The Challenge of Integration and Alignment. Figure 5-2 presents a different graphic arrangement of the core elements of our

Figure 5-2. *The Value, Capacity, and Support Framework*

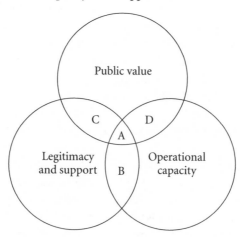

strategic management framework. This Venn diagram draws attention to the degree to which *integration and alignment* can be said to exist among the three core elements for any given public value proposition, regardless of whether that proposition refers to an organizational level strategy or to specific projects or programs that a manager plans to launch.

The idea here is that there are many possible programs or initiatives or actions that managers could pursue using the operational capacities of their agencies and drawing upon their agencies' existing legitimacy and support. Each existing or possible program is associated with a value proposition: an argument about why it might, on balance (net of its costs), create public value. Each is also feasible (or not) given the capacities of the agency (and the capacity of the agency to mobilize coproducers). And each either is or isn't seen as legitimate by the people and organizations whose support is relevant to it.

The Venn diagram defines zones in which particular strategic ideas, or particular programs, could be placed. Each point in the zone represents a different strategic concept or particular program. The location of a program design or idea (inside or outside each of the three circles) indicates whether it exhibits the corresponding characteristic. Differing parts of the diagram thus consist of programs exhibiting different *combinations* of the three central characteristics. Programs that have *all three* characteristics are in area A; areas B, C, and D contain programs with two of the characteristics; and areas where *only one* characteristic applies appear in the remaining spaces in the diagram.

Obviously, the sweet spot in this diagram is the area marked as A. All actions in this zone are already valuable, authorizable, and doable. We call this the "Nike" zone, since every time managers find an initiative in this zone, they should "just do it." There is nothing to prevent them from doing so, and little work is required to initiate or to continue the effort.

Working on projects that lie in this zone should be relatively simple and satisfying. Indeed, these projects may be seductive because they entail little risk and little work. Given the pleasure of working in this zone, it would be tempting to spend all of one's time there and avoid the more difficult but potentially more valuable challenges in other zones. The principal managerial challenge for projects in this zone is to get the work done without spending too much managerial time, attention, and energy on it. Those valuable resources are needed to move projects from other zones to the Nike zone.

As figure 5-2 is drawn, the area composed of strategic ideas or programs that have all three desirable characteristics is relatively small. By contrast, all of the other combinations of characteristics (each with at least one characteristic lacking) present difficult challenges that significantly differ from one another.

Consider the area marked B in the lower middle of the diagram, where operational capacity and legitimacy and support overlap but which lies outside the official's best judgment of where public value lies. This area, too, can be seductive. After all, actions or programs in this area are supported, and the organization has the resources—knowledge, skills, people, money, space, and so on—to carry them out. The only difficulty is that, in the view of strategic public managers, there are convincing reasons to believe that the program does not produce net value for the public. Perhaps legitimacy and support are based on tradition rather than a current justification. Or perhaps a narrow group that benefits from the program, either as beneficiaries or as suppliers, has built a strong political base that has not been contested. Whatever the reason for the continuing support, it is tempting for managers simply to carry forward with the program, leaving to others the moral work of deciding what is valuable and the political case for disrupting the cozy equilibrium.

Alternatively, consider the area where managers' judgment indicates that there would be public value in carrying out the action or program but where the organization has neither the operational capacity nor the support of the public (perhaps because it has failed to establish the program's legitimacy). What should a strategic manager do here? Possibly, the program is a pipe dream, and managers should work on other more practicable ideas. But perhaps with a little (or maybe a lot of) work the program could be made viable. Would it be appropriate for managers to undertake that work? That is, would it be appropriate for them to be, in effect, entrepreneurs for the program? To try to assemble the necessary support and to invent, develop, build, or buy the relevant operational capacities? And, if so—which should they do first?

An obvious answer would be to build legitimacy and support first, on the theory that with support in place the capacities can then be procured. But this has at its root the idea that the missing capacity is something that additional support could easily help the official get the money to procure— like employees with the relevant skills, for example. But what if the missing capacity is the knowledge of how to do some crucial element of the program? In that case, building support first—making promises that the program can be made to work—may be risky indeed. Still it might be worth running that risk, since it would put pressure on the organization to find a way to develop the capacity.

And so it goes. To be successful, managers seek to develop policies and programs in the Nike zone. To do so, they can work in three different ways. First, they can move the strategic concept or the program itself by redesigning it. For example, if the program is initially outside the capacity circle, perhaps managers could redesign the program to fit more neatly within existing operational capacities. Second, managers can work to shift the location of the circles so that the program comes to fall within them. Perhaps they can come up with better arguments for the program, shifting the views of potential supporters so that the program comes to be within the newly positioned support circle. Or perhaps managers can shift resources within the operation, moving the capacity circle so that what was formerly infeasible now lies within the redesigned capacities of the agency.

These moves are all predicated on the idea that managers are sure that their vision of public value is the right one. But perhaps managerial judgment is flawed. On this view, managers might want periodically to review the analysis that supports the value proposition to make sure that they have not made a mistake or that the world has not shifted in a way that makes the program less valuable than they once thought it to be—and this constitutes the third way in which they can undertake the work of producing more value in the Nike zone. There are thus three possible strategic tasks that can be pursued to create more projects within—or to move value-creating actions into—the Nike zone: invent or redesign programs that fit within it; shift capacity and legitimacy and support so that they are more aligned with the value circle, where public value can be produced; or revisit the analysis of public value, checking, correcting, clarifying, and making more reliable the judgments that are serving as the North Star for the overall strategy.

The essential feature of the analytical tool is not that it provides answers to these questions—the questions are highly context specific, and getting the answers to them will depend crucially on the details in each situation, to say nothing of the courage and resourcefulness of the managers and their teams. The utility of the tool is that it suggests, in an organized way, some of the most relevant questions to pursue, observations to be made, and actions to be imagined. To repeat: in democratic societies, successful and durable programs must eventually come to exhibit all three characteristics—value, legitimacy, and support. If a particular public value proposition imagined by a manager lacks one or more of these characteristics, the manager must either abandon the project to the "too hard" or the "too wrong" box or find the means to reshape the project or the concrete conditions in the world so that it meets all three of these tests.

The Fruits of Strategic Analysis

Strategic analysis asks managers to do a lot of work. They have to make many independent observations of the world they inhabit. They have to engage in philosophic as well as empirical examination. They have to keep testing and adjusting their ideas as they try to develop a public value proposition that can find alignment with each of the core concepts. And all this seems to have to happen before a single action can be undertaken. It is all in the imagination of managers and their teams. What could action-oriented managers get from all this other than a headache? It seems that they are in danger of analysis paralysis.

Our answer is that strategic analysis guided by these core concepts and frameworks helps managers in four ways:

—It is an organized way to explore alternative program designs and associated strategic programs to provide capacity, support, and value alignment, thus (we hope!) encouraging creativity and guiding innovation.

—It helps managers avoid characteristic errors in public management.

—It allows managers to gauge the risks of pursuing any value proposition that is different from the status quo.

—It helps identify the specific actions that managers must take to reduce their risks and breathe life into their vision.

Stimulating Creativity and Guiding Innovation. A principal reason to apply this strategic management framework is to provide a systematic, replicable process for imagining value-creating moves. Beginning with a careful analysis of the location of a given program (either current or contemplated) in the Value, Capacity, and Support space (see figure 5-2), the strategic public manager can determine what shifts need to take place either in the conception of the program or in empirical conditions in the world as it now exists. By using judgments made at each point of the strategic triangle to challenge assumptions and constraints at each of the other points, the strategic approach invites brainstorming about the whole and about how the challenges of creating the whole might best be overcome.

Avoiding Characteristic Errors in Managerial Calculation. One major reason to use these strategic management frameworks is to avoid making simple but quite common errors in public management practices. Common managerial errors include at least the following.

First are potentially fatal errors of *diagnosis*:

—Incorrectly assuming or calculating that a given program or action lies within the existing operational capacities of the organization, when in fact it does not. (Oh my God, we thought we could fight and win a conventional land war in Asia against a guerrilla enemy that enjoyed popular support!)

—Incorrectly assuming or calculating that a program or action enjoys or would enjoy legitimacy among, and the support of, the relevant constituencies (on balance, taking into account any opposition), when in fact it does or would not. (Oh my God, we thought the public would support a huge expansion in government spending to ensure medical care for all!)

—Incorrectly projecting that a given program or action would create public value, when indeed it would not. (Oh my God, we thought that it would be valuable to build large public housing projects to house those who could not afford quality housing!)

We refer to these errors as errors of *commission*—because the official who makes these errors is likely to proceed with the program, thus committing the error. These errors are generally visible (and therefore often highly consequential for the careers and reputation of public managers), as it becomes obvious that the program does not in fact have operational capacity, legitimacy and support, or public value.

But similar errors can occur in the opposite direction as well, so we next have three additional errors of diagnosis (less likely to be fatal):

—Incorrectly assuming or calculating that a given program or action lies outside the existing operational capacities of the organization, when in fact capacity exists. (We could never use community health centers to help parents become more committed and better able to manage the overall development of their children!)

—Incorrectly assuming or calculating that a program or action does not or would not enjoy legitimacy and support from the relevant constituencies (on balance, taking into account any opposition), when in fact it does or would. (There is no way we could mount a national program to reduce drunk driving!)

—Incorrectly projecting that a given program or action would not create public value, when indeed it would. (We definitely should not use libraries to supervise latchkey children or the military to help us turn angry young men into disciplined citizens.)

We call errors made in this direction errors of *omission*, because officials who make them leave value on the table. Errors of this kind tend to be less visible—people often are not aware of value that they could have had that they are not receiving—and so tend more often to be survivable for the managers who make them.

Finally, in addition to the foregoing six diagnostic errors, the strategist can make at least three errors in *designing or executing a given strategy*:

—Incorrectly predicting how specific interventions will move capacity or support or provide a more accurate assessment of the location of public value. (If we make schools accountable for improving academic test scores, student performance will improve and the achievement gap will be narrowed.)

—Failing to imagine a line of action that could have taken advantage of an opportunity in the environment. (We can't reach out to teachers' unions and determine whether and how they might help not only to develop teaching as a skilled profession but also to support the goal of demanding strict accountability for academic performance.)

—Failing to reliably and accurately evaluate the success of the strategy as it unfolds and to usefully adapt it to the feedback that comes from the environment as efforts are made to execute the strategy. (If a large majority of schools are failing, the best we can do is to publicize their failure.)

Identifying and Minimizing Strategic Risks. The third key contribution that the strategic management frameworks laid out here can make to managers is to help them, and those who oversee their activities, identify the strategic risks that managers and their enterprises are taking. So far it has been assumed that any particular value proposition would either fit or not fit in the environment in which managers were operating. In fact, no ideas fit perfectly with 100 percent confidence; all ideas carry risk. The important question is how big the risks are and how they can be managed.

The frameworks provide a good way of spotting the particular risks associated with any particular strategic idea. The easiest way to see this is to start the strategic analysis in a place that is most comfortable for purpose-oriented managers—with a vision of some public value that can be produced. Having established that vision, it is possible to "map backward," or "reverse engineer," to the conditions that have to be in place in order for the project to succeed, as outlined above. Such a process produces what can be seen as a gap analysis. The gaps are those places where particular conditions that are necessary for the project to succeed are not now present. (Manager: I want to produce a health financing system that will provide high-quality medical care for all. I'm not sure I have the political support for such an ambitious program. I'm not sure I have the levers to keep costs down even as I am promising to extend coverage and sustain quality.)

The strategic framework not only finds the gaps, it identifies their nature and offers a hint of the managerial work that must be done to close the gap. One might see that a particular project has a lot of political risk but not much operational risk. Or it has operational risks but not so much risk that it won't turn out to be valuable.

Finding the Path Forward: The Dynamics of Strategic Intervention. One standard for effective strategy remains to be met: working out the specific actions that managers and their strategic teams need to take now, and leading into the future, that will allow them to activate the potential they have seen in the environment. Unfortunately, neither tool serves this purpose directly because they focus primarily on *broadly integrating* the core elements of a successful strategy in the near to midterm, not on the actions that are specifically helpful in realizing the potential. To work out the specific actions that managers and members of their teams should undertake to realize a particular public value proposition, they have to take a more dynamic view of the situation—and one that is more concrete and action oriented.

The world that is revealed by trying to integrate value, capacity, and support is far from static. In fact, it is constantly in motion. Both the realities and the beliefs about public value can change. So can the political forces that give legitimacy and support to a particular effort. So do the operational capacities. One important implication of this observation is that timing may play a critical role in developing an effective strategy, and learning to wait and be ready for an opportunity might be an important action tool. Sometimes the best strategic advice is, Don't just do something, stand there and wait for the favorable moment.

But this observation ignores the fact that managers have some agency in shaping how things develop in the world. They can become more articulate and tell a better story about value creation than the one that currently exists.

They can build new operational capacities and show that they can work to deliver valued results that others did not think possible. They can respond to, and help to give standing to, particular political currents that are running in their environments. There are intervention methods that can reshape collective perceptions of the world and what value could be realized within it, that can build new operational capacities through a planned sequence of innovations, and that can activate latent—or redirect existing—political forces.

Ultimately, by understanding enough about where they are today, by imagining where they could be, and by seeing where the principal risks to realizing that grander ambition lie, they can see an action path open to the pursuit of increased public value. The set of actions designed to create these improvements could be called the implementation strategy, and the managerial work laid out in that strategy should be understood as a set of *strategic investments* designed to reposition an enterprise in its setting to produce increased public value. Like all investments, the steps taken now are valued not because they produce value immediately but because managers predict they will produce value in the future, and such predictions are always uncertain.

Application to Englebert's Problem

What, if anything, does all this have to do with Captain Englebert and her problem? What, if anything, does the development of strategic management in government imply for the way we think about public sector organizations and the individuals who work within them on our behalf?

Captain Englebert: Midlevel Bureaucrat or Strategic Public Manager?

Let's look first to see whether the concepts of strategic management have any relevance or utility for Captain Englebert. Is she in any important sense a strategic public manager? Initially, the answer to that question seems to be no. As noted, Captain Englebert is a public servant, embedded in a bureaucracy, with a seemingly well-defined policy mandate and a technical task to accomplish in service of that mandate. Yet it doesn't take much reflection to see that, to carry out her apparently simple technical assignment, she will have to engage in many activities that can only be construed as strategic management.

With respect to public value, she is asked to figure out exactly what "enhanced port security" means as well as how it might best be achieved. She finds that she faces extraordinary uncertainty in both the nature of the threats and what could best be done to deal with them. Consequently, she will be in the business of making guesses and experimenting as well as knowing and executing. She may also find herself addressing complicated value judgments about trade-offs between risks and costs as well as the distribution of both benefits and burdens.

With respect to operational capacity, it quickly becomes obvious that the capacity she needs is distributed widely across many levels of government, many agencies within government, and many private and nonprofit organizations. She cannot rely on her direct authority, or even the authority of the Coast Guard as an institution, but must find the means to mobilize action from others whom she does not directly control. She is enormously advantaged in this by the palpable threat of terrorism and the fact that many other organizations have their own reasons for wanting to take collective action to deal with the threat. But that only gives her a better-than-usual opportunity to mobilize collective action through consultation, deal making, and so on. And this better-than-usual opportunity is very likely temporary; the heightened concern about security in the wake of the 9/11 attacks will ebb over time and, with it, Captain Englebert's leverage.

With respect to legitimacy and support, precisely because she has to innovate at the operational and organizational level, and because she has to mobilize a complex network of largely independent actors, she has to give special attention to the protection of her mandate for action. She has to find a way not only to participate effectively in existing policymaking processes at the international and national level but also to create, enrich, and sustain such processes so that the performance of the whole system can improve over time.

U.S Coast Guard: Organization with a Mission or Platform for Strategic Managers?

An important personal question for Englebert, and the rest of us citizens and taxpayers who are relying on her to help keep us safe, is whether she is operating in an organization, in an accountability system, and in a political culture that will allow her to act like the strategic public manager she needs to be. This is important because organizations create positions in which individuals have significant leverage to produce results. They are guided in this work to some degree not only by their own professionalism but also by a structure of accountability that exists both internal and external to the organization of which they are a part. That structure of accountability is intended to ensure that managers at all levels use their discretion in ways that are oriented to the achievement of value for others rather than themselves: that they are reliable agents of those who have entrusted them with assets.

A key part of being a strategic manager in the public sector is to focus one's calculations and efforts not on personal advancement in the hierarchy, not on ensuring organizational survival, but on producing the best possible results from the assets entrusted to the manager. This is entirely consistent with the business literature on private strategic management. The managerial goal is not to enrich themselves but to serve the interests of shareholders by finding the most valuable use of assets entrusted to them. In the business literature on corporate strategy, and in much of our own presentation, the pursuit of value means finding the best possible use of an organization's assets in a dynamic environment. The unit of analysis is the organization. Finding a successful strategy both guarantees the future of the organization and unleashes its value-creating potential.

In Englebert's case, however, the strategic focus does not seem to be principally on a particular *organization*. The focus is, instead, on *the social problem* Englebert has been commanded to solve. Of course, it matters hugely that Englebert is part of an established organization, that that organization has a mission, and that that organization will be called to account for its performance in its mission. Indeed, at some level her problem-focused strategy can be seen as instrumental to the Coast Guard's strategy of repositioning itself in response to important changes in both the task environment and the authorizing environment.

Still, when the strategic focus shifts from an organization to be positioned to a problem to be solved, a great deal changes in the strategic analysis. The relationship between any given public organization and any given social problem can be very complex. Public organizations often have many purposes—not just one. Public organizations rarely have a monopoly over the capacities to deal with some social problem, and they find themselves both competing with and complementing the efforts of other organizations in trying to solve some social problem. And unfortunately public organizations sometimes forget their purposes and become much more interested in survival than value creation.

This means that when a manager commits herself to a problem to be solved, rather than an organization to be positioned, two important results emerge. First, the strategic manager becomes less preoccupied with the refinement and perpetuation of the organization and more rigorous in aligning the organization's work with the problem it has been assigned to solve. Second, the strategic manager becomes open-minded and opportunistic about engaging other organizations whose assistance may be valuable, or even essential, to the problem's solution.

This creates the paradox that, when midlevel managers in government positions take responsibility for solving new social problems, *they have to operate outside the boundaries of their organization.* And that raises the important question of whether they are operating outside the boundaries of their organization's mission. According to the Coast Guard's website, its mission is as follows: "Safeguard our Nation's maritime interests in the heartland, in the ports, at sea, and around the globe. We protect the maritime economy and the environment, we defend our maritime borders, and we save those in peril. This history has forged our character and purpose as America's Maritime Guardian—*Always Ready* for all hazards and all threats."

This mission statement is broad and inspirational but has enough concreteness that one can imagine taking particular activities that the Coast Guard is currently performing, or some that it is contemplating, and see whether and how they fit into this conception. The difficulty is determining how broad the space turns out to be in practice. The Coast Guard leadership has a significant amount of discretion to decide which activities will be included, which excluded; which will be heavily supported, which given lip service; which new investments will be made, and which old activities repurposed. It is hard to find the single, clear public value proposition that can be used to discipline the activities of the organization. The Coast Guard is more like GE, a multiproduct conglomerate, than it is like ALCOA, a single-product organization. If there is something that makes it a coherent organization, it is less about the purposes it serves than about the kind of operational capacity it brings to situations.

But what is that operational capacity that gives the organization its identity? One answer is that it is a disciplined, well-trained group of individuals arrayed in a hierarchical organization that allows them to operate efficiently and effectively in projects of different scope, that has lots of vessels and bases distributed along America's ports and coastline, and that carries with it the authority of the state. There are lots of valuable purposes that this organization could achieve, including but by no means limited to those noted in the mission statement!

But to say that this organization can make a valuable contribution to these goals is not to say that it is the only one responsible or that it can achieve these goals all by itself. It knows from experience that it shares its responsibilities with many others and that it is dependent on many others to help it accomplish its goals.

This understanding has, over time, developed an additional distinctive capacity in the U.S. Coast Guard: a capacity for orchestrating complex collaborative efforts. Just as one of GE's hallmark competencies became the creation of successful general managers, so too the Coast Guard's trademark is the large-scale and sustained production of managers skilled at aligning both internal and external capacities in innovative and flexible configurations to meet the (often changing) imperatives of an assigned mission.

The U.S. Coast Guard is habituated by its history, and thus equipped by its culture, to deal with whatever comes its way. It is proud to be "Always Ready." Its managers perceive it as normal to take initiative and responsibility and to find ways of developing effective working relationships across organizational and sectoral boundaries. But we submit that many, perhaps most, governmental organizations share, at least latently, this characteristic of the Coast Guard. Governmental organizations can be viewed, like private corporations, as bundles of assets. At any given point in time those bundles are committed to a particular set of purposes and to creating value through the disciplined pursuit of those purposes. But the task of value creation advances not just from incremental process innovations in the service of constant goals but also from the more complex processes of repositioning organizations within a changing world with correspondingly changing goals. Critical to their ability to do that is to develop and support managers, at many levels of the organization, who can be strategic managers, not just midlevel bureaucrats. We think that a highly responsive, legitimate, and innovative government depends on many managers thinking and acting as strategic managers.

Notes

1. Mark H. Moore, *Creating Public Value: Strategic Management in Government* (Harvard University Press, 1995).

2. In this formulation, the focus of strategic thought and action is "an initiative" taken by some strategic actor. The usual focus of "strategic" thought and action in the business world is a business firm. The strategy developed for the firm is a vision of the products and services that a firm will produce and the markets within which it will compete. The strategy also includes the managerial actions that would be necessary to implement this strategy. In the public sector, the focus of strategy is often a particular government organization. But it could also be a policy or project that a manager takes responsibility for authorizing and implementing. There is an important difference between an organization, on the one hand, and a policy or project, on the other. A policy or project can be part of a single organization's activities, or it can cut across many organizations, picking up bits and pieces of organizations within its scope. For example, the Drug Enforcement Administration is an organization with

its own mission or strategy. But it operates as part of an overall federal policy toward drug abuse managed by a drug czar. And DEA has within itself particular policies that seek to manage the distribution of psychoactive drugs—some of which have legal uses, and some of which do not. One can also usefully distinguish between the organizational strategy or policy as it is realized in the actions of a complex policymaking and implementation system and the particular actions that a particular manager needs to carry out to shift current actions toward the execution of the desired strategy or the implementation of the desired program. We imagine that individual managers in positions of authority and influence can leverage their particular actions; the speeches they give, the deals they make with overseers, the decisions they make about the allocation of resources, the ways they measure the performance of an organization, and so on are all designed to give them some leverage over the actions and performance of the larger organization or production system that they seek to influence.

3. R. A. W. Rhodes and John Wanna, "The Limits to Public Value, or Rescuing Responsible Government from the Platonic Guardians," *Australian Journal of Public Administration* 66, no. 4, pp. 406–21.

4. Note that the idea here is that these different level managers are expected to have *thoughts* about ends as well as means and about innovations as well as the continuation of past performances. This is what we assume constitutes the "policy responsibilities" of senior level government officials. It is not that these individuals should act on their thoughts without legitimating their actions through democratic processes. See Moore, *Creating Public Value*, chaps. 4 and 5, for a more extensive treatment of ethical issues and recommended practices.

5. Numerous empirical studies of government policymaking and implementation show just how hard it is conceptually to establish and maintain a clean line between, on the one hand, ends and means and, on the other hand, politics and administration. See James Q. Wilson, *Bureaucracy: What Government Agencies Do and Why They Do It* (New York: Basic Books, 1989). Similarly, many empirical studies show that the problems faced by relatively low-level career public managers often center on both important questions about what values are to be protected and pursued in particular circumstances as well as how legitimacy and support can be built for the efforts that seem consistent with their democratic mandates. See Jerry Mashaw, *Bureaucratic Justice: Managing Social Security Claims* (Yale University Press, 1983); Michael Lipsky, *Street Level Bureaucracy: Dilemmas of the Individual in Public Services* (New York: Russell Sage, 1980). And, as Mark Moore and Archon Fung argue in chapter 9, this volume, there are many reasons to believe that the performance of democratic governments could be improved if there were a closer integration of politics and administration at many different levels of government, from the national level down to the grass roots of local schools, health agencies, and child protective services. But these realities have not forced a significant change in either our conventional thought or necessarily in the practices of public management.

6. Alan Altshuler and Robert D. Behn, eds., *Innovations in American Government: Challenges, Opportunities, and Dilemmas* (Brookings Press, 1997).

7. See, for instance, Ronald A. Heifetz, *Leadership without Easy Answers* (Harvard University Press, 1994).

8. See also Stephen Goldsmith and Donald Kettl, eds., *Unlocking the Power of Networks: Keys to High-Performance Government* (Brookings Press, 2009).

9. On the role of norms in public management, see Mark H. Moore, "On the Office of the Taxpayer and the Social Process of Taxpaying," in *Income Tax Compliance: A Report of the ABA Section of Taxation Invitational Conference on Income Tax Compliance* (Washington: American Bar Association, 1983).

10. For an early treatment of the idea of strategy in the private sector, see Kenneth Andrews, *The Concept of Corporate Strategy* (Homewood, Ill.: Irwin, 1980). For a more contemporary treatment, see Michael Porter, *Competitive Strategy: Techniques for Analyzing Industries and Competitors* (New York: Free Press, 1998).

11. Michael E. Porter, *Competitive Strategy: Techniques for Analyzing Industries and Competitors* (New York: Free Press, 1980).

12. Mark H. Moore, "Policing: De-Regulating or Re-Defining Accountability," in *De-Regulating the Public Service: Can Government Be Improved?* edited by John J. DiIulio Jr. (Brookings Press, 1994).

13. Jeffrey Prottas, *People Processing: The Street Level Bureaucrat in Public Service Bureaucracies* (Lexington, Mass: Lexington Books, 1979).

14. Goldsmith and Kettl, *Unlocking the Power of Networks.*

15. Moore, "Policing: De-Regulating or Re-Defining Accountability." See also Mark H. Moore, *Accounting for Change: Reconciling the Demands for Accountability and Innovation in the Public Sector* (Washington: Council for Excellence in Government, 1993).

16. Altshuler and Behn, *Innovations in Government.*

17. For a vivid account of what we mean by policy politics, see Philip B. Heymann, *The Politics of Public Management* (Yale University Press, 1987); Philip B. Heymann, *Living the Policy Process* (Oxford University Press, 2008).

18. Archon Fung, *Deepening Democracy: Institutional Innovations in Empowered Participatory Governance* (New York: Verso, 2003).

19. V. O. Key, *The Responsible Electorate: Rationality in Presidential Voting, 1936– 1960* (New York: Vintage Books, 1966).

JOHN D. DONAHUE *and* RICHARD J. ZECKHAUSER

6

The Tummler's Task: A Collaborative Conception of Port Protection

Let's start with a scene from the past: Some of the guests on this first day of vacation—the big family groups, the veterans of previous seasons, and a few gregarious newcomers—are already hard at play right after breakfast. Some are on the tennis courts, others cautiously trying to revive horseback-riding skills, others playing the games clustered about the main house, and some just luxuriating in wide-slatted whitewashed chairs. As the sun clears the Catskill ridge and floods the whole resort, all of the right sounds—happy shrieks as old friends reunite, the clatter and clang of disks and balls and horseshoes, cheerful insults issued and repaid—echo through the valley. This is what they came here for. Their day will be good.

But others are stuck in cheerless torpor. A dozen or so are holed up in the game room, which by all rights should be empty on a brilliant morning like this. Others cluster by the pool mumbling mindless pleasantries to the general vicinity or sitting awkwardly alone. There's the sullen seventeen-year-old girl pretending to read a paperback copy of *Siddhartha,* radiating outrage at being dragged to the resort by her parents, whose excruciating voices can be heard all the way from the croquet lawn. There's the widower who has just realized, on the first morning of his first visit without her, that his wife had always been the one to make the plans and find the friends. There's the young rabbinical student—intelligent, kindly, reserved—who came to the resort knowing he needed to relax but now worries he'll be spending the next

We are grateful to the participants in the Smith-Richardson project on networked governance and particularly to the project chair, Mark Moore, for provocative and detailed comments that greatly contributed to our efforts to situate the governmental "tummler" within the broader spectrum of collective-action models.

week working out endgames on the chessboard in front of him. There's the couple trying to rekindle their marriage with a week of fun, though so far they've scarcely exchanged a word with each other. And there are the hopeful singles, who aim to at least make a friend or two, and maybe make a match, on their vacation in the mountains.

Each of these isolated idlers would rather be engaged with others in the group, but they find themselves unable to take that first step to organize interaction. The equilibrium seems perverse; taking the initiative to forge a link might mean a minute or two of moderate discomfort but will yield many hours of satisfying interaction. But it's a step these people—and many of the rest of us—are, for a range of reasons, ill equipped to take.[1]

The Classic Tummler

Suddenly a brightly dressed fellow bursts on the scene. He is balding and somewhere in his thirties—maybe his forties—but he surges among the scattered guests with a toddler's jittery energy. He targets the nearest loner and commences a conversation, uninvited and unabashed. She is peppered with questions—New York, which borough? Which temple? Does she go to the mahjong nights on Tuesday? So she must know our regular, Hattie Strauss! Then he quickly moves on to the next idle guest. As he makes his circuit he continuously doubles back, often towing his current conversation partner to link with an earlier one, cementing the new bond with some shared hobby, or high school, or acquaintance. Like one of those toys in which a magnetic wand drags scattered iron filings onto a picture of a face, the man tugs the singletons and the pairs into larger clumps until the patterns he wants start to emerge.

It's time for Simon Says! The man knows that those who find it hard to strike up a conversation with a stranger will find it impossible to refuse his demands to join the game—lack of skill or a partner is no excuse, as neither is needed—and he soon has a dozen erstwhile loners out of their chairs and on the lawn. Each time he tricks a person into dropping his hands without Simon saying so, there is laughter, perhaps a bit of gentle kidding, and the "loser's" name called out repeatedly and memorably in the man's trumpeting voice. He suddenly stops the game. "Who knows what that big bird is that just alighted on that branch?" Three guests raise their hand. He asks their names and calls on Bernie. "You're right! He is a red-tailed hawk. He hangs around here; we've named him Ralph. Those of you who like birds go down to the meadow, especially the margin where the forest begins."

After twenty minutes of Simon Says, he turns to the day's activities. "I need eight people who know how to play shuffleboard. I'll start with Gerry and George and Louise." All had admitted to him in his initial rounds that they played the game. "Who will join their team? Thank you, Alice." And so it goes. He shrinks the cost of shifting from idle to engaged. "Who is a rider? Come on, I know more of you than that." Ultimately, he coaxes up five hands and tells them to be at the stables at 11 o'clock to meet the hands and the horses. There is a method to his mixing. "Now, who is from New Jersey? You three? OK—tonight you guys are going to be a charades team. Charades is cutthroat here, and there are big prizes, so you might want to get your signals straight in advance." The Jersey contingent—as he had discovered before they had themselves—included the widower and two unattached women of a certain age.

In less than an hour of rearranging people, jump-starting conversations, and a silly game or two, most of the former idlers are connected with promising people and activities. The man scans the scene one last time for lost souls that need immediate attention and decides that the morning roundup is over. He allows himself a wholly genuine private smile. He'll need to reserve some energy for making the rounds at the cocktail hour and tonight's opening dance, but for the moment his work is done. Because this *is* work, the man's job at the resort, and a respected, well-paid profession in this industry. He's the tummler.

The word *tummler* is conventionally—but inadequately—translated as social director. It has origins in Old German, like all the rest of Yiddish. Other linguistic shoots from the same root give us *tumult, tumble,* and the modern German name (*tuemmler*) for the joyously hyperactive bottlenose dolphin. The verb form in Yiddish is *tumlen,* "to make a racket." (You don't have to be noisy to be a tummler, but it helps.) Almost every Jewish resort in the borscht belt from the 1930s through the 1960s employed a tummler, sometimes several. Often the tummler had a sideline doing stand-up comedy on stage in the evenings, but the core job was to forge connections among guests, to ferret out and capitalize on their interests, to create synergies among them—in short, to do whatever it took to make sure a good time was had by all.

Today the borscht belt is no more, Grossinger's and Kutcher's and the Concord and most of the rest have been razed or have fallen into ruin or have mutated into something very different from what they were in their heyday. The profession of the tummler has mostly vanished, and the word itself has become archaic and obscure. Which is too bad, because the tummler's task—to engineer the realization of a latent shared interest while unleashing dormant capabilities—is a timeless one.

Government's Missions and the Tummler Metaphor

We resurrect the term *tummler* and invoke the profession for a specific reason: In an era of complex collective-action problems and cross-sectoral collaboration, the tummler's task is a useful metaphor for some of government's most urgent missions.[2]

This chapter represents variations on a theme we have developed at length in our book *Collaborative Governance: Private Roles for Public Goals in Turbulent Times*.[3] In that book we assert, elaborate, and illustrate several propositions about the use of collaboration with private actors to advance goals conventionally considered to be government's responsibility. Briefly stated, the key notions are as follows:

—The distinction between direct governmental action and delegation to private parties is important, but equally important and far more sparsely studied is the distinction *among* forms of delegation.

—Models for private involvement in public undertakings span the spectrum from simple outsourcing, in which private contractors are paid to follow government's instructions, to voluntarism, philanthropy, and other arrangements in which private parties advance their own conceptions of the public good.

—This spectrum can usefully be characterized in terms of the *allocation of discretion* between the public and private sectors, with government holding all or most discretion in the case of simple outsourcing and the private sector holding all or most discretion in the case of philanthropy.

—The middle range, defined by a significant degree of *shared* discretion, is little examined and poorly understood relative to its practical importance. We use the term *collaborative governance* to designate this realm of shared discretion.

—Private collaborators' exercise of *production discretion* (the ability to innovate, customize, and otherwise deploy production models that are unavailable or awkward for government acting alone) can and usually does promote the creation of public value. Private collaborators' use of *payoff* or *preference discretion* (the ability to tilt benefits to favor the private collaborator at the expense of the public, or to substitute the private collaborator's preferences for those of the public), conversely, undermines public value.

—The positive and negative aspects of private discretion tend to be entangled.

—Government's key responsibility for this category of collective action involves designing and maintaining arrangements that maximize the gains from production discretion, net of the losses from payoff and preference discretion. Discharging this responsibility calls for the simultaneous application of high-order analytical and managerial skills.

We suggest four generic motivations for government to accept the incremental effort and risk that the collaborative approach generally entails. These are *productivity* (the expectation that private actors possess efficiency advantages germane to the accomplishment of a governmental mission), *information* (facts relevant to the production of public value reside outside government itself), *legitimacy* (citizens, for whatever mix of reasons, prefer that the private sector have a role in the pursuit of some task), and *resources* (the belief that a collaborative delivery model will lead to an infusion of private resources to augment the governmental resources devoted to a mission). While it is rare for any real-world collaboration to be rooted exclusively in a single motivation—more than one, and frequently all four, tend to be in play—we find it useful on both analytical and managerial grounds to distinguish among them.

A further overarching theme of our work is that collaborative governance requires continual monitoring and revision as priorities shift and as experience generates evidence about how well arrangements are working. No model of collective action, from the simplest direct bureaucracy to the most baroque collaboration, can be set up once and for all and left to run as is indefinitely. But collaborative governance is especially difficult to get perfectly right up front and is especially prone to fall out of alignment with the imperatives of public value production. Indeed, we stress the importance of a *cycle* of collaboration that begins with an *analysis* of the policy problem or opportunity, moves to the *assignment* of actors to be engaged in the effort, moves on to the *design* of the collaborative arrangement and ends with efforts to *adjust* the collaboration to better meet the mission—and, crucially, returning in an iterative fashion to analysis, and so on around the cycle.

The tummler's task represents an important subcategory of collaborative governance, applicable where the number of private actors is relatively small and (most important) where the interests of the private actors are *closely* but not *perfectly or obviously* aligned with each other's and with those of the public at large. Once established, mutually beneficial collective action is stable, sustainable, and self-reinforcing. But its establishment is not automatic or inevitable. The potential for mutually beneficial cooperation remains dormant—only shallowly latent, but latent nonetheless. In such circumstances government's pivotal role is to make manifest the potential community of interest and to orchestrate its realization, like the tummler helping resort guests achieve their shared goal of interactive fun.

This metaphor is at odds, we are aware, with many more familiar images of the government at work. One classic conception is the *protector*—the soldier, cop, or firefighter—standing between us and malign natural forces or bad guys at home and abroad. Another is the *obligator,* requiring all to contribute money or other resources so that it can spend on undertakings that offer shared benefits. Another is the *enforcer,* demanding that each of us foreswear polluting, double-parking, dope smoking, or other offenses against collective norms. Still another is the *redistributor,* moving resources from the first round's designated winners (whether people or projects) to alternatives whose asserted worth the market misses.[4]

These roles—which call on other capabilities than those of the tummler—endure and indeed make up the bulk of government undertakings, on whatever basis they are tallied. But some governmental tasks, we submit, are closely akin to kindling links among idle guests at a summer resort. Motives are to a substantial degree aligned—but not so completely or so obviously aligned that cooperative action is automatic. A nudge (or at times a shove) is needed to make manifest the latent community of interest. For those more inclined to scientific metaphors, consider a supersaturated liquid requiring only a seed for crystallization to occur.[5]

Some examples are straightforward. Consider the identification and promulgation of technical standards. Or the settlement of the American West, when hundreds of thousands of land-hungry families were eager to extend the frontier—but not all by themselves, without neighbors. (The various Homestead Acts of the late nineteenth and early twentieth centuries can be considered large-scale episodes of tummling.) In Singapore the government takes on an even more ambitious task than the classic tummler, aiming to engineer not just a nice game of tennis but actual matrimony between qualified lonely hearts.[6]

In other instances the tummler's role is less obvious. The federal government's most important contribution to the rescue of the Chrysler Corporation a generation ago—in contrast to more recent rounds of brute-force bailouts—was not so much filling by itself the company's financial gap as it was helping, inducing, or in a few cases compelling a vast network of bankers, lenders, employees, suppliers, dealers, and state and local governments to recognize and act upon their shared stakes in saving the automaker. If and when there is ever a large-scale shift from internal-combustion to electric vehicles, it will very likely involve governmental efforts to coordinate investments in the cars themselves and in the networks of charging stations that will make them feasible. And early in America's history Alexander Hamilton envisioned government as a financial tummler, weaving connections between investable funds and promising projects.

In these and other cases, government's *primary* role is to bring people together to make things better or, as an economist might phrase it, to move to a superior equilibrium. The goal is to motivate voluntary cooperation. Dollars and edicts may be involved, but as catalysts or spark plugs rather than as the main engine of the enterprise. In pursuit of that improved outcome, there are four major tasks: *Define* the latent community of shared interests, *identify* the members' dormant capabilities, *create* a process that can identify outcomes that will be superior for all, and *coordinate* action so that such a beneficial outcome is realized. The Coast Guard's orchestration of a new port protection regime, we suggest, presents a prime example of pursuing these four tasks to produce an improved outcome.

What conditions are helpful, or even essential, if the tummler is to succeed? First, there must exist at least one superior outcome—distinctly superior for some and for all others equivalent (or only trivially inferior) to the status quo—that can be reached via voluntary efforts. This implies that the costs falling on no party can be so onerous that compulsion or large side payments will be required. The tummler's task would be of an entirely different nature, and far more prone to failure, if he had to pay or compel some guests to do things they actively disliked. This governance model applies only when the latent benefits of collective action are large relative to the costs.

Often there are many available mutually beneficial outcomes, which leads to our second condition: the parties must be sufficiently similar in the scale—though not necessarily in the nature—of their burdens and benefits such that none feels that he is getting an unfair deal.[7] Third, it helps if the costs that private parties pay are small absolutely. Otherwise, quibbling over amounts may defeat the deal. If monetary costs are more than trivial it helps if the benefits are also reaped in dollar terms, since parties do not like to pay hard dollars for intangible benefits that go in some measure to other people. Fourth, it eases the outcome if a particular party's efforts visibly advance not just the collective interest but also his own. Thus when the cargo loading facility at the port puts up bright lights to deter terror threats, the facility is protecting its own interests. The lighting deters all-too-conventional pilferage as well as terrorism.

Fifth, the group of participating parties must be small, for two reasons: they have to be effectively coordinated by a single individual, and small size helps them monitor each other and develop a sense of mutual obligation.

The tummler's task, once again, is to coordinate and cajole individual decisionmakers to take (somewhat) costly actions that together produce collective benefits. When is the tummler likely to add the greatest value? Two factors are critical, size (as just mentioned) and the ratio of external benefits relative to private benefits. On both factors, we are looking for a "Goldilocks" solution—group size and the relative scale of public and private benefits must both be not too large and not too small.

When external benefits are modest in comparison to the benefits collected by private parties, the outcome of simple market arrangements is close enough to the social ideal that it's not worth attempting to structure a nonmarket alternative. When the ratio of external benefits to private benefits is extremely high, by contrast, the tummler's task of cajoling and coordination will seldom suffice to overcome the natural tendency to free ride. Government will have to rely on taxing and spending or on regulatory mandates (such as the requirement to be vaccinated or attend school for some minimum number of years) to ensure the right outcome.

The size of the group similarly requires intermediate values if the tummler is to shine. Simple bargaining is superior to tummling when just two or possibly three people are involved. And the tummler's potential to coax a group into a collectively superior one fades when the group gets too large and it becomes hard to verify that others are cooperating. In rough terms, groups ranging from perhaps four to around twenty-five define the tummler's sweet spot. Others of our five factors matter as well. Tummling works better when parties are similarly situated and roughly equal in size. If similar parties get similar arrangements, none can complain of unfair treatment; none can reasonably expect to get a better deal.

Yet one might ask why it should be necessary for some overarching entity—whether the government or a Catskills resort—to take responsibility for ensuring that the tummler's task is fulfilled. Should not the members of the group who stand to benefit be able to recognize and act upon their shared stakes by themselves? What circumstances call for a governmental tummler, as opposed to an entirely private trade association or similar group? The private sector displays endless cleverness in devising guilds, trusts, alliances, franchises, chambers of commerce, and other organizations to advance shared goals. So the question of whether, why, and when this is a role for government—in the person, for present purposes, of Captain Suzanne Englebert—requires some attention.

Government actually possesses significant advantages in playing this role for the particular function of port protection. It is perceived as a natural focal point for coordinating activity. There may be multiple impediments, moreover, to individual parties involved with a port taking the initiative to organize for common advantages. Any single private participant seeking to promote cooperative activity might inspire fears that it is guilefully promoting its own interests more than, or instead of, any shared agenda. From the perspective of the potential group leader herself, she might reason that taking the initiative would signal that she had more to gain than the rest of the group and thus can be expected to bear a disproportionate share of the burden.

The governmental tummler is also a logical focal point because it is different in nature from the parties being coordinated. In an emergency people tend to respond to someone in uniform, whether or not the uniform signals authority or expertise germane to the task at hand. People in a burning building are more likely to follow the lead of a person wearing a Marine officer's uniform than the same person in a business suit, for example. The uniformed person, recognizing this tendency, may feel more responsibility to coordinate activity, even in a venue where he has no responsibilities. In our case study, the government did have a distinctive role (its prime representative wore a uniform), and most participants probably did believe from the outset that it held a privileged position.

The government is also likely to have preexisting relationships with the members of the latent group. Most or all of the private entities associated with a port will have had prior dealings with the Coast Guard or will find it reasonable to respond to an invitation from the Coast Guard to begin a conversation. This network advantage may not be unique to government, to be sure. At every port there is probably some private player known to have a particularly diverse, intense, and lengthy history of relationships with other interests associated with the port. But had he called the meeting, he would be relying on those personal relationships. Those with whom he did not have such links might not come, or might come grudgingly, thinking they would be disadvantaged. A prime asset of the governmental tummler is that it is natural for her to possess and to invoke an extensive set of connections but with the expectation of evenhandedness across the network.

The final advantage of the government, when it takes on the tummler's role, is that it does have coercive powers. Such powers can be important even when they are not invoked (not necessarily applicable to the case at hand)— or indeed not even mentioned. No party would like to be known for having refused to attend a port protection meeting convened by the Coast Guard. It is entirely possible that the Coast Guard would not have the legal ability to apply the slightest sanction to a no-show. But few would want to find out.

We do not wish to suggest that the governmental tummler's task is to simply point to some mutually beneficial solution and get out of the way as the private parties race to implement it. Often the process of realizing some latent store of shared value involves a great deal of time, effort, and risk of failure. Defining, identifying, creating, and coordinating an outcome—the four elements we outline above—can involve many steps. They start with discovery, then move to trust building, and finally move toward the solution. The tummler's second day in the resort week is likely to go more smoothly than the first. The guests already know how to talk to each other and trust each other a little. And so it is with governmental tummlers, as they build what is sometimes called community.

We recognize that our depiction of the tummler's role as someone who conjured collective benefit without coercion might seem Pollyannish. There is an enormous literature on the challenge of promoting shared action, and the baleful term *free riding* gets preeminent attention in this literature. But free riding is not inevitable, as Mancur Olson showed us decades ago.[8] The key, in Olson's formulation, is an appropriate alloy of private and collective benefits. Assembling a coalition to advance a common goal is vastly easier if the coalition's members reap individual gains in the course of the enterprise. Doctors are willing to join the American Medical Association and pay stiff dues to support its lobbying mission in part because membership delivers some private benefit. An AMA card conveys professional gravitas and can be helpful with referrals. (AMA membership as a share of American physicians has fallen significantly since its peak in the 1960s, and the association is trying to ramp up the ratio of private benefits—such as offering discounts on office-management software, or concentrating on newly minted doctors with more to gain from the AMA cachet—in hopes of reversing the trend.)

We view our work as building on Olson's central insight: that the availability of private—or, in his word, "selective"—benefits plays a significant role. But we add three elements. First, we consider explicitly the role of the coordinator. Olson, while technically a political scientist, spent enough of his career consorting with economists to adopt their fabled tendency to assume the existence of some pivotal piece of the collective-action puzzle. Second, we focus on cases where decisionmakers take actions directly to provide a good, rather than contributing resources to a common pot for funding the provision of the good. Third, though Olson's argument could readily apply to organizations such as corporations as providers, his case studies overwhelmingly focus on individuals. We expect tummler illustrations, by contrast, to frequently involve organizations such as government agencies, nonprofit groups, corporations, or even nations as the decisionmakers. In doing this, we recognize that such organizations will often be represented by one or a few individuals.

Protecting American Ports

Given the perceived threat to the ports of the nation after the terror attacks of September 2001, there was plenty of private benefit—bolstered security for shippers, vessels, and port-based facilities, meaning more secure cash flows for their shareholders—to motivate collective action to provide protection. The events of 9/11 alerted officials and citizens to other vulnerabilities that— like tall buildings and fuel-filled airplanes—had not (until that day) occasioned major concern. At the top of any knowledgeable observer's list had to be maritime ports. Over 360 ports open to international commerce dotted America's vast coastal reaches. They ranged from small harbor facilities catering to mostly local commerce to enormous complexes that included factories and refineries, truck and rail hubs and even airports, as well as loading, unloading, repair, and maintenance facilities for seagoing vessels and their cargo. All told, around 95 percent of American imports arrived by sea.[9] It was not hard to imagine all manner of evils slipping into America unnoticed amid the daily tide of oil and toys and oranges and televisions and sneakers, most arriving in sealed containers.

Congress quickly passed the Marine Transportation Security Act, which incorporated the provisions of the International Ship and Port Facility Security Code that had been negotiated, in record time, after the 2001 attacks. The Coast Guard—still adjusting to its recent relocation from the Department of Transportation to the newly created Department of Homeland Security—was tasked with putting the new legislation into effect.

The most straightforward way to respond to this mission—especially, one might think, for a military organization—would be for Coast Guard experts to huddle with a handful of other security specialists and issue stepped-up new security rules to which shippers, operators, and other port denizens would be expected to submit. But to predict this path would be to miss both the essence of the security task and the culture of the Coast Guard. No uniform, top-down, port security regime could work—at least not without strangling port operations, stifling trade, and triggering bankruptcies. American ports were so diverse in size, layout, and function—and hence in security considerations—that no single approach could work for all of them.

Most ports were technically owned by a local government or special authority but were leased to, or otherwise put under the control of, a private (and usually non-U.S.) port operator.[10] Tens of thousands of other private parties—shipping firms, shipowners and insurers, trucking and transshipment firms, and many others—each occupying its own economic niche, were involved in and dependent on the functioning of the ports. Roughly 7.5 million containers—each embodying its own far-flung trade network—entered the United States by sea every year.[11]

Knowledge on how to provide protection was diffused among dockworkers, shipowners and crews, warehouse workers, truckers, longshoremen, and others who—each by playing their own semiautonomous role—permitted the complex entity called a port to function. A port is more like a city—with scores of institutions and interests interacting without central control—than it is like a centrally directed corporation. No mechanism for complete top-down control existed or could easily be constructed.

If top-down would not work, why not bottom-up? Each of the entities involved in the operation of a port, after all, surely has an interest in deterring terror. They are demonstrably competent at cooperating—just look at the balletlike coordination that keeps the cargo flowing. Can't we just count on these separate players to come together to protect the port without government involvement? For the whole range of reasons discussed earlier—including the wrong ratio of private to public benefits, significant real or perceived differences in parties' situations, or the wrong group size—collective benefits that are in principle achievable can be elusive in practice. Even where self-organization is a manageable task, that work can take time. And port protection is a dramatically new task countering a committed and creative external threat. The separate entities that make up a port no doubt *could* figure out on their own how to mount effective defenses against that threat. It would likely take years or decades, however, and the consequences of a successful attack—if defense is ineffective or delayed—could be catastrophic. Most resort guests would eventually find a way to engage with each other, after all, absent the tummler—it just might take twelve of the fourteen vacation days to do so. The tummler's task is to make the connections happen expeditiously—to capitalize on dormant capabilities and coordinate action, quickly enough, around the new collective mission.

These private players had expertise, stakes, and vulnerabilities that the Coast Guard could not hope to incorporate into port protection plans unless the players themselves were brought into the system. Fortunately, a one-size-fits-all security plan imposed by government fiat was also antithetical to the Coast Guard's culture. For a range of reasons—some well understood, others mysterious—the Coast Guard had long been known for flexibility, innovation, and a collaborative mind-set. Its distinctive orientation would prove a perfect match for the challenge of rapidly building the right kind of security system for hundreds of diverse American ports.

A cross-continental series of marathon meetings was organized and moderated by Captain Suzanne Englebert, as other authors have described. At one level these meetings were simply the standard review-and-comment sessions required by the Administrative Procedure Act. But Captain Englebert's intent—and by all evidence the actual outcome of the process—was to identify and implement a security agenda that generated benefits for virtually everyone involved (with the obvious exception of aspiring terrorists). The regime features a significant degree of discretion for private parties, placing it squarely within the broad category of collaborative governance. It has close affinities with approaches taken by the Environmental Protection Agency and the Occupational Safety and Health Administration, among other regulatory agencies, that let regulated firms take the lead in developing plans to protect the public interest, with the government's main role being to assess the private plans and judge their adequacy.[12]

The analogy to organizing a bunch of isolated resort guests into a rousing round of activities, with most directed to their own interests and skills, is only a little strained. Captain Englebert herself, for starters, displays many of the tummler's classic features. She is intuitive, creative, empathetic, tireless—and maybe even a little noisy. She explicitly understood her role to be one of mobilizing other groups to recognize and act on a shared interest. Consider some key characteristics of the outcome:

—*More permissive than coercive.* Once the products of stakeholder meetings and internal deliberations had been distilled into a final plan, what emerged was a security regime in which the Coast Guard took a hard line on the *what* of port security—the performance levels that had to be met—but left its private collaborators lots of discretion on the *how.* An operating company, portside factory, or trucking depot linked to a container port faced a nonnegotiable mandate from the Coast Guard to control access to their facilities to ensure that only screened personnel could enter. But the private parties had almost unlimited freedom to develop their own ways to control access, as long as they could convince the Coast Guard that their plan would do the job and would be faithfully implemented.

—*More tailored than uniform across ports.* There is no single port security regime for the nation but rather an enormous array of interrelated plans customized to each port and to each private party within the port. Individual Coast Guard port officials are encouraged and empowered to learn about and accommodate the specific requirements of the various constituencies involved in "their" port.

—*Embracing, and merging, disparate motives.* Nongovernmental actors involved in ports had a range of motives to support stepped-up security in the wake of 9/11. Some were strictly private—the desire to shrink the risk of financial losses from direct damages and subsequent lawsuits resulting from a terror attack. Some were no doubt entirely public spirited—the urge to help safeguard a country suddenly seen as imperiled. And some motives were in between, such as the hope of burnishing a firm's reputation by visibly participating in a patriotic task or of gaining a position near the center of the action that might yield advantageous information or connections. The Coast Guard's approach invited collaborators to participate without drawing sharp distinctions among reasons for joining the effort.

—*More flexible than rigid at a single port.* Security arrangements can vary not just by port and by the particular configuration of operators, shippers, and other private parties but also by the season, time of day, and type of shipment. A change in the array of shippers and shipments, or the assignment of a new chief port officer, can trigger significant amendments to security arrangements without the need for changed laws or even regulations.

It is important to note that the tummler's task—to define a latent community, capitalize on dormant capacities, and coordinate action toward common benefits—does not exhaust the Coast Guard's role in port security. Some of its functions, such as cruising around on fast boats bristling with machine guns, evoke classic protective roles.[13] Its enforcement responsibilities are meant to head off obvious ways the security regime could fail—deterring free riders from exploiting other private players' security expenditures, for example, or diverting agreed-upon security spending to protect against garden-variety theft rather than terrorism. The constituencies that surround a harbor, after all, have some interests in common but by no means all, as Captain Englebert knows very well. But a Coast Guard strategy that started from or emphasized some other aspect of the governmental repertoire would have produced a port protection regime quite different from and arguably considerably less effective than one rooted in the tummler's task.

Can such a convoluted and shifting system actually work? There have been no noteworthy terror incidents at American ports since the passage of the Marine Transportation Security Act. But terror attacks are, fortunately, rare events, so even a decade of safe operation does not assure us that protection is effective. As Robert Behn (chapter 4, this volume) establishes, there are no perfect metrics—nor even truly reliable proxies—for the level of risk at any one time. And thus there is no good gauge for whether current port protection arrangements have substantially improved upon the status quo ante.

This indeterminacy highlights one of the gravest vulnerabilities of the tummler approach, both in this instance and more generally: the risk of choosing the model because it is the most feasible, even when it is not the most effective, approach to collective action. The model presumes that there is only a narrow gap for the tummler to bridge between potential and actual cooperation—that the confluence of interests is only shallowly latent and that a modest nudge will suffice to make it manifest. If this presumption is wrong, then the tummler approach is misguided—invisibly and insidiously so, since it can masquerade as effective action.

Here Malcolm Sparrow's warning (chapter 3) is particularly germane. American ports confront a diverse portfolio of threats. What if we are mistaken that the most serious bundle of threats is also the set in which public and private interests are most closely aligned? Suppose it were the case that the gravest danger is not an explosion in the harbor but a vial of smallpox virus smuggled through in a tiny corner of some container—to wreak devastation, untraceably, when opened and deployed hundreds of miles inland? If there really *is* no way to secure the ports without forcing private players to incur large costs—the expense of fine-grained inspection, the losses from disrupted commerce—in the name of lowering the risks to the nation at large, then tummling is the wrong role for government. It is thus possible that the current port protection regime is not a success story but a distraction. This is a generic risk not just for the subcategory of collaboration we address in this chapter but also for the collaborative approach to collective action in the broad. The mere maintenance of a partnership ostensibly serving the public interest can be touted as a success—even independent of the empirically elusive production of actual public value.

Yet if the inevitably sketchy evidence can't guarantee that we have gotten port protection right, it also gives little basis for second-guessing the judgment of the public and private actors tasked with the mission. Neutral observers, including the hard-to-impress Government Accountability Office, give the Coast Guard and its network of collaborators generally good marks for progress—while noting that the range of choice left to private players makes the enterprise highly, and inevitably, complex.[14] Captain Englebert and her colleagues and collaborators deserve kudos for creatively improvising a reasonable response to a suddenly urgent collective mission and—in the process—illustrating a collective-action model with relevance to an admittedly finite, but enormously significant, range of tasks.

Notes

1. The situation for our isolated idlers, to invoke the formal terminology of game theory, is that they have two strategies available, idle or engaged. They are all stuck playing idle, since none would find it worthwhile individually to incur the cost to switch to engaged. Yet all would choose engaged if asked to do so or if sufficient numbers of others would have done so. It would be easy to join lively groups around the ping-pong tables or the shuffleboard courts, with the expectation of getting into the next game, or to talk to others with whom you knew you had some minimal connection, or to wander the trail to the waterfall with even a stranger who would like the same experience. The situation has aspects of the dance floor that stands empty, even though it would move to full if it could only start at half full.

2. We thank Mark Moore for strongly encouraging us to expand this section and for his constructive comments pointing out how to do so.

3. John D. Donahue and Richard J. Zeckhauser, *Collaborative Governance: Private Roles for Public Goals in Turbulent Times* (Princeton University Press, 2011).

4. Mark Moore usefully observed that there are also conventional images of government's roles—including the adjudicator, the convener, and the mediator—that are more consistent with the tummler metaphor.

5. We are indebted to Malcolm Sparrow for this image.

6. Singapore's Social Development Unit within the Ministry of Community, Youth, and Sports is profiled in Dan Murphy, "Need a Mate? In Singapore, Ask the Government," *Christian Science Monitor*, July 16, 2002; and on the ministry's website (http://app.mcys.gov.sg/web/corp_orgstruc.asp#5b). Sun Myung Moon, founder of the Unification Church in South Korea, does much the same, sometimes marrying, at the same time, hundreds of couples he has matched up.

7. The nations of the world must find a way to curb their greenhouse gas emissions. Any one of the many cooperative solutions available to reduce emissions would be far superior to the outcomes predicted by leading climate scientists that will otherwise be our fate. Yet the greatest tummler would have trouble getting even the major polluters to substantially curb their activities. The asymmetries are simply too great. China and the United States are the two largest emitters. Any agreement

with teeth that the United States would find acceptable would be rejected by China, and vice versa.

8. Mancur Olson, *The Logic of Collective Action: Public Goods and the Theory of Groups* (Harvard University Press, 1965).

9 Katherine McIntire Peters, "U.S. Port Security Measures Cover the Waterfront," *Government Executive*, September 10, 2004.

10. Anne Khademian, "The United States Coast Guard and a Port Security Network of Shared Responsibility," in *Unlocking the Power of Networks: Keys to High-Performance Government,* edited by Stephen Goldsmith and Donald Kettl (Brookings Press, 2009), pp. 149–50.

11. Ibid., p. 145.

12. Howard Kunreuther and others, "Third-Party Inspection as an Alternative to Command and Control Regulation," *Risk Analysis* 22, no. 2 (2002).

13. Port security jumped from about 1 percent of Coast Guard spending before 9/11 to about 58 percent in the year after the attacks, stabilizing at around 25 percent (ibid., p. 154).

14. "Maritime Security: Substantial Work Remains to Translate New Planning Requirements into Effective Port Security," GAO 04-838 (Government Accountability Office, 2004), p. 4.

STEPHEN GOLDSMITH

7

Toward a Higher Purpose: Captain Englebert Navigates the Choppy Waters of Network Governance

The 9/11 terrorist attacks transformed American perceptions of the world. Until that time, Fortress America had been secure. No one needed to lie awake at night worrying about assaults from abroad. On one horrible morning, all that changed. Instead of being complacently secure, the country would have to be anxiously vigilant. Many wondered what they could or should do to restore the lost sense of security.

Among those who felt most responsible for taking action were federal government agencies with security portfolios. After all, defending the nation from foreign attack was an undisputed core function of the federal government. President Bush demanded that federal agencies responsible for national security—ranging from the military through federal law enforcement agencies to intelligence agencies and the diplomatic corps—should act to "never let this happen again." Officials throughout the federal government wondered how these events would affect them. Would they be commanded or asked to do something new? Would they be invited to think creatively?

The bad news was that no one knew precisely how to "never let this happen again." They had seen one form of attack on the United States, but how many other possible forms could there be? They had seen the defenses breached in one particular area, but how many other vulnerabilities existed?

An equally problematic if less obvious certainty was that the capacities required to identify and meet these potential threats were beyond the federal government's own organizational capacities. It did not matter how mobilized, efficient, professionally competent, or creative federal officials were. If all of the federal agencies were effectively mobilized all at once to meet the threat directly, there would still be significant gaps in security. To meet the threat, they would have had to go beyond the capacities of their own federal agencies. They would have had to leverage the efforts of governmental actors at state and local levels and of actors in the private sector as well.

Fortunately federal government officials were not alone in worrying about and preparing to take action to improve port security. The threat was general. Many actors beyond the federal government felt motivated by some combination of self-interest and sense of duty to do what they could. A second and third army stood ready to act: state and local government officials and the heads of commercial firms that depend on security from terrorist attack. Both waited to see a path forward to improved security that was both worth their while and consistent with their duty.

This situation called for the use of the management techniques that I describe as network governance.[1] The core idea is that there are many public problems that government is called upon to solve but that no single government organization can solve by itself. In response, the most ambitious government officials feel responsible for solving problems rather than presiding over established bureaucratic machinery. To do so, they must find means to outperform the structures they have inherited. First, these officials (elected, appointed, or career) focus on the substantive problem that is to be solved rather than the mission of their organization. Next they envision the solution to the problem and identify those actors who are in positions to contribute to the solution of the problem. Finally, they mobilize and coordinate the capacity of this new network to solve the problem.

While the potential of network governance is clear, it is less obvious how that potential can be identified and exploited. By definition, in these situations there is no individual whose job description explicitly requires her, nor whose authority explicitly allows her, to direct a network. Instead someone must take the assignment, or take the responsibility, to work beyond her mandate. She decides to find the means to exercise influence that goes well beyond her direct authority. Typically, an individual acting as a network manager conceptualizes, identifies, and exploits the latent potential of a network. How that happened within the Coast Guard shortly after the 9/11 attacks is the focus of this chapter.

As noted above, the need—and the opportunity—to create network governance solutions often begins with an obvious problem for which the government's response is essential but inadequate. This is certainly true in the case of port security. There are many possible threats, points of vulnerability, and responses that U.S society as a whole could make to the generalized threat of terrorist attack. Yet a focus on the nation's ports was natural, as ports are vulnerable targets where any damage inflicted could produce wide effects. The ports are also an entry point where it might be possible to interdict threats traveling through toward other domestic targets.

At the time the federal government's capacity to act on port security could be found primarily in the United States Coast Guard. The USCG had long assumed responsibility for port security and had constructed relationships with the myriad private and public actors who used and operated the ports. Indeed, each port had a Coast Guard official assigned as captain of the port. These officials took responsibility not only for directing the activities of Coast Guard personnel at the port but also for enforcing regulations that the Coast Guard had developed to ensure the smooth functioning of the port (a form of network governance, as it were). The captain of the port also facilitated communication among the many commercial and other actors within the port community and ensured its efficient operation (another form of network governance). President Bush's charge to government agencies to "never let this happen again" led to the Coast Guard's activation, which in turn led to a mandate for Captain Suzanne Englebert.

This chapter uses Captain Englebert's actions to examine the what, who, and how of network governance from envisioning through design to implementation. It tackles foundational questions of network formation and management, including

—How will the mission and strategies of the network be defined?

—What elements of the existing landscape of actors, resources, and capacities might best be recruited into the network?

—How should the network be called into existence, made self-conscious, and structured to define and do its work?

—From what sources does the network manager derive or construct her authority and influence over the operation of the network?

—What mechanisms could the network manager or convener use to ensure participation among network players?

—How might the network manager navigate the primary tension of competing accountabilities?

—What are the individual leadership skills and techniques demonstrated by a successful network manager?

After introducing the concept of network governance, I then apply its core principles to the captivating and illustrative story of post-9/11 port security as envisioned by the U.S. Coast Guard. This exercise provides not only a useful exploration of the leadership lessons from Captain Englebert but also a useful analysis of the network governance theory of twenty-first-century public management.

Basics of Network Governance

I use the term *network governance* here to mean any effort involving sub-stantial government participation initiated to accomplish public purposes through complex arrangements that combine the existing capacities of many private and public organizations. Rather than reaching public goals through single government agencies or through efforts fully financed and controlled by government (and characterized by the hierarchical structures and processes one might expect), network governance relies on complex mechanisms to coordinate private and public resources. It animates multiple efforts toward a shared view of an important public purpose.

Network governance is a common approach to dealing with important public problems. As of 2004 the federal government was already spending approximately $100 billion more on outside contracts than on employee salaries. Federal agencies like NASA and the Department of Energy were spending up to 80 percent of their budgets on outside contracts. Some forms of public-private partnership—albeit generally less sophisticated than the multiparty arrangements we refer to here as network governance—have been used for a long time. In fact, government has often used its varied tools to spark and guide the actions of both private and public actors to address public problems rather than rely only on direct government pro-duction of desired social outcomes. The federal government relied on pri-vate companies to explore the Western frontier and to build the railroads that made it inhabitable. It also relied on private individuals to maintain security in the West long before local government could pay for police departments. Local government required that children attend school long before it built public schools. It is hard to think of any important social or public problem that some combination of private and public action is not meeting (or attempting to meet).

What makes the idea of network governance seem new is the increased complexity of problems, which highlights the limits of direct government action to accomplish important results. Government agencies cannot pro-duce domestic security, or economic prosperity, or equal opportunity for children without depending critically on private individual and collective capacities. Public managers and policymakers have become interested in the previously underrecognized contributions of private actors to social welfare. Government also hopes to leverage those contributions by finding ways to work with rather than against private desires and capacities.

Why Networks?

There are many advantages to network governance.

—Tapping into private motivations to act on public problems can enlarge the effective stock of resources that government can use to achieve its objectives. This is particularly important in a world in which citizens are less willing than before to part with their hard-earned money or their right to live without intrusion from governmental restrictions.

—The varied social actors recruited to a network often bring a variety of approaches and relationships, which can improve the performance of government. This occurs partly because the solutions are more tailored to particular individuals, communities, or market niches and in part because what first seems like a customized innovation turns out on occasion to be a robust method for the field as a whole.

—Relying on networks allows particular members of the network to do what they do best. It also amplifies their effect by ensuring that complementary capacities needed to parlay the contributions of one organization to a larger social effect can be relied upon.

—Networks enable mangers to be more nimble by bypassing some of the stultifying rules and procedures, to more quickly scale up or down in terms of both staff and participants, and to personalize individual solutions when a one-size-fits-all solution is counterproductive.

—Resourceful managers mobilize networks when they need the financial or intellectual capital of the private sector to reach beyond what they could do alone with their current materials and technical resources—whether helping a greater percentage of constituents, crossing jurisdiction lines, or connecting to actors in closely related but structurally distant issue areas.

Challenges of Network Governance

While network governance offers advantages, creating and leading a network poses significant challenges. These challenges include the effort made to create a shared sense of opportunity and obligation among network participants and maintaining effective communication and coordination among a potentially large number of actors. They include managing the tension between competition and collaboration. Other challenges include creating data systems that can help the network see how it is acting and finding ways to plug gaps in capacity so that the whole can be significantly more than the sum of the parts.

Most important, potentially, are challenges the network manager faces around goal congruence and accountability (which are explored in greater depth below). Policy goals can be fuzzy, hard to measure, and long term—which in turn makes it hard to hold a network and its individual actors accountable. As discussed above, the mission and goals of individual organizations may simultaneously overlap and compete or conflict. Network managers and members are also likely to find it hard when their organization's interests are hindered by the interests of the network or of the public more broadly.

Network managers find it challenging to navigate the minefield of oversight: if it is too prescriptive and rigid, the benefits of the network model are lost, whether in the form of licensing, code enforcement, or second-guessing; if oversight is too loose, the network falls apart from internal or external pressures or both, from cost overruns, from service failures, or from illegal behavior. Government's typical reaction to a breakdown of any type is to overcompensate, adding heavy reporting requirements for all providers—for example, after a well-publicized error or scandal by a single actor.

The Government Accountability Office found that more than a third of federal programs are at "high risk" of experiencing significant problems with their large procurement operations or with large programs delivered mainly by third parties. In particular, public officials are not trained to manage the complicated webs of the new network governance model, nor do adequate numbers of them have sufficient experience in such management.

Collectively, in order to optimize its problem-solving networks, government officials need new skills. For example they must be able to understand which combination of public, private, and nonprofit actors will produce the best solutions to particular public problems. I introduce here basic but helpful rules and concepts in network design and later address the necessary competencies to make these concepts work effectively.

Design Phase: Envisioning the Network

The first step in exploiting the potential of a network governance model is for the system manager to envision the network in relatively concrete terms. She must then help each member of the network come to see roughly the same set of possibilities. At the outset, the network potential is only latent, hidden so to speak within the current arrangement of assets, capacities, and commitments of many social actors. The challenge is to see what that latent network could accomplish if organized and how one could galvanize it into action.

Defining the Purpose of the Imagined Network. The network manager's starting point is the problem to be solved. The operations follow the outcome to be achieved. The network's imagined capacity to achieve an important social goal is what gives it a raison d'être, not the mission of any particular organization within the network. Being clear about the problem is crucial to knowing whom to enlist and with what priority and urgency. It is also the first step in trying to persuade these network actors to join.

The purpose that the network manager has in mind for her network is unlikely to be a purpose to which network participants feel accountable in any substantial way. They each have their own purposes, missions, and structures of accountability that may or may not align with the purposes of the network. The more overlap there is between the actions they feel duty bound to take and the aims of the overall network, the easier it will be to recruit and sustain participants' engagement. What makes potential recruits attractive then is not that they already share a common purpose but that they have some capacity that would be useful to the network and that might be molded into a new shared purpose. The network's goal has to become important to each member's existing organizational mission.

To accomplish this goal, the network manager can appeal to some higher authority that can direct participants to adjust their existing purposes and activities. Alternatively, the network manager can persuade the participants that the goal of the network is not inconsistent with the mission of their organizations. In this case, she might argue that they ought to willingly participate because their participation is sufficiently inexpensive while the benefit for society as a whole is great. This approach is more effective if some higher authority (like the president, in this case—or even the entire nation) declares this calculation to be true. The network manager might also persuade participants that achieving the goal of the network is indeed necessary to achieving their own core missions. Finally, the network manager can call on norms of mutual assistance and reciprocity to engage the network actors.

Captain Englebert, as the manager and integrator of a network, found that her major challenge was shifting her participants' view of accountability from fulfilling the mission of their individual agencies and of their authorizers or overseers (likely based on completing a series of predetermined functions) to solving or at least making progress on the problem of port security.

Envisioning the Right Partners. The central task of the network manager is to develop the operational capacity required to move the needle on an important public problem. Consequently, in determining whom to recruit as network participants, network managers depend on a functional logic of production. In order to achieve social goal A, the manager figures that first X, Y, and Z will have to be accomplished. Her diagnosis of the situation shows us that particular social actors are in a position to do X, Y, and Z or to create conditions under which other actors will do X, Y, and Z. The network manager judges the importance of potential members on how their organizational capacities—technology, experience, skills, and resources—match the network's operational requirements. The right set of actors will make a substantial difference once animated and directed toward the goal.

After determining the network's purpose, the second step is to search for social actors and organizations that have the capacities that a manager identifies as necessary. In some cases these actors may not even be using the capacities now for the purpose driving network managers. These partners must be able to devote capacity in a way that does not compete with other mission-critical assignments.

Exploring Potential Structures for the Network. Configuration of the network follows. While common network structures include service contracts, supply chains, and ad hoc models, there is no single, exhaustive list of network structures.[2] Quite often network structures blend together among multiple, interrelated partnerships, as with the case of Captain Englebert, which does not fit any neat typology.[3] Keith Provan and Patrick Kenis write that the rough outline of a network is born of an analysis of the problem at hand, the size and scope of the network required, network-level competencies of potential partners, trust level among partners, and degree of goal consensus among them.[4] Context of course is also important in selecting a structure: strategies and parameters vary to fit distinctly challenging landscapes and environmental factors, including system stability.[5] A list of eight dimensions follows for the consideration of the leader ready to determine her ideal network structure.

The first dimension is the overarching purpose of the network and its organizational congruence. Congruence among partners can provide an impetus for cohesion within networks, as they can be thought of as "efforts to adapt existing organizations, through practical partnerships, to pursue public purposes."[6] Indeed, the public purpose itself is an important structural factor begging analysis. The stronger the ties between the partners' organizational purpose and the overarching purpose convening the network, the greater likelihood that it can operate successfully. In other words, the likelihood that each partner can be induced to commit to the network's mission plays a role in its shape. Similarly, cultural similarities (that is, organizational values) can induce partners to work with one another.[7] Captain Englebert likely enjoyed a high level of cultural compatibility among the actors already involved in maritime commerce—and in port security in particular. If her network was more of a supply chain model, like collaboration between two auto parts companies, then she would have instead looked for commonalities among partners in terms of how they viewed trade-offs among price, quality, and time.

The second dimension is the required duration of the network. Varying scenarios call for a range of expected life spans for networks. The less time a network is required to operate, such as in cleaning up after a natural disaster, the greater the likelihood that participants can overcome organizational, ideological, and operational differences so as to work together. Further, the network manager might spend less time examining conflicts between potential participants. Long-term networks like Captain Englebert's, however, demand continued operational output from participants despite the prospect of dynamic environmental factors. While informal bonds might suffice in temporary networks, longer life spans might require more formal contractual bonds. A second duration-related distinction, worthy of mention but whose exploration is outside the realm of this chapter, is between the length of time the network is activated and the length of time over which one would expect to see progress on the policy outcome.

The third dimension is number of participants in the network. The number of network members required for success has bearing over structure. As the number of participants grows, so does the number of potential conflicts. Thus wide-reaching networks often require structural leadership and well-defined operational parameters. Smaller networks can suffice with more distributed governance, since each participant can more easily gain informal access to the others, allowing for more tacit accountability. The network manager must keep this trade-off in mind as she seeks to organize participants, set network operations expectations among players, and eventually manage the work. For example, a federally financed interstate highway project requires a vast array of federal and state agencies, construction companies, and environmental groups. As network manager, the U.S. Department of Transportation would tightly manage the project to prevent contractual abuse among participants and to ensure prompt delivery of the proposed service. A loose network with widely distributed governance would lead to disorganization, redundancy, and project complications.

In the case of port security, however, the network is large—global in fact—and involves large numbers of participants. But Captain Englebert organized networks locally when possible so that she could avoid well-defined operational parameters and a command-and-control approach unsuitable to the nature of ports.

The fourth dimension is the balance between uniformity and flexibility. Network managers balance uniformity and fairness with the flexibility they can offer to network participants. These participants, especially those subject to rules from the lead agency, want to be treated fairly but are often nervous about overly prescriptive regulations. As participants are more likely to be open to a plan that maintains their autonomy, the promise of flexibility is an important tool that network managers can use to draw participants to the table. As was the case for Captain Englebert, navigating the balance between treating commercial and other actors equally or fairly across the network, while allowing them to adjust to the local environment and to the local capacities, was necessary to keep them at the table.

The fifth dimension is the balance between efficiency and inclusiveness. Despite the logic of the production approach to selecting partners based on needed capacity, network managers might also invite a certain organization into the network specifically, and only, for conciliatory purposes. This step could appease outside pressures, but it also has the potential to divert valuable time and attention from the network's smooth operations. The downside of this move is that it might incite opposition or frustration among partners who were drawn to the network with assurances of efficiency.

The sixth dimension is the balance between accountability and flexibility. In determining the proper type of network, the manager must examine another potential network tension. Whether it is operational structure, the proximate relationships of network participants, or public scrutiny, a major determinant of proper network formation and functionality is the manager's ability to structure a network that is both nimble and efficient. Some networks are scrutinized intensely by the media, policymakers, and the public at large. To maintain legitimacy, the network manager may need to show evidence of progress, possibly through well-defined performance incentives and contractual agreements. Well-defined and predetermined performance goals can translate into prescriptive regulations and rules that hamstring participants. Other networks—for example, those that face less outside scrutiny—can allow a greater flexibility in order to accomplish their goals. Flexibility can also be a useful motivational tool, showing trust in participants and providing them with ownership over solving the process-related problems essential to the targeted public value. In the end, managers must discern how the structure will hold partners accountable to their missions, maintain flexibility for network adaptation, and encourage a healthy rapport with and among partners.

The seventh dimension is network-level competencies. The ability of participants to function within the scope of the network is important to their ability to add value beyond their individual capacities. Two critical issues determine how these network-level competencies are directed to attain network goals: the nature of the task being performed and the external demands faced by the network.[8] Some tasks require regular interaction among partners, for example. Without a healthy rapport and effective collaboration skills among participants, the network manager is forced to more closely monitor and facilitate the work of the network actors. Similarly, external demands such as those from a funder or overseer also have bearing over network-level competencies—and subsequently on the network structure. If a foundation provides a grant for a public service project with strict demands on how the money is spent, the ability of network actors to identify, understand, and incorporate shifting mandates becomes important. The same can be true with a narrow mandate from a legislative body like Congress, one of the external entities to which USCG reports. Without these competencies, someone in Captain Englebert's position might be required to adopt a tightly managed structure in order to pivot network activities to meet the funder's demands.

The eighth dimension is the availability of resources. Public sector agencies often have multiple statutory missions, each of which is represented by a manager who competes with other managers for funding, authority, and overall departmental influence. Captain Englebert and other officials who execute a network approach must examine the relevance of the network's mission to the existing purpose and mission of their agency through the lens of resource availability. The risk of shifting inter- and intra-agency priorities is real. Networks require diligent oversight and significant attention to this issue. Network managers must also convince members that the network is a high enough priority within her convening agency to ensure proper resourcing.

In sum, determining a distinct network mission, and considering the eight dimensions, allow managers to design an effective network approach. Having envisioned the network, however, the difficult task of bringing the players together and securing their commitment to the new network mission remains.

Initiation Phase: Developing a Sense of Interdependence and Opportunity

Early on, Englebert spent considerable time participating in discussions. To create a network, the manager must make visible the members' shared capacity and shared interest in solving the problem. The network manager has to develop some level of self-awareness among network partners about their interdependence. Initially that means just getting them together to talk and develop a shared consciousness of what they could do together.

While the aim is information sharing and consciousness-raising, some effective action may nonetheless occur. They might choose to act unilaterally to adjust their actions in light of being exposed to a new problem or opportunity that ought to be higher on their agenda. Seeing the situation in a new light, a network recruit might decide to make arrangements with another network recruit. These types of mutual and bilateral deals can help realize some of the potential of the network, but they can only go so far. To exploit the potential of the network, participants have to begin thinking and acting more like a corporate unit with a common purpose that disciplines and guides their actions.

A leader must bring partners to the table and propose a network structure to organize them. These steps require either implicit or explicit authority vested in the manager. The network manager's authority does not however spontaneously generate from the soup of existing public agencies, nonprofits, and industry participants. Where does it come from? It is obvious that not all potential network participants have the power to convene, but what separates the ones that do from the ones that do not? The following five sources of authority provide public agencies with the necessary authority to step into a leadership role.

Widely Accepted Public Need. A common source of authority to convene a network is a widely accepted public need. In the face of either a glaring public value problem (poverty, crowded prisons, crumbling highways) or a catastrophe (like a natural disaster), organizations often feel an impetus to band together. This cohesive force is embodied in the manager, who synthesizes the public need in its relation to potential network partners and illustrates an understanding of the breadth and depth of the problem. A proper assessment of the surrounding conditions can inspire groups to work with others—providing an opportunity for network managers to make contact and form the network for public purposes. Of course the September 11 attacks provide the backdrop for a call to action among the network actors who worked together around the port security issue.

Statutory Authority. The law may provide a public agency with the authority to convene a network. Statutory authority is an important guide for public policy administrators—providing them with the credence to work with others to solve public problems. Yet this statutory authority can produce myopia as well. Some of the greatest risks result from a failure of agency leadership to think broadly, outside their current activities. Statutory authority can prove to be both a critical source of nominated position and a limitation.

Deft Navigation of Inevitable Conflicts of Interest. Ensuring the functional capacity of a network is essential for its successful operation. But what if a participant is unable, or even unwilling to perform its role due to preexisting conflicts of interest? Intranetwork political issues could include preexisting bad blood or competition among participants. A network manager's authority is vested in the ability to understand and overcome the myriad and often conflicting interests of potential participants. One potential conflict that conveners cannot underestimate is the risk of other public sector or private organizations vying for convening and managing authority. Efforts to convene can initiate conflict among other agencies, whose leadership may, justifiably or not, view their own organization as the logical integrator. A broad understanding of legacy missions, perspectives, and viewpoints is essential to weaving together the network while navigating the politics of participants.

Preexisting Relationships. Preexisting relationships are a source of authority for convening a network. Managers can use operational arrangements from past projects as building blocks for future network endeavors. Successful work with another agency could have built personal connections and cultivated trust for a future network setting. Additionally, previous work arrangements can produce foundations that facilitate new network arrangements with very little tweaking. Preexisting networks at the local, state, or federal levels can ease the front-end convening work by providing structures through which the network manager can communicate efficiently with participants. USCG port captains were used to working closely with local industry and other actors.

However, having a preexisting relationship also is a potential liability. If the structures and processes within a preexisting network are well established or entrenched, it can be challenging for the manager to evaluate participants individually and define new network roles for them. In extreme cases, plugging network players into a new network could render them inoperable, due to their dependence on the previously well-functioning network.

Credibility/Reputation. Perhaps most important, managers must be perceived as trustworthy to draw competent partners to the table—that is, they must have an established reputation. If a network partner sees the manager as less than competent, the perception will extend to the value of the network. This credibility can be drawn from several sources. First, the manager's technical ability allows partners the confidence that she will see and understand what the challenge is and will know how to optimally deploy network participants. Not only do participants need to trust the management of the convening authority to be functionally competent, they also must trust the manager's ability to select and draw the proper participants. To some extent participants will be sharing reputational risks, so they need to be confident that the manager will attract enough quality participants and capacity to be successful. In the situation discussed here the Coast Guard was respected as an agency with considerable talent and professionalism in the relevant areas.

Further, partners will be concerned with the level and intensity of their and others' participation. As a result, they must trust that the network manager will organize the work fairly, equitably distributing the burdens as well as any benefits, such as political credit. Similarly, network managers build credibility based on holding all actors accountable. Potential partners need to trust that the network manager won't allow free riding but instead will ask everyone to do their fair share.

Activation Phase: Creating Ties That Bind

I have explored how Captain Englebert in theory would have begun by envisioning a network based principally on being clear about the substantive purposes of the network and a logic of production that indicates which actors will be important parts of the network. Next, according to the network governance model, she would have called the network into existence by developing a sense of interdependence and opportunity among network actors. She would also have thought about the sources of power that she might draw upon as a leader. Further, the act of convening the network may have both revealed and helped to build the sources of influence that she possesses. But Englebert would still have been a long way from being able to sustain, animate, direct, and exploit the potential of the network to improve port security.

A variety of resources can help the government draw people to the negotiating table: money, legislative authority, and powerful sponsors. Over time, in order for the network to be effectively sustained, managed, and focused, the governing capacity of the network has to be able to commit network participants to concrete action to achieve the desired goals. This capacity is first held by the network convener as she calls the network into existence; later it might spread more widely across network participants through both formal and informal means. The network has to be able to raise resources, shift commitments, and invent new capacities among network participants.

It is worth mentioning again that the network's governance capacity has to be strong enough to cause network participants to shift some of their sense of accountability and purpose to the network from their own organizational missions. Network actors have their own prior personal and cultural commitments. Their organizations have purposes and established working relationships. Developing sinews strong enough to replace, or at least dislodge, these settled commitments and relationships was Englebert's toughest leadership challenge.

Network participants are held to these prior purposes not only by tradition and culture but also by strong systems of accountability. However important the goals of the network might seem to be, whether network partners can give themselves over wholeheartedly to those purposes depends crucially on how tight their current accountability system is and how congruent the purposes of the organization are with the mission of the network. One of the critical tasks facing the network manager is to create a different kind of accountability, one that is tied to the network's purposes rather than the purposes of member organizations. This new system must be able to compete in the minds of the individuals joining the network with their old system of accountability.

In the unlikely scenario that the network manager has vast amounts of money and formal authority over network members, the rules of direct, hierarchical government are more relevant than network governance. The money and authority simply buys or compels all the actions needed from network participants. Network managers often will goad potential participants with the opportunity to win a contract. For example, when the Air Force is acquiring a fighter plane, it will take bids from potential participants. In this case, the Air Force is both the manager and the buyer. Most often, the defense contractor that wins the bid will manage a supply chain network while being managed by the buyer. Conversely, costs to network participants, or the threat of losing money, can bind a network.

Leaders within convening agencies can also use rule making or legislative influence as a tool to draw together a network. While this is not available to every agency, those closely aligned with their legislative overseers can influence lawmakers to structure laws that catalyze network formation. Network managers also can use rule making as leverage to draw together uncooperative participants, helping them see a possibility of punitive rules if they don't cooperate. Clearly, this power must be used with discretion, as exercising too much leverage can result in operating tensions later on. Similarly, a powerful sponsor can lend credence to the network effort. This is especially useful for public officials who themselves do not have name recognition to attract attention but who can often gather momentum from the promotion and legal authority of a sponsor, such as an influential person in the White House or the head of a relevant congressional committee.

More often than not, however, sufficient money and authority are not at the manager's disposal. In the USCG port security case, Captain Englebert had to form the network through different processes. Without enough money or authority to buy or coerce cooperation, the sinews that bind the network depend more on feelings of obligation. The network manager, in this case, had to rely on the willingness of network participants to make contributions that they were not, strictly speaking, either paid or obligated to make.

One can think of this as a kind of mutual accountability. Mutual accountability—or agreement among actors who participate in the network—develops as each partner wants to keep the promises they've committed to. Each has agreed that the network mission is important, each has made specific deals regarding who is going to do what, and each has agreed how to hold one another accountable. To fail to keep one's end of the bargain is to be shamed within the group. Mutual accountability differs from both hierarchical accountability (in which one actor sets the purposes and coerces the action of others) and contract accountability (in which actors are bound by a formal contract). Mutual accountability is closer however to contract accountability than to hierarchical accountability, because the actors have to agree to the proposed joint action. They cannot be coerced.

The difference between contract accountability and mutual accountability is the degree to which the relationship is structured by a formal written contract with legal rights and obligations on both sides. In mutual accountability, the terms are looser than in contract accountability and are usually unwritten and tacitly (rather than explicitly) understood. There is the expectation that things might change in the future, in which case a new understanding will have to be created. Mutual accountability is also important in network governance when there is a less detailed calculation about how the benefits and burdens will be distributed and a less adversarial proceeding when things do not go well.

Individual Leadership Techniques for Network Formulation and Management

Network managers can help ensure hierarchical or contractual accountability by relying on some well-documented lessons, including writing values into the original contract or memorandum of understanding (for example, diversity of vendors, environmental sustainability, transparency), and investing in more work time, in more training, and in more expertise for public employees to ensure proper oversight of a network approach. How to create and sustain an operational sense of *mutual* accountability requires different but equally important skills. It is preparing the human capacity to lead effective network governance in its many forms that most burdens government.

Traditionally, the skill sets of public sector managers do not necessarily align with the demands of managing a network. Top-down, hierarchical government agencies breed managers focused on the internal workforce, not on the effects of their actions on public values. As a result, it might be necessary to bring on additional, specialized staff, or it might become apparent that, with training, the existing staff is capable of handling the new responsibilities. Either way, convening a network requires the ability to intensely focus on the overall public value while balancing the demands that the new network responsibilities place on agency partners. This capacity will also send a message to prospective network actors and help cement trust. Is the network manager capable of shifting her focus from top-down management to a network view? If circumstances shift, either financially or environmentally, can her agency adapt? Does she have the skills she needs at different stages to overcome the challenges of network management: indifference, free riding, internal competition, communication meltdown, gaps in capacity, and divergent accountability systems?

To move from a fairly straightforward job managing a program or service to managing a loose network of actors surely requires a different set of leadership techniques. No longer is success based on advising on policy, on managing more and more staff, or on applying rules in a standardized and highly structured way. Network leaders spend less time managing employees and more time attracting and deploying others' assets. This new set of competencies includes setting goals, aligning values, building trust, structuring incentives, analyzing and sharing risk, measuring and monitoring performance, and negotiating, mediating, and managing change.

The network manager, meanwhile, must have a broader view of government's purpose and view her job as producing value (results oriented) rather than managing activities (process oriented). Public employees at the management level who coordinate networks must also learn to tackle problems unconventionally. They must be comfortable working with more flexibility and more discretion than they find in the traditional command-and-control, rule-based environment. Successful network managers must have strong oral communication skills, be highly organized and creative thinkers, be adept at resolving problems, and know how to create win-win situations. They must act fairly and firmly, attracting the respect of private partners. As "connectors," network managers must appreciate the assets of others, build relationships across sectors, and operate flexibly across enterprises.

Moving into a network management role, for example, a social worker would require education and training to move from case management to vendor management. Recruitment of staff with management and business skills, as opposed to technical skills, is also important to building the leadership pool within the public sector. Further, reforms to civil service rules could encourage employees to move more easily between the public, private, and nonprofit sectors, through which they could pick up an understanding of the needs and motivations of network partners. At the chief executive level, meanwhile, most public leaders focus their attention on providing political or stakeholder support for existing nongovernmental structures and putting out related fires. To prepare for network approaches, executives must supervise and foster partnerships rather than push that role down the ranks to contract administrators. A higher-level view of all external relationships affords a more objective evaluation of what works and what doesn't, a better assessment risk, and a better view to spot opportunities for improvement.

Captain Englebert as Network Convener and Manager

How could this theory of both the conditions that make network governance important and possible, and the methods that network managers must use to exploit their potential, be of use to Captain Englebert? How could it help her diagnose her situation and act effectively within it?

Why Network Governance? Why Englebert as Convener?

Perhaps the first contribution that the theory of network governance could offer Captain Englebert is to help her see more clearly the nature of the work she had to do, why it came to her, and what resources she could have engaged.

Four dynamics brought Englebert to the position in which she found herself. First, the objective conditions of the world changed in a way that created an urgent new task for many actors inside and outside of government. This task, of course, was the construction of an effective defense against terrorism; to "never let this happen again." Second, those objective conditions mobilized a strong political commitment at all levels of government to support any potentially effective actions in dealing with the problem. Third, the legal mandates, the mission commitments, and the capacities of the USCG thrust the agency forward as one of the important agencies in the area of port security.

Fourth, Englebert was given the responsibility of leading not only the Coast Guard's response but also the nation's and even the world's response to keeping U.S. ports secure and interdicting attacks headed elsewhere. In short, she was delegated authority from society as a whole. The job fell on Englebert to do whatever she could think of to do to enhance port security.

It was only once Englebert had the job clearly in view that it became apparent that her work required her to act as a network convener and manager. There is simply no way that acting alone, even with the existing resources and powers of the U.S. Coast Guard, could she hope to accomplish this goal. Englebert's mandate was particularly important in convening other parties, but her authority was limited. Further, Englebert's mandate for action— rooted in shock and dismay—was probably a wasting asset. The felt urgency would fade as time passed, as the difficulty of the task increased, and as conflicts proliferated over what should be done and who should do it. Englebert could have used the moment to call a network into existence, perhaps, but she would also have to find the means for sustaining it, helping it to act, and helping it to learn.

Mission and Strategy

The USCG leadership understood that establishing a port security network would require cooperation from a multitude of players in both the private and public sectors. To foster cooperation, the USCG relied upon a coalescing purpose: the need for security requirements in the vulnerable maritime commerce sector. Upon review of security requirements in ports, USCG leadership, among other agency leaders, was shocked to find out how little coordination was occurring between industry leaders and agencies charged with security. And while port and vessel operators also were interested in port security, they relied upon efficiency for their business. Indeed all ports are interested in efficiency, yet maintaining that efficiency while improving security is challenging due to their wide variety of operating procedures. Some ports, such as those that import automobiles, store cargo on the premises for extended periods. Others, such as ports concentrated on shipping food, must unload cargo quickly and transport it from the port immediately. The variance in port operations presented a complex issue for the USCG: how could it issue regulations that fit each port?

Choosing the Right Partners and Design

The USCG had sufficient authority and credibility to work with the various players in port security. Yet it still needed to design a network response that capitalized on the strengths and mitigated the risks brought to the effort by the participants.

Savvy public officials offer as much flexibility as is feasible to network participants in how they fulfill their function. Captain Englebert and the USCG adopted this flexible approach for port operators. Operators largely were responsible for imagining, financing, and implementing security mechanisms to prevent maritime terrorist attacks. In this new paradigm they would maintain their ability to make decisions regarding details like the height of fences and screening of incoming vehicles, as long as the USCG approved them.

The length of duration for improving port security standards was an influential factor in the overall network design presented by the USCG. The problem of port security was not going to dissolve quickly. Put plainly, the network needed to last forever, making paramount not only flexibility but sustained cooperation among partners. The stakes were high—one attack and the network would be deemed a failure. With these forces acting in concert, as network designer Captain Englebert was left with a stark choice: accountability or flexibility? Could she achieve both?

To add to the complexity, Englebert had to focus on building an international network for port security, since ships arriving in the United States originate in foreign ports. But USCG leadership was hamstrung—it could not regulate foreign ports due to sovereignty issues. Instead it reached out to the international community through the International Maritime Organization.

Developing a Sense of Interdependence

From where did the USCG derive its power to convene actors outside its traditional authority? What emboldened its leadership to rise above other agencies with security jurisdictions and convene the network? The USCG's experience is a powerful example of how public sector leaders like Captain Englebert use their authority to establish trust among potential participants and communicate internal capacities to govern.

The USCG possessed many of the attributes listed above on convening authority. It had an excellent reputation of working with private industry to solve public problems. In the 1950s the USCG was tasked with decreasing the number of accidental deaths in the maritime industry. After working with private companies and establishing regulations, it solved the problem. The relationships resulting from prior experiences working together lent credence to the USCG's candidacy as a network convener. The USCG was also aptly equipped to convene a port security network immediately. It had "boats and boots" in the harbors and on the ground, ready to work with port operators and manage various industry participants. Additionally, the USCG possessed statutory authority on port security.

The USCG's role in port security found its beginnings during World War I, and since the enactment of the Magnuson Act of 1950, the agency has been responsible for port security, even in peacetime. Before 9/11 it had a presence in all the major ports through its captain of the ports program, which places regional ports under the jurisdiction of a Coast Guard officer to enforce regulations and to protect vessels, harbors, waterfront facilities, and so on. Judging from the USCG's previous responsibilities, it was clear to other agencies and industry participants that the USCG was adept at managing competing missions. With its many separate missions, some called the USCG "the United States government's maritime utility infielder."

The USCG is also known for its competent leadership, flexible work structure, and rapport with partner agencies, other branches of the military, and private industry. This rapport was evidenced by its industrywide meetings with port authorities, terminal operators, shipping company representatives, and other stakeholders to develop a port security network. As a port security liaison officer reported:

> To ensure that crucial security concerns were addressed the USCG included all port stakeholders in the rule making process. For example, seven MTSA outreach and feedback sessions were held throughout the U.S. Discussions from these meetings and comments from other interested organizations aided the USCG in determining the types of vessels and facilities that posed risks of being involved in a transportation security incident, and in identifying security measures and standards to deter such incidents.[9]

Simply put, the USCG had a great familiarity and positive working relationships with the various players in port security.

The USCG's reputation for effective collaboration was matched by its actual network-level competencies. Remember that the purpose of the network is unlikely to be a purpose to which network participants feel accountable. To reconcile organizational mission with network mission, and to subsequently harness the strengths of the network partners, the USCG decided to involve them in the initial design phase. Englebert approached public officials in other agencies, like Customs and Border Protection, and asked them to join early on in the policy formation process. Such actions communicated to network participants that they would not simply be subject to network governance but, instead, would be part of it.[10] The importance of reaching out to regulatory partners before the network was designed cannot be understated. Englebert and other leaders from the USCG relied upon information from agencies like Customs and Border Patrol to avoid redundancy in their regulations going forward.

Ties That Bind

Eventually the USCG decided to establish new regulatory requirements for all ports and vessels. Port and vessel operators would be required to gain certification that they met regulations. The costs to port and vessel operators for not obtaining this certification would be immense, encouraging industry participants to attend initial meetings and help form future regulations. But before presenting their plan to international operators and other stakeholders through the International Maritime Organization, Englebert did her homework.

To prevent the lack of accountability inherent in the USCG's troubled Project Deepwater, for post-9/11 port security they struck a plan that allowed flexibility without sacrificing accountability. Englebert incorporated input from the shipping industry on how to create flexible rules that port operators and shipping companies could abide by. The plan conducted industrywide meetings to learn the current security operations of ports, how they can be changed, and what kinds of changes would maintain efficiency. Ultimately, in collaboration with industry partners, the USCG created pragmatic security requirements for port and vessel operators. Approval by the USCG that a port was meeting security standards would allow it to continue efficient operation; without such approval, it would face steep economic costs.

Outside the United States, each nation represented by the International Maritime Organization would develop and implement its own plans. The USCG would provide consultation for compliance. It would also facilitate working groups on methods for mitigating risk in the maritime sector.

In this case, perhaps most notable from a network governance perspective was how intentional Captain Englebert was in ensuring an inclusive and well-considered network design phase. Early on, Englebert made clear that she considered the role of the USCG to be network integrator. Before the network was activated, the USCG contacted relevant partners in security and leaders in industry and requested their input in the network design phase. The resulting network design was pragmatic and flexible but also comprehensive. It codified requirements for ports and shipping companies and allowed them to meet the requirements on their own terms. To ease into network operation, leaders from the USCG were available to port and vessel operators to answer questions on security compliance.

The actions of the USCG signaled to network participants its interest in the overall public value. By including partners in the design phase, the USCG gained trust as an integrator and included skin in the game for operating partners. The clear emphasis on network design paid dividends.

Individual Leadership Techniques

When we look closely at Captain Englebert's managerial techniques and practices in the creation of this network, two things stand out.

First is the degree to which Englebert could use herself and her position to embody the challenge the network was being called upon to solve. For this Englebert did not seek to consolidate power but instead to keep everyone's attention on the problem to be solved. She had to be the embodiment of the task, not the authoritative leader of the effort. Key to success in this approach was her presence and her persistence. Everywhere there was a group meeting, or when two or more people gathered to worry about port security, Englebert had to be there. Where there were no meetings, she had to create them. Englebert had to doggedly stay in the game at the operational level as well, while reflecting modesty and professionalism at all times. Her essential work was convening when necessary and helping when a group convened on its own.

Note that the above work describes the techniques of campaign managers and community organizers more than the work of chief executives. It is a set of techniques designed to encourage the initiative and leadership of others rather than to ensure control over what is being done. Effort by others in the right general direction is considered more important than precision, guidance, and control over what is being done—at least in the short run, when the principal task is to mobilize attention, resources, and thought.

The second key is the program management skill Englebert displayed. This was exemplified in her success at organizing and running the large meetings in which network partners participated. Critical to the success of such meetings was accomplishing two apparently quite conflicting goals. One was to make sure that those who attended the meetings felt that Englebert protected their rights to participate, to raise their voice, to make their suggestions, to criticize proposals made by others, and so on. Think of this as a kind of due process protection. Each person had to believe that he or she could make a useful contribution to the effort that would be heard and taken seriously. The second goal was to ensure some kind of quality in the discussion. By quality I mean both in the technical sense, that the contributions were substantive and important, but also in the sense that the contributions were efficient, short, and clear. Many efforts to mobilize the collective effort needed to make network government work fail because they do not guarantee both due process and quality in the discussion.

Captain Englebert built a system and developed a style in which this work could be accomplished. When presiding over a meeting, she was careful to be more a listener than a talker. She developed a system that ensured participant access to the floor. But there was also a strong discipline that came from a timer and a scowl if the contributions did not seem germane. Englebert gave up a significant amount of control over the focus of the agenda, and allowed many to speak, but kept enough control that the discussions didn't dissolve into either set speeches or sharp conflict. This style conflicted with the usual methods of running meetings, which pack their agendas with speeches from authoritative individuals. Englebert's style in truth made the USCG nervous. But over time a network did form that took responsibility for managing itself.

It is not clear whether Englebert has yet developed the techniques and skills that would allow her to discipline the network when it falters in performance. And that is presumably the ultimate test of whether the network governance system she has convened can do its work. But she has made a start, and it is at least imaginable that some kind of executive capacity will emerge along with the deliberative capacity she has created.

Conclusion

Public officials who decide to convene a network are undertaking a great responsibility. Yet with changing expectations of how governments operate and how they deliver services, networks may be the only option to achieve a pressing or lingering public value. As Captain Englebert illustrates, officials must conduct their due diligence during the network design phase to ensure that proper details are secured. These details include the identification of participants, of the structure of contracts, of the duration of the network, of the resources to pay for it, and of its manager. Network managers must determine which actors, in which ways when brought together, can produce more positive results per dollar and unit of effort than government can produce alone. Network managers must also work to inspire and motivate network participants to commit to and act upon a new purpose—one that goes beyond the purpose of their organization.

Further, even if an agency gets all of these factors correct in its design and activation phases, it still must stay nimble and able to adapt to dynamic changes. The circumstances catalyzing network formation are seldom static. In fact, networks are an effort to harness the value of collaborating organizations to achieve an agreed-upon public value amidst dynamic environmental factors. As circumstances change, so must goals. Convening agencies must have the facility to adjust simultaneously. A network convener must be sensitive to avoid using her position of authority to preserve power but should instead use it to identify new and problematic situations. Such scenarios can call for reallocations of authority through avenues such as providing targeted institutional funding, outsourcing to civilian contractors, paring down or adding network partners, or even relinquishing leadership authority to a partner better fit to serve in that capacity. The flexibility required to convene a network requires competent managers who are willing to self-evaluate and synthesize criticism from network players.

As these are difficult tasks, there are success and horror stories from each level and sector of government. Each tale offers new lessons for conveners. To me, it seems that Captain Englebert and the U.S. Coast Guard applied these lessons well as they set about protecting the country in the period after 9/11.

Notes

1. See Stephen Goldsmith and William D. Eggers, *Governing by Network: The New Shape of the Public Sector* (Brookings Press, 2004).

2. For a separate taxonomy, see Robert Agranoff, "Leveraging Networks: A Guide for Public Managers Working across Organizations" (Washington: IBM Endowment for the Business of Government, 2003); Keith Provan and Patrick Kenis, "Modes of Network Governance: Structure, Management, and Effectiveness," *Journal of Public Administration and Theory* 18 (2007): 229–52; John M. Kamensky and Thomas J. Burlin, *Collaboration: Using Networks and Partnerships* (Rowman and Littlefield, 2004), p. 13.

3. Keith Provan and Patrick Kenis, "Modes of Network Governance and Implication for Network Management and Effectiveness," communication to the PMRA, Los Angeles (2005).

4. Provan and Kenis, "Modes of Network Governance: Structure."

5. John M. Bryson, Barbara C. Crosby, and Melissa Middleton Stone, "The Design and Implementation of Cross-Sector Collaborations: Propositions from the Literature," *Public Administration Review* (2006).

6. Steve Goldsmith and Donald Kettl, eds., *Unlocking the Power of Networks* (Brookings Press, 2009), p. 7.

7. Peter R. Monge and Noshir S. Contractor, *Theories of Communications Networks* (Oxford University Press, 2003), p. 62.

8. Provan and Kenis, "Modes of Network Governance and Implication for Network Management."

9. T. Schneider, "Maritime Security: A Collaborative Responsibility," paper prepared for the International Conference on the Accession of Bulgaria to the European Union, November 17, 2006 (www.docstoc.com/docs/45877877/What-do-ISPS_-MTSA-_-the-USCG-have-in-common).

10. Much of the information in this section is from an interview with Mike Brown, Office of Governmental and Public Affairs, USCG, January 14, 2010.

ELAINE C. KAMARCK

8

Improving Port Security: A Twenty-First-Century Government Approach

Twentieth-century government conducted its business largely through bureaucracies—the governmental and organizational equivalent of assembly lines. And for most of that time, in America and in other developed countries, the organizational structures of the private sector and the public sector were pretty much the same. Until late in the century the primitive nature or actual absence of information technology—especially large computers for storing and analyzing records and data—meant that many organizations, from the Social Security Administration to private insurance companies, spent much of their time collecting and organizing records. The employees of these large organizations consisted largely of clerks and those who supervised them. The federal government and most state and local governments were, for most of the century, governments of clerks.

Origins of the Postbureaucratic State

But toward the end of the twentieth century the private sector was changing. Thanks to surging investment in ever-improving information technology, business was able to offer better service and better customization. But many governmental structures stuck to rigid rules and inflexible procedures. It was no surprise that the contrast between the two had an effect on the way citizens saw their government. This manifested itself in a paradox. In the world's most advanced democracies, citizens who lived in countries whose governments had, by many objective measures, done a pretty good job of delivering on public goods were getting more and more critical of government.[1] Nowhere was this as apparent as in the United States, where over a period of four decades—in which the United States was prosperous and mostly at peace—Americans grew less and less trustful of government.[2]

Politicians were not oblivious to these changes. Ronald Reagan, Brian Maloney, and Margaret Thatcher made impressive careers out of dissatisfaction with late-twentieth-century bureaucracy.[3] Stories about the stupid government fueled not only conservative political revolutions but late-night television as well. Distaste for the bureaucratic state got to the point at which people couldn't imagine that anything they liked and valued was actually done by the government. President Bill Clinton used to tell of meeting an old woman who pressed his hands intensely in hers and pleaded with him, "Please, please Mr. President, don't let the government get its hands on my Medicare."

Dissatisfaction with government manifested itself in more concrete ways in a tax revolt that spread across the United States beginning in 1978 with passage of Proposition 13 in California. Prop 13 put a ceiling on property taxes, and it was quickly copied in other states. People refused to pay more taxes or voted with their feet by moving to lower-tax jurisdictions. Even liberal politicians became reluctant to raise taxes, and conservative politicians came to use lower taxation as a mantra for all the ills that ailed the country.

In the meantime, however, no one seriously suggested that government actually do less. Local governments were expected to fix potholes and run school systems, state governments were expected to manage public health systems and fund universities. With Newt Gingrich's 1994 Republican takeover of the House of Representatives (the first time in more than forty years), conservative political elites hoped for great changes, and liberal political elites feared them. But even then, with the wind at their backs and decades of pent-up antigovernment sentiment, the conservative revolution failed to deliver any substantial reduction in government. A conservative, antitax, antigovernment majority governed Congress for more than half of the past two decades, and with the exception of changes related to 9/11 such as the creation of the Department of Homeland Security, the government doesn't look appreciably different now than it did then. The most notable change, in fact, is that it is bigger.

In the meantime, in the face of citizen distrust and doubts about policy implementation, elected politicians and civil servants still had to govern; they still had to use public authority to run a more and more complex society. Late twentieth-century political culture presented those who governed with an interesting dilemma: How do you govern in an era when the public yells "Do something!" at regular intervals about problems ranging from bad meat in hamburgers to terrorists in the subways. And yet as soon as the public is demanding that you do something they are yelling yet again, "And don't let the government do it!"

This barrage of contradictory messages begat one of the most creative periods in the history of governance. The movement to "reinvent government," as it was dubbed in the United States, or the "new public management," as it was called in the other English-speaking countries at the forefront of this movement, began in Great Britain in 1982, in New Zealand in 1984, in American statehouses in the 1980s, and in the American federal government in 1993. It affected all levels of government and all aspects of policy.

Today in America and in some other information-age economies, public authority is exercised through a vast array of new arrangements. Over the years many authors have described these new governance arrangements, the first and still the most well known being David Osborne, author of the best seller *Reinventing Government*. But academics were chronicling the emergence of these new governmental forms as well—most notably Lester Salamon, *The Tools of Government: A Guide to the New Governance*, and B. Guy Peters, *The Future of Governing: Four Emerging Models*.

In my own work (*The End of Government . . . As We Know It*) I describe the new governmental forms and then try to do two things that I hope improve our understanding of twenty-first-century government: describe the policy problems that these new forms are best suited to and describe the problems to date.

A Brief Description of the Postbureaucratic State

As the twenty-first century and the information technology revolution dawned in conjunction with each other, it was (briefly) fashionable to talk about the end of the state. But one decade into that century and those discussions sound naïve indeed. The decade began with the 9/11 attacks on America and the resulting need for increased security in a war on terror; it ended with an economic meltdown and the need for governments all over the world to serve as economic stabilizers and providers of social safety nets.

After flattening briefly in the late twentieth century, government spending in the United States and in many other developed countries is increasing again, driven by the 2008 economic crisis and by aging populations. Thus the twenty-first century has not begun with a decrease in the overall amount of government; nor has it begun with a decrease in the authority of the state to oblige people to do things. But it has begun with a dramatic change in the means—as opposed to the ends—of government. Government implements policy differently than it did in the bureaucratic century that preceded it. Modern government exercises public authority in three ways: through its power to coerce, through its power to spend, and through its power to create markets where none existed before. These translate roughly into three new tools of government: reinvented government, government by network, and government by market. A brief description of each follows.

Reinvented Government

I use the term *reinvented government* to refer to modernized public sector bureaucracies. Public sector bureaucracies implement the state's power to coerce; we must have a passport to travel, we must have a driver's license to drive, we cannot receive state-provided benefits without meeting certain legal requirements. But these bureaucracies operate without much of their twentieth-century trappings. Performance measures attempt to act as market proxies, allowing government to compete against measures set for it and against other, similarly situated, governments (or in some cases, against similar private sector institutions). Reinvented bureaucratic organizations, in their ideal form, trade the dominance of central control mechanisms such as budget rules, personnel rules, and procurement rules for enhanced flexibilities. In these modernized bureaucracies, customer service is used to model organizational behavior vis-à-vis the citizen, even though it is clear that the citizen is not exactly a customer. Finally, in these organizations information technology is used to increase productivity. In other words, reinvented government is a traditional government bureaucracy that has borrowed modern management tools from the private sector to enhance its efficiency and effectiveness.

The reality, of course, does not often live up to the ideal. For instance, it is clear that modernized bureaucracies often have performance standards laid on top of the older, rule-based control systems. As Robert Behn points out in chapter 4 in this book, "Unfortunately, many of those who rise to positions of authority in large public agencies do so by assiduously following the rules, not by producing results." But with each increment of progress toward the ideal, reinvented government attempts to deal with the lack of flexibility, low innovation, and unsatisfactory results that constituted so much of the critique of twentieth-century bureaucracy.

Government by Network

In government by network, traditional bureaucracy is replaced by a variety of other kinds of institutions, most of which are fueled by governments' willingness to spend money on a particular problem. In government by network, the government stops trying to do everything itself and funds other organizations, which in turn do the actual work that the government wants done. The variety of organizations that can constitute government by network is immense. Churches, university research labs, private research labs, nonprofit organizations, for-profit organizations—in the modern state all have been called upon to perform the work of the government.

When the state opts to create a network it is because its leaders (political or career) want things to happen that would not occur to the same extent without the resources and direction of the state. There is a great deal of confusion over this point, as some persist in seeing this change as a withdrawal of the state. Yet as the 1996 shutdown of the U.S. federal government illustrates, there exists a vast array of private sector entities whose work comes to a grinding halt when the federal money stops. Far from being powerless, the state is still very much in the center of the action, since without its resources there would not be the same degree of activity. Networks can be composed of other public organizations, such as state and local governments, or they can be composed of nongovernmental organizations. The defining characteristic is that they are all engaged by a state entity, using state money, for the production of something that the private market would not produce, to the extent desired by the state, on its own.

Government by network, of course, has its problems. As any student of these arrangements admits, many government-by-network schemes suffer from poor design. In part that is because government by network was not a conscious decision but rather emerged as a sort of default mechanism for when government ran up against problems (such as the treatment of drug addiction) that did not lend themselves to standard operating procedures. But government by network, like reinvented government but to a greater degree, is a radical attempt to deal with the lack of innovation inherent in traditional bureaucracy.

Government by Market

Reinvented government and government by network are both different from bureaucratic government and yet they both involve a significant amount of government as we know it. In reinvented government organizations, public work is done by people who work for the government. In government by network much of the public's work is paid for by the government and directed (more or less) by the government, even though it is not performed by people who work for the government and not constrained by all of government's protocols and central control mechanisms. In the third category of implementation—government by market—the work of government involves few, if any, public employees and little or no public money. In government by market, the government uses state power to create a market that fulfills a public purpose. By definition, that kind of market would not exist in the private sector. Often this involves taking into account what economists call externalities. If reinvented government is government all dressed up to look like the private sector and government by network is government that hides behind much more popular organizations, government by market is so well disguised that most people aren't even aware that it's government in operation.

Government by market is by far the newest of these modes of government. When it is possible to design a simple, transparent market, it succeeds; when there are too many moving parts or an incomplete market, it fails. Government by market works best on those policy problems that require hundreds, thousands, or millions of individuals or organizations to act in such a way that the total result is something of public value. Those who are old enough to remember Lady Bird Johnson (wife of President Lyndon Johnson) are old enough to remember that she waged a battle to clean up American's highways, which in the 1960s were beginning to be overrun with beer cans and soda bottles. By the 1970s beer and soft drink bottles were posing serious problems for public cleanliness and for landfills. The solution to this problem came from government. But instead of creating the Bureau of Clean Highways and hiring workers to pick up bottles, government did something unusual—it created a market. Bypassing laws that required deposits on bottles and soda cans, government created an economic incentive to keep people from throwing bottles out of their cars. In 1971 the state of Oregon passed the nation's first bottle bill; other states quickly followed. And for the hard-core litterbugs who persisted in throwing bottles away, the laws created an economic incentive for other people to pick them up.[4]

Similarly, in the 1991 Clean Air Act, Congress decided to put a price on sulfur dioxide emissions from industrial plants. Sulfur dioxide (SO_2) is the primary cause of acid rain. Essentially, the government determined how much sulfur dioxide the environment could handle and then developed a trading system to allow clean plants to "sell" permits and dirty plants to "buy" permits. Most analysts feel this system has worked. In the last thirty years, emissions trading (and other improvements) have caused nearly a 50 percent drop in the amount of SO_2 in the air.[5] The price was high enough to encourage plants to get new equipment for cleaner air but low enough that companies could determine their own timetable and their own technology.

As in the example of government by network, the success of government by market is dependent on its original design and on that design being robust against manipulation, gamesmanship, and unintended consequences. More than a decade ago, the state of California set out to design an electricity market that would (presumably) result in cheaper, cleaner energy. Instead it resulted in a summer of severe blackouts across the state of California and in numerous accusations of fraud and market manipulation that are still being sorted out.[6] The California experience ended, for the time being at least, the world's interest in laissez-faire electricity markets. The attempt to create a cap and trade system for carbon dioxide (CO_2) emissions is an example of a very ambitious attempt at government by market. And yet three versions of cap and trade have failed to pass through Congress. Complexity and fear of market manipulation have been major impediments to attracting support for this sort of solution to the climate change problem. And yet, despite their shortcomings, the very efficiency of markets and the fact that they allow for millions of adaptations to solve a public problem make government by market an attractive option for policy implementation.

Matching Policies to Implementation

Today, modern American government (federal, state, and local) is a confusing hodgepodge of the above three models and of variations on those themes. At the local level, counties have been creating networks of contractors for everything from social service delivery to the management of municipal golf courses. At the state level, bottle bills have created markets for used beer and soda cans. At the federal level, markets have been created for the reduction of sulfur dioxide, and networks have been created for all kinds of research, from weapons to cancer. At all levels, electronic government flourishes and allows for transactions that used to be completed by clerks to be completed by a click on a computer screen. Sometimes this new, postbureaucratic state performs well, as it did when the government by market model used in the SO_2 trading market essentially got rid of the problem of acid rain and when the government by network model used in the welfare-to-work program produced a reduction in welfare dependency. And sometimes it flops, as it did when California repealed its electricity market after a summer of unexplained brownouts in 2000, and when the attacks of 9/11 proved that airport security really could not be contracted out effectively. This should not be surprising; these new modes of policy implementation are still evolving, and we are just beginning to learn how to use them.

Table 8-1. *Optimal Implementation Tools, by Characteristics of Policy Problems*

Reliability/uniformity of outputs needed for optimal outcome	Degree of innovation and flexibility desired		
	Low	*Medium*	*High*
Low	. . .	. . .	Government by market
Medium	. . .	Government by network	. . .
High	Reinvented government	. . .	. . .

The first step in making these new policy tools work is to understand when and where they work. This means looking at a two-step policy implementation. First, a problem needs to be broken down into its components; second, each component needs to be matched to the most appropriate implementation mode. For some pieces of a policy problem, the public goal requires a high degree of reliability, or (to put it another way) it requires a high degree of uniformity in outputs in order to achieve the outcome.[7] For other pieces of a policy problem the public goal requires a high degree of innovation and flexibility in the outputs in order to produce the outcome. Table 8-1 illustrates how the characteristics of a policy problem can dictate the best governmental approach. For instance, some components of a policy problem have unambiguous goals and are therefore subject to routinization. Others require a high level of security. When the two occur together, the objective can be best met by reinvented public sector organizations. Issuing passports, drivers' licenses, or other forms of legal identification and determining eligibility for government benefits are examples of policy that can be routinized.

In theory these functions could be performed by a network of organizations under contract to the state. But given how important legal documents are to identity and security, the problems associated with allowing any entity but the public sector to have a role in this process are enormous. And given how important it is for the state to control the amount of benefits it pays out and the fairness with which those benefits are paid, it makes sense that the public sector should control this process as well. The public interest here is in reliability and uniformity of outputs. The public interest in innovation is in fact low. Innovation in the awarding of government benefits (My brother-in-law gets a social security check; yours does not) is certainly not in the interest of the modern state. Thus when outputs need to be uniform and reliable and when the need for innovation and flexibility is low, the best implementation tool is probably reinvented government.

But just because a function is best implemented within the public sector does not mean that it cannot incorporate modern business practices—especially customer service—in its routines. Hence the term *reinvented government*. It used to be that if you had to go abroad at the last minute and your passport had expired you were required to go through a rather elaborate explanation and show the urgency of your trip in order to get an expedited passport. These days you simply show your travel dates, pay more money, and the U.S. consular service will renew your passport quickly. User fees, online information and transactions, Saturday and evening business hours all help make the reinvented public sector more efficient and more responsive to the citizen while not sacrificing the important public purpose of treating citizens equitably and according to the law.

On the other hand, fishing and hunting licenses—while mandated by the public sector—are not nearly as important to the state as are passports. State governments often allow them to be purchased at bait shops or at campgrounds. Thus in those instances the government requires the license but allows a network to do much of the actual work of processing and selling the license. The difference? Most governments don't think a fishing license, unlike a passport, entails a high degree of security.

Benefits are another area where reinvented public sector organizations should, and most often do, retain control. Access to government benefits is intended to be universal under the law: all citizens should be able to get benefits if they qualify. And governments have an interest in trying to control the costs of benefit programs by reducing fraud. A network system of determining social security or pension or welfare eligibility would be hard to police and probably open to even more fraud than exists today. But even though the state has an overwhelming interest in maintaining control over the issuance of government benefits, it can use modern technology and modern customer service techniques to ease the distribution of those benefits to the citizen and to reduce its own costs.

Other public policy problems require flexibility and innovation. We do not want flexibility in determining whether poverty-stricken mothers are entitled to welfare benefits in the first place; but we do know from experience that what works to get one welfare mother into a job may require a substantial amount of flexibility and innovation and may differ from what works for another welfare mother. Getting welfare mothers to work is one of many governmental problems to which there is no *one* answer. Government by network allows the public sector to provide a range of options to certain policy problems. For this reason many social services in the United States have traditionally been provided through some form of network, where the providers of the services take different and often innovative approaches to the problems. People problems—or "sticky" problems, as they have been referred to in political science—do not lend themselves to standard routines.

Nor does the state care particularly about reliability or uniformity in the actual outputs. For instance, it doesn't matter to the state why a previously drug-addicted mother of two goes straight and gets a job, whether it was because she found Jesus or because she took a sewing class. What matters is that the outcome—getting people off welfare and into productive lives—is achieved. The bureaucratic model has never worked well in these kinds of policy areas.

Similarly, government has played an enormously important role in society by sponsoring pure research. Although government labs have been prolific, the U.S. government's implementation choice for basic research has never been bureaucracy; it has always been some form of network. When it comes to research, government by network has two major attractions. Unlike bureaucratic government, it has the potential to be flexible and to innovate, characteristics in short supply in traditional bureaucracies. Second, government by network is often used in those cases in which the government values innovation so much that it is willing to give up a certain degree of control. Reliability presupposes that a result can be defined ahead of time—a ridiculous requirement when the public goal is breakthrough research.

Implementation of a single policy can move between the various modes. For instance, before 9/11 airport security was a classic example of government by network. The FAA (Federal Aviation Administration) mandated that the airlines pay for screening procedures at each airport. They also set standards and rules to be followed by those companies. The cost was borne by the airlines, which up until 9/11 had had years without a terrorist incident or hijacking in the United States. Since security was not perceived to be a problem and because it was not tied into the airlines' bottom line, the money spent on security was minimal, and it showed. Quickly following 9/11, Congress passed a law creating the Transportation Security Administration

(TSA), placing airport security under the control of the federal government. Airport security moved from the government by network model back to the realm of traditional government (and it is still trying to reinvent itself).

Finally, government by market is the best and sometimes only realistic implementation option when a policy goal is formulated that requires many hundreds of businesses or many thousands of people to change their behavior. Government by market is especially important in societies in which citizens place a high value on personal choice. It is also appropriate in the information age, in which scientific and technological change happen so quickly that they often outstrip the ability of the law to keep up. For instance, one of the lessons of the 1960s and 1970s was that government job creation for the poor did not work very well. In fact, as a policy option it has been largely abandoned in favor of a tax subsidy (the earned income tax credit) for people who have low-income jobs in the private sector. Instead of trying to *create* jobs for the poor through the government, a more successful antipoverty strategy has been to *subsidize,* through the tax system, the low-paying jobs that poor people most often find for themselves.

In the field of environmental regulation, policymakers have increasingly turned to setting performance goals and away from dictating technologies for the achievement of those goals. Individual chemical factories and plants can be far more creative than legislators and rule writers can be when it comes to figuring out ways of reducing pollution. One of these programs, the Environmental Protection Agency's 33/50 program, achieved its goal of fifty percent reduction in releases and transfers of seventeen targeted chemicals one year ahead of schedule.[8]

And in a free society, any public policy whose goal is to change the behaviors of millions of people must, almost of necessity, rely to some degree on government by market. The degree of coercion required to police bottle disposal or gasoline consumption is simply unthinkable outside of an extreme emergency or a police state.

To successfully meet the challenges that confront them, modern governments have taken to using nearly all of the above models in an attempt to introduce flexibility and innovation into the governmental equation. This is no simple task. As citizens ratchet up their expectations for these new demands, they retain traditional demands for reliability and uniformity in the output of government activity. In an ideal world, dimensions of complex problems are sorted out according to this trade-off between reliability and innovation, and the appropriate governmental tool is chosen.

Applying Twenty-First-Century Government
to the Problem of Port Security

So now we turn to Suzanne Englebert's challenge. How can these organizational and transactional technologies of twenty-first-century government be used to improve port security? The situation she inherited was certainly challenging—371 ports, each involving a constellation of state and local government agencies as well as multiple federal agencies and private shippers. For all practical purposes, port security had been left to the discretion of the thirty-five captains of the port. Thus on September 10, 2001, security at American ports was similar to security at American airports—a low priority item for both the governmental and private sectors. To make matters worse, when it was clear on September 12, 2001, that port security had to become a priority, policymakers realized that the federal government agency with the clearest authority for the ports, the United States Coast Guard, had been systematically starved of resources for years. In part for that reason and in part because port security had previously consisted of law enforcement problems like cargo theft, security at ports had come to mean, in the words of Joe Cox of the Chamber of Shipping of America, "three guys and a dog."[9]

The attacks of 9/11 elevated port security to the highest possible level. It was clear that a new and more rigorous security regimen was called for. When a policy problem demands high levels of security, responsibility must reside with government. Thus following 9/11 airport security was returned to the public sector. By the same token, no one suggested that port security be contracted out to Kroll Associates or to Blackwater. The U.S. Coast Guard was in charge. Military preparedness planning had already established a central role for the captains of the port:

> In May of 1986, the Coast Guard, in accordance with a recommendation from the National Port Readiness Working Group, directed Coast Guard Captains of the Port to take the lead in establishing Port Readiness Committees (PRCs) throughout the United States. Captains of the Port were selected to serve as permanent chairpersons because of their broad port safety and security authority and responsibilities, and because of their presence in all U.S. Seaports of Embarkation.[10]

Thus it was the captains of the port who were called upon to form port security committees and to undertake their own portwide assessments.

But before we go any further it is important to understand the limits of the Coast Guard's control over security issues. There are two pieces to the port security problem, of which only one is under the control of the Coast Guard. The first piece is prevention, and that is primarily an intelligence problem. The Coast Guard is by and large a customer of intelligence agencies, mostly the FBI and the CIA. The Coast Guard does not have its own spies abroad, as the CIA does; it does not monitor suspicious conversations, as the National Security Agency does; and it does not wiretap the phones of suspected criminals, as the FBI does. When it comes to preventing terrorism, Captain Englebert had to rely on the quality of information coming from organizations over which she had no control. But as we know from the all too numerous examples of missed signals and failures to connect the dots, prevention of terrorism is a very difficult business.

Thus for the Coast Guard the issue is not prevention but preemption. The question is, What can the Coast Guard do to thwart acts of terrorism at both U.S. ports and foreign ports where ships are bound for the United States? The only way to test each port's capacity to actually preempt an attack is to red-team each port on a regular basis and then compare one port's vulnerabilities and reactions to another port's.

Red-teaming involves mounting simulated threats to test the strength and probe the weaknesses of a security regime. It is the best way we know to test for threats and then to train for responses to them. The CIA and the military have used it for years, and more recently the TSA has used it to test airport security. The Coast Guard uses PortSTEP scenarios and AMSTEP scenarios for training, and it also participates in the Asymmetric Warfare Initiative with the navy, the FBI, and local law enforcement.[11]

Red-teaming, in this case, involves simulating an attack on a plane, an airport, a ship, or a port. The bigger the attack the better. But it is expensive, which means that many locations are left out of the exercises, making it difficult to compare them . Sometimes the governments sponsoring such exercises place absurd conditions on the attackers—that they don't break any laws in executing the attacks, for instance. And government agencies have been known to halt red-team activities or attempt to suppress their findings in order to avoid embarrassment. But for all the flaws of red-teaming, it is a way of constantly testing security procedures and of getting those involved in security to test their responses.

Like the PerformanceStat programs described by Robert Behn in this volume, the point of red-teaming is both testing and learning. Given that there are 371 U.S. ports, the results of port security tests can be usefully compared. If properly structured, the results of these exercises can be used as tools to improve security. Learning comes from both competition and evaluation.

Competition from the results of red-team exercises would go a long way toward identifying vulnerabilities. Decades ago, during the cold war, the famous air force general Wilbur L. Creech reorganized the Air Combat Command so that each jet loaded with nuclear weapons had its own team, which was composed of everyone who worked on that plane, from the pilot to the mechanic to the cleaning person. Persistent testing of the system led to dramatic increases in readiness, defined in this instance as the ability to get the jet into the air as soon as possible. The teams that did the best job received not only symbolic rewards but also more tangible rewards, such as extra days of leave.

In the above example, competition increased performance. But competition should also be combined with evaluation. The United States Army is continually practicing its skills in war games. After those games it engages in what is known as an after-action review, in which everyone involved, regardless of rank, discusses what happened and why. Likewise, the U.S. Coast Guard needed to make sure that the personnel at each port have the chance to reflect on red-team attacks and to share those reflections with the broader port community.

Regular red-teaming exercises provide a proxy measurement for outcome measures and, as mentioned at the beginning of this chapter, outcome measures are an extremely important means of accountability in twenty-first-century government. Without a pretty clear outcome measure, it is impossible to tell whether or not the reinvented public sector, or the network, or the market is actually accomplishing something of public value. In the case of terrorism, outcome measures are especially unreliable, since the absence of incidents does not necessarily mean the presence of good security. The case is similar for fraud. As Malcolm Sparrow points, "Fraud also belongs within a class of risks that involve conscious opposition: risks which have a *brain* behind them. . . . In this regard, fraud perpetrators belong more naturally with drug smugglers, terrorists, computer hackers, and thieves. Such groups constantly study the relevant defenses, adapt quickly to changes in those defenses, and thrive on novelty and surprise."[12]

The cat-and-mouse nature of the terrorist threat makes measurement especially tricky. Measuring the performance of airlines' ability to catch contraband in checked baggage—a protocol set up after the Pan Am 103 bombing over Lockerbie in 1988—would not have helped prevent 9/11. In this case, the output measure (the degree to which every bag was examined to make sure it corresponded to a passenger on board) could not have achieved the outcome (prevention of a terrorist act on a plane). Every bag in the world

Table 8-2. *Optimal Implementation Tools, by Characteristics of the Port Security Problem*

Reliability/uniformity of outputs needed for optimal outcome.	Degree of innovation and flexibility desired		
	Low	*Medium*	*High*
Low	. . .	. . .	Insurance policies for shippers and cargo
Medium	. . .	Creation of port security plans; C-TPAT	. . .
High	Security clearances for personnel at ports	. . .	. . .

could have been examined and it would not have prevented those planes from flying into the World Trade Center and the Pentagon.

Since it is impossible to develop performance metrics around extremely infrequent events, a program of continual testing and (one hopes) shared learning is the best that can be envisaged in a situation in which the danger—a terrorist attack on a port—has never yet happened.

Tackling the Port Security Problem Using Twenty-First-Century Tools

Complex problems do not lend themselves to only one policy prescription, and therefore, like managers in other complicated policy fields, Suzanne Englebert found herself having to manage a variety of systems. These are summarized in table 8-2.

Reinvented Government

As noted earlier, there are a large number of governmental and nongovernmental agencies at every port—not to mention private sector shippers. In addition, the Coast Guard is heavily reliant on intelligence information from other government entities. But intelligence agencies are loath to share their data with those who do not have the proper security clearances. And yet for a piece of intelligence to be effective in preventing an incident it usually needs to be shared widely. Thus the first challenge Suzanne Englebert faced was to get security clearances for enough people at each port so that any potentially useful intelligence could get to the people who could use it.

This sounds like a simple and straightforward task. But even within the intelligence community, standardizing security clearances across agencies is both time consuming and complex and is frequently cited as one of the biggest impediments to fighting the war on terror. There are two issues: one is simply the time it takes to get a security clearance. As of 2005 it took nearly a year (347 days) to get a top-secret clearance and nearly half a year (155 days) to get a secret/confidential clearance.[13] Progress has been made—by 2009 these numbers had been cut substantially; but it still takes time.

The second issue is whether or not a clearance granted by one agency (customs, for instance) will be recognized by another agency operating at the port. As an OMB task force on the topic writes, "There is an inconsistent understanding among the agencies with respect to when reciprocal recognition of an existing clearance is required."[14] Yet on this aspect of the problem, progress has been slow even within the intelligence community, prompting Senator George Voinovich to comment at a 2009 hearing, "I am particularly concerned about the lack of progress being made regarding reciprocity, because I still consistently hear from individuals who have problems having one agency accept another agency's clearance."[15]

Since the security clearance problem has been a major problem within both the intelligence community and the Department of Defense, imagine how much more of a problem it is for the captains of the port, who might need to share intelligence with local police and private sector shippers. Security clearances need to be dealt with by the government itself; the standards need to be consistent from one agency to the other and highly reliable. There is no need for innovation or for flexibility in the granting of security clearances, but there is need for innovation in the process by which they are granted and in the standards for reciprocity. Security clearances are thus an area in need of reinvented government.

Government by Network

The first and most obvious examples of government by network are the port security plan that each captain of the port is mandated to create. As table 8-2 illustrates, government by network attempts to balance standard outputs related to security with innovation. Hence Suzanne Englebert's challenge was to guide the creation and implementation of these plans so that they possess the level of innovation and flexibility necessary to take into consideration differences in ports and yet create a certain threshold of preparedness.

The network option is critical here for the reasons pointed out by John D. Donahue and Richard J. Zeckhauser in chapter 6 in this book. "No uniform, top-down, port security regime could work—at least not without strangling port operations, stifling trade, and triggering bankruptcies. American ports were so diverse in size, layout, and function—and hence in security considerations—that no single approach could work for all of them." Hence the first important network here to be created and managed was the network articulated in the port security plans.

The second important network is an even wider one; it takes into account nongovernmental entities engaged in the work of the government. Manufacturers of exports to the United States, shipping companies, and cargo ships are key to increasing security, since even with a robust budget it would be impossible for Coast Guard personnel to inspect each of the ships bound for a U.S. port, even if they had the authority to do so. The U.S. Customs and Border Protection has purview over freight; it uses intelligence and a risk-based strategy to screen cargo before it is loaded onto vessels bound for the United States. Customs can deny the loading of high-risk cargo while the vessel is still overseas. But this is a fairly severe sanction. To avoid it, exporters are encouraged to join C-TPAT (Customs-Trade Partnership against Terrorism), a public-private international partnership that works with customs to provide baseline security standards for supply chain and container security. In theory the government reviews the security practices of the company shipping the goods as well as the security practices of the companies providing them with services. Companies with a good history of compliance with customs laws and procedures were granted membership in C-TPAT, and membership means less-frequent inspections.

This example of government by network is not without some big problems. In other governmentally led networks, the members of the network receive most or all of their funding from the government. Financial dependence is an incentive sufficient to induce reasonably good performance in most instances. In the case of port security, however, shippers and exporters are not paid by the Coast Guard to fill out forms and otherwise adhere to security procedures. Thus the incentive to participate in the network is the real possibility that failure to participate will result in denial of access to ports and in cargo being ruined because it sits on a dock somewhere, awaiting passage to the United States. (This is an especially difficult problem for exporters of perishable items like fruit and flowers.)

But stopping goods from being sent to the United States poses an enormous economic—and thus political—problem. All government-by-network arrangements suffer from a political challenge. One familiar case is defense contractors whose cost overruns are tolerated because they have the protection of powerful members of Congress. Similarly, social service providers often have their contracts renewed year after year either because they have powerful political patrons or because they are the sole provider of that service and hold, therefore, a monopoly position. In the case of port security, powerful economic interests are at work as is the broader public policy goal of free and robust trade. A too-aggressive strategy on the part of C-TPAT could result in trade sanctions that would reverberate throughout the world's economy.

No wonder Congress has been nervous about the security of the millions of containers coming into the United States. And so in 2006 the program began the move away from a sampling approach and toward 100 percent screening of goods at high-risk ports such as Port Qasim, Pakistan. This has been problematic on several fronts. The technology is not well enough developed to solve the massive problem of screening every container, and importers to the United States are frustrated by delays and angry at the cost. But more fundamental to the government-by-network problem is that the countries and the exporters singled out for 100 percent review of their cargo are insulted at being chosen. The message seems to them to be that the United States doesn't trust others to perform security screening. At a more basic level, this has been viewed as a protectionist barrier to trade.

Government by network works well when there is mutual trust and when incentives are aligned to keep everyone in the network performing well. The port security network involves hundreds of nation-states, thousands of shippers, and many more exporters. Barring some breakthrough technology to efficiently scan cargo, the reliance on a network to provide port security when that *same* network is the backbone of international trade is challenging to say the least.

Finally, while Suzanne Englebert was in control of ports, she was not in control of C-TPAT, which is under the purview of U.S. Customs. While they both reside in the Department of Homeland Security, the fact is that customs, one of the oldest agencies in the U.S. government, has its own world. Thus once again, as in the case of intelligence, Captain Englebert's job was dependent on a piece of the federal government over which she had no control.

Government by Market

Government by market works best when the state uses its power to attach a price to externalities, whether positive or negative, and thus to nudge private incentives more closely into line with public value. Ever since 1989, when the *Exxon Valdez* spilled more than 10 million gallons of oil into the ocean and created one of the worst ecological disasters ever, the importance of shipping safety—especially when carrying hazardous products—has been recognized. And so shipping companies carry insurance and take care to maintain safety standards in order to avoid increases in the cost of insurance or to become uninsurable.

But safety is different from security. The market does a fairly good job of assessing safety. The metrics for measuring the safety of ships, aircraft, trucks, and trains are known and can be predicted with some degree of certainty. In the aftermath of 9/11 there was a great deal of talk about making insurance companies take security into account in their assessments of everything from companies to office buildings. And yet relatively little has happened in this respect. And for the reasons laid out earlier (short of the artificial metrics created by an intensive and continuous program of red-teaming ports), there is simply no way to know who is doing a good job and who is not doing a good job at preventing terrorist activity at ports.

But the recent increase in piracy in the Gulf of Aden is forcing the insurance industry to rethink its policies. The first effect is, of course, to raise premiums on ships going through waters where pirates are known to operate. In May 2008 premiums were running 0.015 percent of a vessel's value; a year later they were as high as 0.15 percent, a tenfold increase.[16] This has meant that some ships have been taking long routes in order to avoid the dangerous waters and the insurance premiums. If the extra cost of the longer journey in terms of fuel, crew time, and wear and tear on the ship is less than the probabilistic value of piracy averted—as seems likely—this is an example of market efficiency at work. Ironically, however, while insurance companies such as Lloyd's of London have covered the risk from piracy since the 1800s, acts of terror are generally not covered under standard insurance policies. So the first challenge is to get insurance companies to cover terrorist acts as they cover piracy.

The second challenge then is to begin to suggest to insurers that they offer rates for shippers based upon the precautions they take to prevent terrorist acts. This is a well-established practice in the insurance industry. People who have good driving records pay lower rates for car insurance than those who don't, people who do not smoke pay lower rates for health insurance, and so on. By building in certain precautions, shippers can increase their own security and the security of the ports they enter, while receiving lower premiums.

For instance, terrorism experts worry about employees on large vessels who might be recruited to attack the vessel from the inside. Insurance companies could offer discounts for shippers who prove that they have undertaken extensive background checks of their employees. Another source of potential terrorism is disgruntled employees who leave but who take with them the insiders' knowledge of shipping operations. A shipper's participation in a system that tracks former employees could also lead to an insurance discount.

The most frequent terrorism worry is smuggling a "weapon of mass destruction" (such as a dirty bomb) onto a container ship. But radioactive material is difficult to smuggle. Insurance companies could offer discounts to those shippers who train their employees to identify potentially dangerous cargo. A second frequent worry is LNG (liquefied natural gas) containers. Again, insurance companies are in a position to insist upon high levels of security in return for lower insurance premiums.

With ships and shipping companies numbering in the thousands, it is impossible for any governmental entity to actually inspect cargo and crew on all of them. Yet just as there exists a substantial financial incentive to avoid piracy, it is in principle entirely possible to establish a substantial financial incentive to avoid terrorism. The solutions should be as varied and as innovative as the ships and as the cargo and the crew they require, and enforcement should be the financial incentives stemming from the need for insurance. Hence government by market becomes a useful model.

Conclusion

Traditional bureaucracy, with its emphasis on rules and regulations, does not provide the flexibility and innovation needed to meet a terrorist threat. To address port security, the U.S. Coast Guard needs to employ a variety of modern, twenty-first-century forms of government. But modern forms of government are, in one way or another, based on the ability to measure performance. And in the case of extremely low-probability events like terrorism, a proxy needs to be created to take the place of normal performance metrics. Without it, both government and the complex network of private actors involved in port security are flying blind. Until a better measure is invented, the ports need to employ aggressive red-teaming in order to consistently test their security procedures and learn from their mistakes. With the aid of this proxy measure, the Coast Guard and the Department of Homeland Security can employ a wide variety of new forms of governance—including those discussed here—better positioned than traditional bureaucracy for tackling complex problems that require the cooperation of multiple stakeholders.

Notes

1. See Donald Inglehart, "Post-Modernization Erodes Respect for Authority but Increases Support for Democracy," in *Critical Citizens: Global Support for Democratic Governance*, edited by Pippa Norris (Oxford University Press, 1999).

2. See Joseph S. Nye Jr. and others, *Why People Don't Trust Government* (Harvard University Press, 1997).

3. For a wonderful history of these leaders see Donald Savoie, *Thatcher, Reagan and Mulroney* (University of Pittsburgh Press, 1994).

4. By 1987 ten states, accounting for 25 percent of the nation's population, had passed some form of bottle bill (www.bottlebill.com).

5. See Robert N. Stavins, "What Can We Learn from the Grand Policy Experiment? Lessons from SO_2 Allowance Trading," *Journal of Economic Perspectives* 12, no. 3 (1998): 69–88.

6. See "Disaster by Design: California's Experience with Electricity Restructuring: The Origins," Kennedy School of Government Case Study 1632; "Disaster by Design: California's Experience with Electricity Restructuring: The Storm Hits," Kennedy School of Government Case Study 1633.

7. I use *outputs* to refer to the actual day-to-day results of an organization's work: for instance, the number of welfare-to-work clients placed in job training programs. I use *outcomes* to refer to the actual longer-term public policy goal, such as an increase in the number of welfare recipients who become self-sufficient enough to not return to the program after a significant period of time.

8. See www.epa.gov/oppt/3350/33fin01.htm.

9. Zachary Tumin, "From Safety to Security: The United States Coast Guard and the Move to a Global Network of Secure Ports, Cargos, Crews, and Vessels," Working Paper (Harvard Kennedy School of Government, 2009), p. 8.

10. "National Port Readiness Network" (www.globalsecurity.org/military/agency/dot/nprn.htm).

11. CRS Report for Congress, "Maritime Security: Potential Terrorist Attacks and Protection Priorities," May 14, 2007, RL33787.

12. This passage occurs in an early draft of chapter 3, this volume.

13. Office of Management and Budget, "Report of the Security Clearance Oversight Group" (www.fas.org/sgp/othergov/omb021507.pdf).

14. Ibid.

15. Testimony of Senator George Voinovich before the Senate Homeland Security and Governmental Affairs Subcommittee on Oversight of Government Management Hearing, September 15, 2009.

16. See "Shipping insurance up 10 fold due to piracy" (www.gnp.com.mx/gnp/clientes.nsf/(catalogoPDF)/0010/$file/World%20Finance.pdf).

MARK H. MOORE *and* ARCHON FUNG

9

Calling Publics into Existence: The Political Arts of Public Management

How best to integrate democratic politics into the management of public enterprises has been a central question in public administration for over a century.[1] On the one hand, all writers in the field recognize the critical importance of democratic political processes in legitimating state action—not only the state's use of public authority in regulatory and enforcement activities but also its use of tax dollars to provide goods and services. On the other hand, the processes of democratic legitimation create significant problems for the efficient and effective management of government in both practical and philosophical terms.[2]

Politics and Public Management: The Debate

At the practical level, the processes of democratic legitimation expose government managers to a continuing, contentious public debate about the important public values that should be *pursued by,* and *reflected in,* government operations. This debate occurs in *advance* of government action, as citizens and their representatives argue about whether and how government should act to deal with a particular social condition nominated as a public problem to be solved. The debate continues *subsequent* to government action, as citizens and their representatives call the government to account for its performance.[3] The debate focuses not only on the proper *ends* of government (the ideas of the good and just that provide the raison d'être for government action) but also on the best and fairest *means* for achieving those collectively established ends.

The continuing debate undermines effective public management in two key ways. First, responding to the continuing debate distracts managers from the important task of running their agencies. Second, the debate introduces uncertainty and vacillation among those whom managers are trying to rally to do the necessary work.

At a philosophical level, focusing on democratic legitimacy raises important questions about the fairness and justice of government operations as well as their efficiency and effectiveness.[4] This makes accounting for the public value produced by the government both different and harder than answering the simple question, what works?[5] Managers must also answer the question of whether the government is acting fairly, is protecting individual rights, and is helping to create more just conditions in the wider society.

Given the normative desirability of imbuing government action with democratic legitimacy, on the one hand, and the obstacles that processes of legitimation can pose to successful executive management, on the other, it is not surprising that theorists of public administration and public management have tried to sweep the problem of politics under the rug. They did so first at the turn of the twentieth century by trying to establish a reliable temporal distinction between *policy* on one hand, and *operations* on the other.[6] Policymaking was understood to be the realm within which debate occurred about the ends and means of government and were resolved in relatively clear and coherent articulations of the will of the people. Implementation was understood to be the sphere within which administrative experts found the means to achieve the desired purposes with the available resources as efficiently and effectively (and as fairly) as possible.

They did so again in the late 1980s and early 1990s effort to create a "new public management" that focused on creating a "customer oriented government."[7] In this view, "focusing on the customer" promised to bypass the problem of politics by seeing the body politic not as a collective that had to find some way to become articulate about its collectively defined purposes and commitments but instead as a collection of individuals who, like customers in the private sector, retained their right to decide what was valuable in government policy operations to them as individuals. On this view, the arbiter of public value was not the collective formed through the messy processes of democratic government but instead was each individual in society who was entitled to his own views of value. Just as the private sector created value by satisfying the desires of individual customers, so the public sector could create public value by satisfying the desires of individual citizens and clients. To accomplish this goal, government did not have to engage in the arduous political task of creating an articulate collective; it simply had to make its operations transparent to citizens and its transactions with individual citizens attuned to their individual desires. Public value would register in the individual valuations made by individual citizens and clients.

The Crucial Role of Democratic Politics
in Achieving Managerial Success

In our view, neither of these efforts to exclude democratic politics from public management can succeed. Fortunately, we are not alone in thinking this. At the beginning of the twentieth century, in the midst of the Progressive Era that sought to banish politics from public administration, John Dewey argued that if public managers—and society more generally—were to succeed in deploying publicly authority and money to achieve publicly valued results, they had to learn how to "call a public into existence having a common interest in controlling" the negative consequences of their interactions together.[8] We agree with Dewey. In our view, bringing the techniques of successful democratic political engagement to the public manager's work is crucial for both normative and practical reasons.

Normatively, we think that the important processes of democratic elections can only go so far to legitimate government action. Elections are too rare and too crude to provide useful guidance for the broad range of government action. If it is a virtue for *all* government action to be legitimated by explicit expressions of public support, then creating more forums in which citizens can participate in important choices about how to use state authority and money will advance the cause of democratic government. Beyond elections, and beyond the formal consultative processes of legislatures and administrative rule-making legislatures, lie many opportunities for governments to reach out for consultation and advice about how public assets might best be deployed in particular domains.[9] The use of such mechanisms might help to close the legitimacy gap that is experienced in many democratic governments, even those that are relatively far advanced. They might also help to solve problems of governance and accountability in countries in which democratic traditions are less well established.

Practically, we think that these consultative mechanisms can make democratic government more efficient and effective in the pursuit of its mandated goals. The reason is simple: in democratic governance, individual citizens are important not only because they *authorize* the government to pursue a particular goal but also because they help the government *operationally achieve* the desired goal.[10] They do so by putting their own shoulders to the capstan. This is true every time the government asks citizens to pay taxes (on pain of legal prosecution if they do not). It is true every time the government asks individuals to protect their own health (and reduce the financial and economic burden that their ill health creates for others) by driving safely, eating better, and exercising more. It is true every time the government seeks to manage the threat of global warming by requiring firms to reduce their polluting activities or by subsidizing the use of clean technologies. And it is true every time the government seeks to improve the impact and fairness of educational opportunities by reaching out to parents to work with the schools to leverage the school's influence over their children. If individual citizens cannot be mobilized to contribute actively to the achievement of public purposes, they will not be achieved.

In our view, there is simply no way to sweep politics under the rug. Public managers in democratic societies have to deploy the arts of political as well as administrative management. This is the theory we have been developing. And it is the utility of that theory that we mean to test by applying it to the problem faced by Captain Suzanne Englebert.

Captain Englebert's Problem

At the outset, it seems that a theory that emphasized engaging political processes to legitimate government action would have relatively little to offer Captain Englebert. After all, at the outset of the case, Captain Englebert had no formal authority to deploy that would require democratic legitimation! No body of public law required citizens to protect the security of the ports. No public money could subsidize or directly purchase private efforts to enhance port security. Indeed, many social actors who had interests and capacities related to port security were not even citizens of the United States! If Englebert were only a small part of the U.S. government, if the U.S. government were only one actor among many, and if the solution of the problem required action from those not subject to U.S. law, then the problem she faced could not be simply the problem of legitimating U.S. government action. Instead, she had to identify processes that used her position in the government *to mobilize actors who are largely independent of government authority.*

In chapter 7 of this volume, Stephen Goldsmith argues that Captain Englebert should think of herself as managing a network rather than a hierarchical organization. That is helpful insofar as it points to the fact that the operational capacities needed to improve port security are distributed across many organizations. But Goldsmith's view of a network focuses more on the operational challenge of realigning capacities to achieve goals than it does on precisely how large numbers of largely independent actors might be motivated to cooperate in a joint task. As a mayor, Goldsmith routinely used the authority of his office to focus the attention of multiple government organizations on a single complex problem.[11] He also used his wider political powers to engage the civic and for-profit sectors in the doing of public work. But he always started with both the formal powers and the informal political influences of an elected chief executive.

In Englebert's case, however, the network was more diffuse than those described by Goldsmith, and her position was much weaker. The organizations she needed to mobilize formed a network only in the loosest sense. They were functionally bound together by their combined interest in, and capacity to produce, improved port security. But they may not have been fully aware of the details of their functional interdependence nor how those could be exploited to create joint value. They had worked together in the past to take advantage of functional interdependencies associated with maritime trade, so they had some experience of working together. But they had never faced this particular task before. These facts together established them as a *latent* network that could be motivated and able to act to improve port security. But it was by no means clear whether or how the latent potential of that functional network could be activated. No one was assigned the responsibility or had the authority to take the lead in defining a purpose, committing independent actors to that purpose, finding effective means of achieving that purpose, and distributing the burdens and benefits of achieving the purpose in a fair as well as efficient and effective manner. No one was given a pot of money to spread around to attract commitment and effort.

These observations suggest that Captain Englebert's problem was less the narrow political challenge of legitimating government action taken by a powerful executive agency than it was to perform the more complex task of "calling a public into existence that can understand and act on its own interests."[12] Her challenge was at once *prior* to the use of executive authority (in the sense that she had to create a context in which a collectively constructed shared urgency for dealing with a problem can substitute—functionally— for the existence of formal authority) and *subsequent* to executive decision-making (in that it sought to ensure effective implementation by actors who were not under her administrative control). Her bureaucratic position could be used to convene a wider public deliberation to mobilize and guide action, but if so, it would be through the mobilization of an informal collective agreement that hardened into shared expectations (and perhaps negotiated regulations), not through the immediate and direct use of state authority. In short, *it was precisely because she lacked formal authority to get the job done that she had to rely heavily on wider political processes that mobilize social action above and beyond what government could order.* She had to think of herself as leading a social movement, not just as changing an organization.[13]

To say that she had to think and act as a leader of a political movement is not to take her away from her job. She is an officer of the U.S. Coast Guard, not a civil rights leader or a community organizer. But the paradox is that her administrative job required her to become a skillful political mobilizer. She could not achieve the goal she was assigned without finding the means not only to aggregate the capacities of different organizations into an effective machine for enhancing port security but also to find the means to motivate and mobilize those she did not control. To make that stretch, she had to rely on some kind of political process to mobilize both consent and a capacity to act that existed independently of her particular formal authority. She could be helped along in this by the existence of some formal authority that gave her a platform to use—a kind of bully pulpit. But if she were to build a sufficient governance capacity to guide the network actors toward improved performance, she had to construct the influence and authority of that governance structure through persuasion and exhortation as well as through the use of the government's money and authority.

Similarly, to say her task was largely a political one is not to say that she did not face a technical and operational problem as well. Indeed, what made her task so hard was that she has to, in the end, meet a demanding set of technical and operational challenges. Together, she and others in the latent network had to figure out the practical means for improving port security. Unless they could meet the operational requirements of this challenge, she would have failed. And it is this part of her job that remained operational, managerial, and technical. A good sound bite would not protect the ports. Lots of general enthusiasm would not lead to the particular actions that could improve port security.

The particular combination of political and technical challenges that Captain Englebert faced could be relatively rare; if so, this experience is better seen as a special case than one that can illustrate the general burdens on public managers. Yet many public management scholars are beginning to view situations in which public managers' formal authority falls well short of being sufficient to achieve the desired results as the rule rather than the exception.[14] If public authority is often limited in this way, then the political techniques associated with both legitimating the actions of government and mobilizing effective action from many independent actors will become much more central to effective managerial action. All public managers may have to learn to use the bully pulpit. This, at any rate, is the argument we wish to make.

We begin by rehearsing the managerial justifications for political engagement on behalf of both democratic legitimation of state action and the mobilization of effective social action. Along the way, we discuss actions taken by Captain Englebert that seem to be consistent with the theory we are developing. We then present a way of thinking about the tools available to managers for engaging their political environment—ways of calling a public into existence that can legitimate governmental action, extend its influence, and produce important social results. Finally, we conclude with observations about the strengths and limitations of our theory in helping Captain Englebert do her important public, governmental work.

Democratic Political Management: Why Building Legitimacy and Support for Public Action Is Important

An important trend in the theory of public management has been to encourage public managers—those entrusted with the authority and money of states—to focus more attention and effort on engaging rather than avoiding the political currents that swirl around them, their agencies, and their efforts to create the good and just society.[15] Some have viewed this advice as antidemocratic, as an invitation for public managers to subvert democratic politics for their own self-interested purposes.[16]

Our view is the opposite. A principal task confronting all public managers is to find ways to legitimate, in the eyes of the public, the actions that they and their agencies take. They cannot legitimate their actions without engaging the political world in ways that help public managers understand and enact what the public wishes them to do. Moreover, in a world in which public managers are called to account for achieving purposes that go well beyond their formal authority and depend on their capacity to mobilize a large number of formally independent social actors to help them achieve their goals, they must turn to the methods of political engagement to meet the expectations placed on them.

The Legitimacy Gap in Democratic Governance

In the past, we hoped that the task of legitimating government action could be left largely to the machinery of public administrators, directed by elected representatives. In this conception, elections and the choices made by those elected provided all the legitimacy that a democratic government needed.

But modern realities have shown that this ideal is wrong.[17] Politicians of many stripes have come to understand that there are real limits to the kind of legitimacy that can be delivered through periodic but still rare public elections. There are always issues ignored in electoral politics that surface in the course of governing and that require a different kind of legitimation. Conditions in the world often change rapidly so that commitments made in elections seem to be less compelling over time. As experience accumulates about the success or failure of particular governmental efforts, there are always reasons to reconsider established government policies. And while it has never been quite true that elections were about purposes and administration was about means, there are always enough detailed technical questions as to means (and their consequences for individual citizens and groups!) that need a closer and different kind of consulting than is typical of elections.

As a result of this legitimacy gap, public managers must often be concerned with political consultation and the mobilization of legitimacy and support as well as with the technical execution of well-defined, stable, policy mandates warranted by elections. Governments of many kinds have increasingly sought to reduce the legitimacy gap by surveying citizens about their experiences and views and by relying on and experimenting with new methods of public consultation and deliberation.[18] This is largely in the interest of increasing the responsiveness of government operations not only to individual clients of government but also to political and social communities that are smaller and different than the political communities that come into existence during election campaigns.

But moves to close the legitimacy gap are also important in mobilizing action from those who can make useful contributions to the solution of public problems. Sometimes, as in the case of port security, the problems are international and multisectoral. Other times, as in the case of public education, the problems are more local and more narrowly focused on government action alone. But whether large or small, the problems all depend on a certain amount of quasi-voluntary, public-spirited action to get the job done. Englebert had to rely on the willingness of the port communities to see what could be done, to share that knowledge, and to take the necessary actions. A local school superintendent has to rely on parents and other community-based organizations to create an environment of high academic expectations and performance to achieve her goals. None of the quasi-volunteer action is available for use without doing the political work of building a strong sense of interdependence and mutual responsibility.

To provide clear operational guidance about the nature of this work, it is useful to distinguish the role of political management for two broad strategic purposes: building political legitimacy and support for managers and their causes, on the one hand, and building the operational capacity needed to achieve their goals, on the other.[19] Further, with respect to building legitimacy and support, one can distinguish among the challenge of meeting routine demands for authorization and accountability, of making special efforts to expand one's own individual position, and of creating political room for innovation and experimentation.[20] With respect to building operational capacity, one can distinguish between the challenge of building effective influence across organizational boundaries (a kind of inside game often involving relatively few actors, all of whom are organizations) and the challenge of mobilizing action by thousands, even millions, of decentralized individual actors (a kind of outside game that involves different forms of public marketing).[21] These specific challenges that must be met to close both the legitimacy gap and the performance gap in modern government are discussed in more detail below.

The Political Challenge of Building Legitimacy and Support for a Public Cause

Building legitimacy and support for officials and their causes assumes great importance right at the outset, with the obvious but fundamental point that public officials have to be sure that the goal they seek is something that is, in fact, *publicly* valued, and not some self-interested or idiosyncratic goal of their own. Viewed from this perspective, democratic political management begins with the idea of being accountable to the body politic, in the case of governmental action, or to the society at large, in the case of wider social action. Public managers in democratic societies are duty bound to make accurate reports about their aims and accomplishments to what has been described as their "political authorizing environment."[22] This requirement helps ensure that their aims are closely aligned with the more or less clearly expressed aspirations of the body politic.

Creating Legitimacy and Support by Being Accountable. Although we don't often think of accountability as a form of political engagement, on reflection, it seems as though it is one of the most important forms of political dialogue among managers, politicians, and the public.[23] It is through the processes of calling an organization to account that the public has to speak clearly about what it wants from the organization and that those who lead public sector organizations can talk about what they think they should be trying to achieve.

As a commissioned officer of the U.S. Coast Guard, Captain Englebert was, in the first instance, accountable to her immediate bureaucratic superiors. She was assumed to be competent and resourceful, an asset in any mission that might be assigned to the Coast Guard, but she could not undertake any assignment that was not given to her. Her immediate bureaucratic superiors, however, were accountable to the statutes that authorize (and require) the U.S. Coast Guard to pursue certain purposes with appropriated money and specific authorities, the expectations and demands of political officials in the legislature and the executive branch, and the interests of many other social actors who have concerns about both the actions and inactions of the USCG. The broadest description of Captain Englebert's authorization is that she was expected to do what she could and was required to do to help her superiors achieve the legislatively mandated mission of the Coast Guard in today's changing circumstances.

That environment was changed by the 9/11 attacks on the World Trade Center and the Pentagon. A new and unexpected threat appeared in the world. She and her superiors were duty bound to think about how that new threat might best be met. Consistent with her understanding of her duties, Englebert immediately started to work on creating a position within the USCG that could provide some leadership in helping the USCG and other social actors search for and make a suitable response. Having put herself forward in this way, her bureaucratic superiors assigned her the job. She got what Richard Neustadt called a "hunting license" to see what she could do in the wider political environment to advance the mission of the Coast Guard.[24] This both authorized and required her to offer some form of leadership to the USCG and the wider society.

Arguably, this first step did not require much political management. To no small degree, the objective conditions in the world did the political work of creating an urgent need to which Englebert was responding. To calibrate the importance of the 9/11 attack in creating the political authorization for action, all one has to do is imagine how Englebert's effort to create a position focusing on port security would have fared had the 9/11 attacks not occurred. If she had simply been an officer in the Coast Guard with an intuition that the ports were at risk of a terrorist attack, she could have worked long and hard to "sell" her superiors on this vision and failed to do so.

Still, it is worth noting that the ordinary processes of politics, like the ordinary processes of the market, can play an important role in helping society make a useful response to changing material conditions in the society—and that a portion of that response comes from inside the bureaucracy as well as from politicians. It is also worth noting that, while the crisis created the opportunity, Englebert would have to do a great deal of work over time to *sustain* her license and to ensure that the license was *used* to enhance port security. That means remaining accountable and responsive not only to her immediate superiors but also to a much larger public that has an interest in, and a capacity to act to improve, port security.

Building Legitimacy to Enhance Personal Influence. Public managers have to be engaged with their authorizing environments to ensure both account-ability and responsiveness. But if they are assigned tasks that greatly exceed their formal authority, they have to find the means to widen the effective scope of their personal and positional influence. This means finding ways to legitimate the goals they seek in the eyes of those whom they hope to persuade to contribute to the cause. As noted above, that puts lots of pressure on the capacity of managers to persuade independent actors that the purposes the managers seek to accomplish are sufficiently important that the other actors will agree to cooperate even though they are neither required, nor paid, to do so—at least not at the outset. As Neustadt observes, "The essence of a [pub-lic leader's] persuasive task is to convince [public officials over whom the leader has no direct authority] that what [the public leader] wants of them is what they ought to do for their own sake and on their own authority."[25] We can extend this idea to include the idea that public officials have to persuade private officials and other individuals that *it is their duty to help achieve col-lectively desired goals.* It is through this kind of activity that a purpose acquires a legitimacy that is beyond the formal authority of a given manager.

Captain Englebert, for example, was given the task of orchestrating a large, highly decentralized effort to improve port security. In that effort, her personal authority and legitimacy seemed quite limited. She probably could not effectively reach an existing, coherent structure of authority, because there was none. Even if she could have acted with the full sovereign powers of the president, she would have commanded only one level of government, would have had limited influence over private parties, and would have been second-guessed by Congress. And that power alone would have had little sway with the international governments and private corporations that she had to influence. There is no election that could have been held that would have given her democratic legitimacy over the actors she needed to influence. She had to build her legitimacy in order to secure their cooperation.

Fortunately, she was not without resources to do this. Most important, she had the acknowledged urgency of both the collective task of increasing port security and the specific material concerns of the actors, who could easily have imagined themselves as victims of a terrorist attack. To some degree, she could also claim to represent the interests of the United States as a whole (as long as her mandate held) and could have suggested that government might eventually have to regulate private action or come up with some money pay for port security enhancements. But the important question for her was whether this set of assets would provide enough legitimacy and effective influence to get the job done. This is particularly important, because the material tasks associated with enhancing port authority would almost certainly have required some social actors to absorb losses as well as enjoy gains, and all those who were called upon to do the work would have had views not only about the best way to do the work but also about the fairest way to divide the costs and benefits. She needed a great deal of legitimacy to begin the game; even more to be influential in the game; even more to become the broker and guarantor of a bundle of agreements that could constitute a fair and effective regime for producing port security from a large number of independent contributors.

Legitimating Innovations in Governance and Operations. Building legitimacy and support become particularly challenging when public managers are forced to innovate and to experiment with untried methods. In our view, democratic politics is entirely consistent with the idea of innovation in government policies and operations. What is a democratic election about if it is not about the voters listening to new ideas about how to use the assets of government to improve individual and collective conditions in society? That is why each election results in pressures on reluctant bureaucracies to innovate in furtherance of their new mandate. Operating managers are politically appointed so that they can reach more deeply and more reliably into government operations and exploit the new ideas and pursue the new values that were ratified by the election.

On the other hand, democratic politics challenges innovation.[26] Citizens do not like to think that their officials are experimenting with methods whose results are uncertain. They don't like gambling with the state's money and authority and with the welfare of individuals and collectives who are affected by the uncertain choices about how to use these assets. Indeed, one of the reasons that bureaucrats have some independent standing and legitimacy in proposing government action is precisely because their expertise is viewed as a bulwark against uncertainty. We need bureaucrats to be expert. Otherwise the terror of the unknown will come over us. Even though citizens might be dissatisfied with mediocre results, even though they might understand that improvement requires an uncertain search for the elusive production-possibility frontier, even though they accept the necessity for risk and innovation in the private sector, when it comes to authorizing government managers they prefer the status quo or the application of tried and true (but low-performing) measures to new situations.[27]

For Captain Englebert, the aversion to innovation created two distinct problems. The reason is that she was responsible for leading two distinct innovative efforts. First, she was responsible for introducing an *innovation in the governance.* Before 9/11 the government relied on a particular set of policies and institutional arrangements to ensure the security of the ports. Following 9/11 those institutional arrangements became subject to review and no longer seemed adequate. They did not require enough attention or coordinated effort from all the network players whose contributions were necessary to solve this problem. Her challenge was to figure out a new process or structure of governance that could turn a latent network into an effective action network. Think of this as an *institutional* innovation in the structures and processes of governance.

Second, as Malcolm Sparrow suggests in chapter 3, she had to orchestrate a complex learning process to find the appropriate technical and operational means for ensuring port security. As noted above, Englebert and her collaborators did not know whether the objective was to protect the ports from attack, to use the ports to thwart attacks headed elsewhere, or some combination of the two. They did not now know, and could never be quite sure, whether they had imagined all the specific threats they faced nor the measures that would be cost effective in dealing with the full set of specific threats. They could not know for sure, then, exactly what actions taken by particular actors would be effective in dealing with the threats, nor could they be fair in distributing the burden of reacting to the threats. Think of this as the family of substantive *programmatic* innovations that could use material assets to successfully ward off the various threats to port security.

In this world of threat uncertainty, the task of politically legitimating the actions becomes particularly difficult. The relative power of expertise to dictate a desired result goes down, and the relative power of deliberating and reaching agreements in a world of uncertainty goes up. This created a particular problem for Captain Englebert, because she probably correctly assumed that her legitimacy rested in her technical knowledge. The idea that it would have to be created by a capacity for leading a *learning effort* among her colleagues and collaborators rather than the application of technical knowledge she already had imposed a special burden and stretched her professional skills beyond what is usually required.

Legitimacy for Operational Capacity

So far we have focused on the role of politics and political engagement in building legitimacy, support, and commitment to a particular policy initiative and for searching for the effective institutional and substantive means for enhancing port security. This focus on accountability, on building one's personal influence, on creating room for innovation is the part of political management that is concerned with defining and legitimating the *purposes* of public managers. This is important because it ensures that public managers are doing the right thing and because it generates a flow of fungible resources they can use in their work. It is less preoccupied with the operational question of how best to deploy those resources in particular policies, programs, and activities designed to produce material changes in the world.

Yet a little reflection reveals that successful political engagement and management is crucial not only for building support and guaranteeing a flow of resources for a particular conception of public value but also for efforts to *produce* that value. Two conditions make political management crucial to successful implementation as well as successful policy development.

Mobilizing across Organizational Boundaries. As the government has developed over time—as it has made significant changes in the basic structure of government by changing its overall scope, decentralizing responsibility from national to state and local and grass-roots levels, and shifting many of its functions to private sector organizations—the nature of the managerial work that focuses on operations and implementation has also changed.[28] As Elaine Kamarck observes in chapter 8, some of these changes have been made in accord with principles of the "new public management," which has sought to reduce the role of politics in the system by increasing the role of private sector organizations and markets and to turn the government into a market organizer and regulator rather than direct producer. But none of these changes alter the basic fact that, when government uses public money and authority to shape production systems that produce goods, services, and conditions in which the public has an interest, democratic politics must once again appear to give legitimacy and substantive guidance to government as it carries out its purposes.

Indeed, to many writers it seems that the more distributed systems of production for public goods and services have *increased* rather than reduced the role of political acumen and action in ensuring that the public's goals are achieved. The private sector has many ways of making its private interests felt in the halls of government in ways that might end up costing the government more money and producing less public value if public managers cannot defend the interests of the public. In order to do so, public managers have to build some bulwarks against the influence of private sector actors and legitimate those bulwarks as protectors of democratically established public interests. That involves significant political sophistication and action. It requires public managers to work politically to be sure they can resist private interests when they are advanced as though they were identical to public interests.

This trend has also been exacerbated by changes in the scope and character of the problems that government seeks to solve. Part of the problem is that many of the more pressing issues now span organizational boundaries. The existing structures do not fit; not all the resources and capacities required to act on a given problem are held within a coherent structure of authority that can act operationally to achieve the desired results. This means that managers have to find ways to operate *outside the structures in which they are placed.*[29] As they move across boundaries trying to engage other more or less independent agencies in the doing of their work, the key role of the political context and the utility of methods of political mobilization become apparent. In simply making an approach and seeking an operational partnership, managers are to some degree undermining or transforming the structures of political accountability that previously existed and that largely guided the actions of existing agencies. The only processes that can simultaneously weaken old systems of accountability and create new ones that guide public action more reliably to public goals are political processes.[30]

Operational partnerships can require both political permission and political assistance in transforming the previously existing structures of accountability into forms of accountability that recognize both the new work they are doing and the new results they are achieving. They often benefit from having a political current running that can get them into the discussions and keep them there long enough to build more effective working partnerships. In sum, successful political management could help to create a context in which agency managers could approach key partners for assistance in the achievement of their mandated objectives, where the work of the agency could be supplemented by contributions made by other independent social actors to the achievement of the manager's goals.

All this is on display in Captain Englebert's case. The threat of a terrorist attack on or through the nation's ports was a new problem. One could say it has always been a theoretical possibility. One can also say that it has existed all along, in the form of pirates and enemies who threaten U.S. security through its ports.[31] But surely the threat represented by terrorists willing to sacrifice their lives while delivering technologically sophisticated blows to life and property is a new one.

It is not only that the threat is new, and not only that the new threat challenges the old institutional framework, but also that this new threat would likely end up challenging *any* plausible institutional framework. The reason is an effective counter to the position that the uncertain threat of terrorism to the ports will inevitably outrun the functional capacities of any single agency. Core constitutional boundaries will have to be breached. Any response will involve state and local as well as federal governments. It will involve private companies as well as governments. The response will likely be strung together through a set of complex agreements, both tacit and explicit, among many actors. The adequacy of that set of negotiated deals to deliver real safety will always be a bit uncertain until we see it succeed or fail against anticipated or unanticipated threats.

Because port security is exactly the kind of problem that requires a networked government, or a collaborative governance response, it seems likely that political management would have been particularly important for Captain Englebert. It is only through the work of continued dialogue leading to tacit and explicit understandings that a real capacity to protect can be constructed.

Legitimacy to Mobilize Decentralized Coproducers. Beyond mobilizing partners in other public or nongovernmental organizations, another kind of political management seeks to motivate coproduction that reaches out to large numbers of individual decentralized actors as potential contributors to social activities.[32] The paradigm here is the mobilization of individuals to contribute to solid waste recycling by sorting their own garbage.[33] But other obvious examples are encouraging citizens to lock their cars in efforts to reduce auto thefts, or to get flu shots to help halt an influenza epidemic, or to participate in a designated-driver program to reduce the chance of auto fatalities.[34]

There are two key ideas here. First and most obvious is the idea that we shift from a relatively small group of actors, who have to coordinate relatively large actions taken by the organizations they guide, to a very large number of decentralized actors who are never in the same room with one another and do not engage in face-to-face negotiations. They are targets of political mobilization, not collaborators . Second (and probably more important for the particular case of port security) is the idea that reluctant social actors are being persuaded to do something out of a sense of public duty. In short, they are the foci of socially created obligations that pressure them to do their duty rather than actors who are entirely free of social obligation.

The easy part of this idea is that individuals need to be persuaded to do something that is simultaneously in their own interest and the interests of the wider public. The question is how best to inform, how best to teach, how best to motivate.

The harder part has to do with remembering that individuals receive not only services from government organizations but also obligations. For citizens on whom government imposes duties—that is, citizens who are asked to do something that is not in their self-interest and not something that they would voluntarily choose to do on their own but that are nonetheless required by government—an important task becomes not just helping the citizens act in their own immediate best interests but also convincing them of the necessity of compliance.[35] Obligatory encounters between the state and individuals go more smoothly if individuals can be sure that their sacrifice is important and appreciated and if the imposition is fair.[36] This is a special kind of public sector marketing, the kind that focuses on obligatees rather than beneficiaries.

In the case of Captain Englebert, she had no direct authority to deploy. To succeed she had to find some means of imposing unwelcome burdens on the private and public actors who make up the port community and whose resource commitments and actions could play a decisive role in strengthening or weakening the defenses of the ports and in their capacity to thwart attacks aimed elsewhere. There is no small amount of self-interest she could call on to motivate actions to increase port security. The lives and property of private agents are at stake in port vulnerability, and the self-interest in protection can be animated, to say nothing of their desires to appear as good citizens in shouldering a public burden. But in the language of economics, the production of port security has many externalities and public good aspects that make it difficult to organize the production of port security through a kind of market system, in which a desired level of port security is specified, a responsibility to pay for this level of security is distributed among the beneficiaries (according to their benefit), and then individual actors are invited to bid for the bits of work that will add up to the desired level of security, with the resulting level of financial surplus or burden distributed once again. Moreover, there is a great deal of technical uncertainty about, for example, the nature of the threats facing the ports and the opportunities the ports have for thwarting other attacks.

This means that some kind of collective discussion and negotiation had to occur as the port community struggled to find a way toward more security at a cost acceptable to those being asked to accept the financial or operational burden of making the changes. That negotiation would have been shot through with material self-interest. But it would also have been conditioned to no small degree by the public spirit created within the group.[37] A cost-effective and fair way to produce port security depended to no small degree on each of the parties coming to think and act as citizens of the community seeking to pool their knowledge and their resources to achieve the collectively desired results. Captain Englebert had to help to create a forum that emphasized the importance of collaboration and that allowed members of the community to search for the particular solutions that would simultaneously meet the technical demands of increasing port security at low cost and that fairly distributed the benefits and burdens of executing the particular solution that emerged.

On this view, Captain Englebert's problem was precisely that described by Dewey: to succeed in her important public task, she had to call into existence *a public* that could recognize and then act upon its own individual and collective interests. She had to help create and strengthen the capacities of the imperfect community that existed in the ports and to guide this community through a process that kept the common problem in front of it as it sought a joint solution. She could not have created a governance capacity to enhance port security without offering assurances at each step along the way that the governance capacity being built and used was *of* the community, *for* the community, and *by* the community that she sought to create and to mobilize.

How to Convene a Public: The Democracy Cube

Exactly how this legitimacy gets created, and how citizens more or less well organized in particular interest groups can be mobilized to act on behalf of public goals, are crucially important questions for government officials trying to achieve mandates or to seize opportunities to create public value. To no small degree, legitimacy comes from following procedures that are both culturally and legally understood to confer legitimacy on government action. Processes of consultation, respect for individual rights in both policymaking and operations, compliance with established rules, and so on are all important ways of building legitimacy and therefore public moral support for particular actions.

But legitimacy can also be constructed from technical expertise and practical effectiveness in achieving particular results. Indeed, there is sometimes a conflict between the form of legitimacy that comes from following rules, on the one hand, and on the other hand, the kind that comes from producing outcomes effectively. Both can exist in real political processes, and the usual problem facing public managers is to try to amass legitimacy from both sources.

Finally, legitimacy can come from satisfying the particular interests of either discrete individuals or of individuals formed into like-minded groups. Individuals and voluntarily formed groups who like the consequences of government policies when evaluated in their own terms are more likely to view government policies as legitimate. When pressed, such actors might feel obligated to say more than that their particular material interests have been satisfied. They may have to say that they had a right to be consulted and to have their interests either considered or protected as a matter of democratic process. Or they may have to construct an argument about why their particular interests should be considered worthy of public concern against all others. But the practical point is that many social actors confer legitimacy on governmental actors if the actions the government takes satisfy their interests.

Through a combination of past experience—in particular, creating the oil spill control regime around SOLAS—and through an individual aptitude, Captain Englebert seemed to possess a knack for political leadership in the sense described above. She crafted a framework document and facilitated initial agreement by a wide array of disparate actors over whom she had little formal authority. In this section, we consider a general framework for mapping the major dimensions along which a public—or minipublic, as one of the authors has called it elsewhere—can be convened and collective decisions made.[38] Though Captain Englebert probably didn't have such a framework in her head, others lacking her natural facility might benefit from this more structured schema. The framework has three primary dimensions: who participates in this public, how they communicate with one another and make decisions, and how much formal authority they have to command the disposition of resources or behavior.[39]

Participant Selection

One feature of any public decisionmaking venue is the character of its franchise: Who is eligible to participate and how do individuals become participants? In the universe of direct participation, there are five common selection mechanisms.

—*Open to all.* The vast majority of public participation mechanisms utilize the least-restrictive method for selecting participants: the process is open to all who wish to attend. The public meeting at the International Maritime

Organization (IMO) that Englebert hosted had this formal character. Actual participants are a self-selected subset of the general population. While complete openness possesses obvious appeal, those who choose to participate are frequently quite unrepresentative of any larger public. Individuals who are wealthier and better educated tend to participate more than those who lack these advantages as do those who have special interests or stronger views.[40]

—*Open to all with selective recruiting and random selection.* This describes two participant selection methods. Some mechanisms that are open to all selectively recruit participants among subgroups who are less likely to engage. In this case, for example, it would have required special efforts to elicit the participation of residents who lived in port communities, or perhaps of the smaller nations that would be affected by maritime regulation. Randomly selecting participants from among the general population is the best guarantee of descriptive representativeness. Though it would not have been appropriate in this situation, initiatives such as deliberative polling, citizens' juries, and planning cells randomly select participants to discuss various public issues.[41]

—*Lay stakeholders.* A fourth method engages lay stakeholders in public discussions and decisions. Lay stakeholders are unpaid citizens who have a deep interest in some public concern and are thus willing to invest substantial time and energy to represent and serve those who have similar interests or perspectives but choose not to participate. Many neighborhood association boards and school councils, for example, are composed of lay stakeholders.

—*Professional stakeholders.* Finally, some governance processes that have been described under such labels as regulatory negotiation, grassroots environmental management, and collaborative planning bring together professional stakeholders. These participants are frequently paid representatives of organized interests and public officials. Most of the participants in the post-9/11 effort to secure the ports were professional stakeholders. Many of them came from other public organizations, outside of the Coast Guard, who had a stake in decisions and plans for port security; others came from private organizations such as shipping firms.

Communication and Decision

A second crucial dimension of institutional design specifies how participants interact within a venue of public discussion or decision. Informed by images of the Athenian forum or the New England town meeting, many treatments of political participation and deliberation implicitly conjure up idealistic deliberation: participants engage with one another directly as equals who reason together about public problems. But the vast majority of institution-alized public discussions do not occur in this way, nor is it clear that they should. For example, if the main reason for direct participation is one that John Dewey once gave—that the man who wears the shoe, not the shoe-maker, knows best where it pinches—then participants need do no more than complain to policymakers.[42]

There are six main modes of communication and decisionmaking in par-ticipatory settings, and these vary according to the ways that individuals par-ticipate in the discussion and the degree to which an effort is made to forge a collective view. We consider first the different ways in which individuals can participate; second the ways that individuals can be organized to speak as a collective.

Different Forms of Individual Participation. The vast majority of those who attend events such as public hearings and community meetings do not put forward their own views at all. Instead, they participate as spectators, who receive information about some policy or project; and they bear witness to struggles among politicians, activists, and interest groups.

But there are few public meetings in which everyone is a spectator. Almost all of them offer opportunities for some to express their preferences to the audience and officials there. Think of the citizens and activists who line up at the ubiquitous microphone to pose a pointed question or say their piece.

Other discussions are organized in ways that allow participants to explore, develop, and perhaps transform their preferences and perspectives. They encourage participants to learn about issues and, if appropriate, trans-form their views and opinions by providing them with educational materi-als or briefings and then asking them to consider the merits and trade-offs among several alternatives. Participants usually discuss these issues with one another (often organized into small groups) rather than only listening to experts, politicians, or advocates.

Mechanisms to Forge Collective Agreements. Mechanisms employing these first three modes of communication often do not attempt to translate the views or preferences of participants into a collective view or decision. In most public hearings, for example, officials commit to no more than receiv-ing the testimony of participants and considering their views in their own subsequent deliberations.

Some venues, however, *do* attempt to develop a collective choice through some combination of three methods of decisionmaking. The most com-mon of these is aggregation and bargaining. In this mode, participants know what they want, and the mode of decisionmaking aggregates their preferences—often mediated by the influence and power that they bring—into a social choice. The exploration and give and take of bargaining allows participants to find the best available alternative to advance the joint preferences they have. A decision at a New England town meeting operates in this mode when the townspeople have polarized over some heated issue ahead of the meeting and use the final vote simply to reckon their antecedent views.

Deliberation and Negotiation. This is a second mode of decisionmaking. Participants deliberate in order to figure out what they want individually and as a group. In mechanisms designed to create deliberation, participants typically absorb educational background materials and exchange perspectives, experiences, and reasons with one another in order to develop their views and discover their interests as individuals. In the course of developing their individual views in a group context, deliberative mechanisms often include procedures to facilitate the emergence of principled agreement, the clarification of persisting disagreements, and the discovery of new options that better advance what participants value.

Two features distinguish the deliberative mode. First, a process of interaction, exchange, and—we hope—edification precedes any group choice. Second, participants in deliberation aim toward agreement with one another (though frequently they do not reach consensus) based upon reasons, arguments, and principles. In political theory, this mode has been elaborated and defended as a deliberative ideal of democracy, while scholars of dispute resolution describe such processes as negotiation and consensus building.[43]

Captain Englebert and her colleagues seemed to engage in a mix of deliberation and negotiation with port chiefs, private shipping companies, and IMO members in crafting a framework document that these parties could use as a foundation for increasing domestic and international port security. Though the case lacks details in this regard, the parties seemed to view security and the prevention of attack as a common goal and all were willing to take action to secure that objective. Some of the specifics—for example the technologies and requirements that private shippers would have to adopt and the question of performance standards for varied ports—were settled through some combination of reasoning and bargaining.

Many, perhaps most, public policies and decisions are determined through neither aggregation nor deliberation but rather through the technical expertise of officials whose training and professional specialization suits them to solving particular problems. This mode usually creates less room for citizen engagement. It is the domain of planners, regulators, social workers, teachers and principals, police officers, and the like. As the legitimacy of expertise has waned, however, and the legitimacy of individual and political consent for the actions of government has waxed, this method has become less reliable as a method for producing governmental choices that are acceptable as legitimate by those affected.

Authority, Power, and Influence

The third important dimension of design gauges the impact of public participation. How is what participants say linked to what public authorities or they themselves do?

—*Participating without impact.* In many, perhaps most, participatory venues, the typical participant has little or no expectation of influencing policy or action. Instead, he or she participates in order to derive the personal benefits of edification or perhaps to fulfill a sense of civic obligation. Forums that principally affect participants rather than policy and action employ the first three communicative modes (listening, expressing preferences, and developing preferences) and not the three more intensive decisionmaking modes described above.

—*Participating to shape wider public opinion and build political pressure.* Many participatory mechanisms exert influence upon the state or its agents indirectly by altering or mobilizing public opinion. Their discussions and decisions exert a communicative influence upon members of the public or officials, who are moved by the testimony, reasons, conclusions, or by the probity of the process itself. For example, while the 9/11 Commission (the National Commission on Terrorist Attacks upon the United States) was created by Congress to offer recommendations to lawmakers, its principal source of influence was arguably the enormous public interest and support that the final report generated. Providing advice and consultation is a third common mechanism through which participatory forums exert influence upon public authority. In this mode, officials preserve their authority and power but commit themselves to receiving input from participants. The stated purpose of most public hearings and many other public meetings is to provide such advice.

—*Participation for direct political power.* Less commonly, some participation mechanisms exercise direct power.[44] It is useful to distinguish between two levels of empowerment. In some venues, citizens who participate join in a kind of cogoverning partnership with officials to make plans and policies or to develop strategies for public action. Each public school in Chicago, for example, is jointly governed by a local school council composed of parents, community members, and the school's principal and teaching staff.

Figure 9-1. *Democracy Cube*

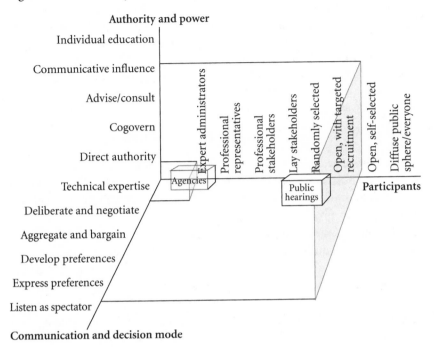

At a higher (though not necessarily more desirable) level of empowerment, participatory bodies occasionally *exercise direct authority over public
decisions or resources.* The New England town meeting provides the classic example of direct participatory authority. In urban contexts, neighborhood councils in some cities in the United States control substantial zoning
authority or financial resources that allow them to control, plan, or implement sublocal development projects.[45]

The Democracy Cube

Putting these three dimensions of participant selection, communicative
mode, and extent of influence yields a three-dimensional space—a democracy cube—of institutional design choices according to which varieties of
participatory mechanisms can be located and contrasted with more pro-
fessionalized arrangements. Figure 9-1 plots two familiar mechanisms of
governance on this three-dimensional space. In the typical public agency,
trained experts utilize their technical expertise to make decisions that they

are authorized to execute. The typical public hearing is open to all who wish to attend. While many in the audience listen to educate themselves, a few participants express their views in the hope that these preferences will be taken into account and thus advise the deliberations of policymakers. These two mechanisms lie on nearly opposite sides of the cube in terms of who participates, how they communicate, and the extent of their influence on public action.

Conclusion: Looking Forward to Creating Publics

Captain Englebert's basic challenge to enhance port security exceeded the parameters normally thought to circumscribe the task of public management. She could not solve the problem solely by properly mobilizing and organizing people and resources under her Coast Guard command. It was clear from the outset that she was responsible for trying to produce a material outcome in the world that required far more resources than she directly controled.

In the business world, this is the classic definition of an entrepreneur: a person who pursues purposes regardless of the availability of resources.[46] Someone who becomes an entrepreneur assumes responsibility for mobilizing resources as well as deploying them. But Englebert was a captain in the U.S Coast Guard. She had her own command structure to deal with. And in trying to mobilize action to protect U.S. ports, she had to confront a huge array of different actors. These actors were functionally able to help and had more or less interest in doing so but who were not her direct subordinates. They were accountable to others and pursued other purposes.

The challenge of port security, furthermore, was complicated by three critical problems. First, it was not at the outset clear what the most important challenge was. Was it to find ways to protect themselves from terrorist attack? Or was it to take advantage of their strategic locations and capacities to spot and thwart terrorist threats headed elsewhere? Second, it was by no means clear what would be the best means for dealing with either problem. Third, all ports were different.

This meant that there would have to be a continuous learning process. Englebert needed a strong regulatory initiative to get people's attention and begin doing the work. But that regulatory initiative had to be flexible enough not only to serve the political function of keeping independent individuals engaged but also flexible enough to adapt and change as the actors in the system learned about the threats and possibilities and what constituted an effective approach.

Unlike many other contexts, this one benefited Captain Englebert through its plentiful stock of good will and public spirit. In the wake of the 9/11 attacks, all of the individuals leading and working in organizations that she relied upon realized that they faced a common threat. She also benefited from a prior history, in which many of these organizations worked together on other issues, such as maritime safety. Part of that prior history included the construction of international forums and routines in which shippers, port authorities, and naval organizations had become accustomed to cooperating with one another.

While favorable, these factors did not create the legitimacy and cooperation that Englebert required. Instead, they formed a promising basis upon which she was able to facilitate agreement on a more specific sense of shared interests, a common articulation of goals, mutually agreed commitments, and a sense that this network of organizations would move forward together. Captain Englebert seemed to have a remarkable intuitive capacity for creating this far-flung collaborative effort around port security. Someone less skilled, or less outwardly oriented toward the network of necessary partners, would likely have been less successful.

The approach sketched in this chapter sets out several conceptual guideposts that help to orient public managers to operate more effectively in contexts such as Englebert's. Generally, our emphasis on the importance of legitimacy and external capacities stresses a fundamental but easily overlooked aspect of Englebert's job: she had to mobilize legitimacy and support from a wide variety of actors in addition to the more familiar public management challenges of maintaining the confidence and goodwill of her superiors in order to ensure the flows of internal resources and discretion that she needed to operate effectively. Second, the mobilization of independent actors to help her achieve the mission assigned to her focused her attention on how best to organize a process that would engage those independent actors not only in politically supporting choices she made but also in doing the work that was required to enhance port security even when she could not directly pay them for doing the work—and where the regulatory regime that could require them to do the work was still developing and fragile.

The democracy cube could have been useful to Englebert's thinking about the kind of engagement process that would help her achieve her objectives. With respect to the issue of how much *power and influence* to delegate to participants, she probably would have seen what she intuitively grasped: namely, that the usual expert mode of decisionmaking was simply not going to work in this case. She had too little expertise, and too little formal authority, to be able to make this decision on her own. This meant that she had to be willing to organize a process of decisionmaking that gave the participants influence. She needed their knowledge and their cooperation. The price was to give them influence over the choice.

Similarly, with respect to *communication and decisionmaking*, she could not afford to run a process in which individuals were silent or simply presented their own views. She had to stretch for a process that drew the interested individuals and capable parties into a dialogue with one another that was focused on exploring what each could do to contribute to port security and that built a sense of connection, interdependence, and mutual commitment.

Finally, with respect to *participant selection*, it would have seemed clear that she needed, at least in the short run, professional stakeholders who had either political influence to exert, money to spend, or (most important) some direct capacity to act effectively to enhance port security. She did not need a mass political movement of lay participants, since the attack itself would have done the political work of focusing everyone's attention. What she needed was the group of actors for each port, and for all the ports together, who, if they could reach an agreement, could enhance the security of that port and contribute to an understanding about how all ports might be made secure.

These strategic judgments about how best to organize a political, participatory process to help achieve her goals would have located her in a particular part of the democracy cube, the part that calls for the following: participation by professional stakeholders; and a form of communication and decisionmaking that not only pushed interested and capable individuals to learn, to change their views, and to develop a collective perspective about how to act but also that gave the participants a significant amount of power and influence over the actions to be taken by them and by government.

In sum, we hope these pages show that wide support and collaborative action from other public and private organizations as well as citizens themselves are important, albeit overlooked, dimensions of public management and leadership. To secure that support is to secure a kind of legitimacy, which can underwrite not just consent but also active endorsement and engaged cooperation. If we are correct, then public managers should adopt a perspective that encompasses the need to create legitimacy and collaboration beyond the walls of their formal authority. Making good on that perspective will require them to master a range of skills and methods beyond the conventional public management repertoire, including an understanding of the possibilities for fostering democratic engagement.

Notes

1. For the early discussions of the role of politics in public administration that established the distinction between policy as the proper role of politics in government administration and administration as a nonpolitical part of public administration, see Woodrow Wilson, "The Study of Administration," *Political Science Quarterly* 2 (June 1887); or Frank J. Goodnow, *Politics and Administration* (New York: Russell and Russell, 1900). For more recent commentary on the indefensibility of this idea, see Frederick C. Mosher, *Democracy and the Public Service* (Oxford University Press, 1968).

2. Mosher, *Democracy and the Public Service.*

3. The first part of this process is often described as the policy development process, and it can happen in both legislative and executive branches of government. For a vivid account, see Philip B. Heymann, *Living the Policy Process* (Oxford University Press, 2008). The second part of the process is often described in terms of the operations of a public system of accountability. For a discussion of accountability in government, see Judith E. Gruber, *Controlling Bureaucracies: Dilemmas in Democratic Governance* (University of California Press, 1987).

4. For compelling, detailed accounts of how public bureaucracies manage their encounters with citizens, and the degree to which these encounters meet the standards of justice and fairness, see Jerry L. Mashaw, *Bureaucratic Justice: Managing Social Security Disability Claims* (Yale University Press, 1983); Jeffrey Prottas, *People Processing: The Street Level Bureaucrat in Public Service Bureaucracies* (Lexington, Mass: Lexington Books, 1979).

5. On the problem of evaluating government performance and what can be done about it, see Mark H. Moore, *Recognizing Public Value Creation: Strategic Uses of Performance Measurement in Government* (Harvard University Press, forthcoming).

6. See n. 1.

7. David Osborne and Ted Gaebler, *Reinventing Government: How the Entrepreneurial Spirit Is Transforming the Public Sector* (Reading, Mass: Addison-Wesley, 1992), pp. 166–94.

8. John Dewey, *The Public and Its Problems* (New York: H. Holt and Co., 1927), p. 126.

9. For examples, see discussion of effort to increase the legitimacy and support of citizens for public schools and policing in Archon Fung, *Empowered Participation: Reinventing Urban Democracy* (Princeton University Press, 2004).

10. John Alford, *Engaging Public Sector Clients: From Service Delivery to Co-Production* (New York: Palgrave Macmillan, 2009).

11. Stephen Goldsmith, *Governing by Network: The New Shape of the Public Sector* (Brookings Press, 2004).

12. Dewey, *The Public and Its Problems,* n. 8.

13. Kelman develops this idea in a different context in his efforts to transform the procurement processes of the federal government. See Steven Kelman, *Unleashing Change: A Study of Organizational Renewal in Government* (Brookings Press, 2005).

14. Stephen Goldsmith and Donald Kettl, *Unlocking the Power of Networks: Keys to High Performance Government* (Brookings Press, 2009).

15. For a view of managers working in the politics of the policymaking process, see Philip B. Heymann, *The Politics of Public Management* (Yale University Press, 1987), and his more recent work, Philip B. Heymann, *Living the Policy Process* (Oxford University Press, 2008). For a discussion of the wider role of political management in public administration, see Mark H. Moore, *Creating Public Value: Strategic Management in Government* (Harvard University Press, 1995).

16. R. A. W. Rhodes and John Wanna, "The Limits to Public Value, or Rescuing Responsible Government from the Platonic Guardians," *Australian Journal of Public Administration* 66, no. 4 (2007): 406–21.

17. Archon Fung and Erik Olin Wright, eds., *Deepening Democracy: Institutional Innovations in Empowered Participatory Governance* (London: Verso, 2003); Fung, *Empowered Participation.*

18. Archon Fung, *Full Disclosure: The Perils and Promises of Transparency* (Cambridge University Press, 2007).

19. The distinction between the function of building legitimacy and support for a public enterprise, on the one hand, and building and deploying operational capacity to achieve the desired result, on the other, is a key distinction in the theory of strategic management in the public sector. See Moore, *Creating Public Value;* Herman Leonard and Mark Moore, chap. 5, this volume.

20. Moore, *Creating Public Value,* chap. 4.

21. Laurence Lynn developed the idea of levels of the game to suggest a widening scope of political mobilization in policy development processes. See Laurence E. Lynn, *Managing the Public's Business: The Job of the Government Executive* (New York: Basic Books, 1981), chap. 6. More recently, the idea has been extended to include the idea of public marketing as an important tool of public management for creating behavior change in large populations. See Janet Weiss, "Public Information," in *The Tools of Government: A Guide to the New Governance,* edited by Lester M. Salamon (Oxford University Press, 2002), pp. 217–54.

22. Moore, *Creating Public Value,* pp. 118–34.

23. Moore, *Recognizing Public Value Creation,* chap. 3.

24. Richard Neustadt, *Alliance Politics* (New York: Columbia University Press, 1970), p. 116.

25. Richard Neustadt, *Presidential Power and the Modern Presidents: The Politics of Leadership from Roosevelt to Reagan* (New York: Free Press, 1990), p. 30.

26. Alan Altshuler and Robert D. Behn, eds., *Innovation in American Government: Challenges, Opportunities, and Dilemmas* (Brookings Press, 1997).

27. The concept of a production possibility is a basic idea in economic theory. It describes the locus of points describing a specific combination of product and service attributes that can be produced by a producing firm with a given budget constraint

using currently available technologies. See Edith Stokey and Richard Zeckhauser, *A Primer for Policy Analysis* (New York: Norton, 1978), pp. 23–28.

28. Eugene Bardach, *Getting Agencies to Work Together: The Practice and Theory of Managerial Craftsmanship* (Brookings Press, 1998).

29. Goldsmith and Kettl, *Unlocking the Power of Networks*.

30. Bardach, *Getting Agencies to Work Together*.

31. Zachary Tumin, "From Safety to Security: The United States Coast Guard and the Move to a Global Network of Secure Ports, Cargos, Crews and Vessels," Working Paper (Harvard Kennedy School of Government, 2009).

32. Moore, *Creating Public Value*, pp. 117–18; Weiss, "Public Information."

33. Howard Husock, "'Please Be Patient': The Seattle Solid Waste Utility Meets the Press," Case #C16-91-1058 (Harvard Kennedy School of Government Case Program, 1991). For an analysis of this case, see Moore, *Recognizing Public Value Creation*, chap. 5.

34. Weiss, "Public Information."

35. Tom R. Tyler, *Why People Obey the Law* (Yale University Press, 1990).

36. Ibid.

37. This is part of the difference between negotiation and deliberation. See discussion above.

38. See Archon Fung, "Recipes for Public Spheres," *Journal of Political Philosophy* 11, no. 3. (2003): 338–67. The material in this section is drawn from Archon Fung, "Varieties of Participation in Complex Governance," *Public Administration Review* 66 (December 2006): 66–75.

39. Fung, "Recipes for Public Spheres."

40. Morris P. Fiorina, "Extreme Voices: A Dark Side of Civic Engagement," in *Civic Engagement in American Democracy*, edited by Theda Skocpol and Morris P. Fiorina (Brookings Press and Russell Sage, 1999), pp. 395–426.

41. James Fishkin, *The Voice of the People* (Yale University Press, 1995); Ethan J. Leib, *Deliberative Democracy in America: A Proposal for a Popular Branch of Government* (Pennsylvania State University Press, 2004); Graham Smith and Corinne Wales, "Citizens' Juries and Deliberative Democracy," *Political Studies* 48 (2000): 51–65.

42. Dewey, *The Public and Its Problems*, p. 264.

43. See Joshua Cohen, "Deliberation and Democratic Legitimacy," in *The Good Polity*, edited by Alan Hamlin and Philip Pettit (New York: Basil Blackwell, 1989), pp. 17–34; Amy Gutmann and Dennis F. Thompson, *Democracy and Disagreement* (Cambridge, Mass.: Belknap Press, 1996); Roger Fisher and William Ury, *Getting to Yes: Negotiating Agreement without Giving In* (Boston: Houghton Mifflin, 1981); Lawrence Susskind and Jeffrey L. Cruikshank, *Breaking the Impasse: Consensual Approaches to Resolving Public Disputes* (New York: Basic Books, 1987); Lawrence Susskind, Sarah McKearnan, and Jennifer Thomas-Larmer, *The Consensus Building Handbook: A Comprehensive Guide to Reaching Agreement* (Thousand Oaks, Calif.: Sage, 1999).

44. Fung, *Empowered Participation;* Archon Fung and Erik Olin Wright, eds., *Deepening Democracy: Institutional Innovations in Empowered Participatory Governance* (London: Verso, 2003).

45. Jeffry M. Berry, Kent Portney, and Ken Thomson, *The Rebirth of Urban Democracy* (Brookings Press, 1994).

46. Howard H. Stevenson, "A Perspective on Entrepreneurship," in *The Entrepreneurial Venture,* edited by William Sahlman and others (Harvard Business School Press, 1994), pp. 7–22.

Index